WELCOME TO THE MAYA WORLD!

With this *Travelog*, we have put attempted to include every route that you could take while exploring the Mayan world. We hope you like this new format. It should insure that the *Travelog* you get is as current as we have to offer. Folks have told us they glance over the *Travelog* the night before, to look for possible side-sorties that they might not have taken on the spur of the moment. The "navigator" shouldn't read too far ahead (more than 3 or 4 entries), or it'll be confusing to the "pilot". All cities, *ejidos* and danger spots are bolded — but I can't get **every** tope (speed bumps, also called vibrators or vibradores), so watch for 'em at the entrances to towns.

TYPOGRAPHIC CONVENTIONS

The top of the page looks like this:

JULY, 1992   1 of 2   186-E-3
            SCENIC RATING = 1

The date I travelled the highway is at the top left corner of each log, or in the case of Eat & Stray's, the date we changed information. The center (1 of 1) tells you how many pages there are to that particular log. 1 of 2, for instance indicates there are two pages to that particular stretch of highway. The log number is on the top right corner. It consists of the highway # (180, for example), the direction you are travelling (E for east, etc.), the section number of that highway (3, or sometimes 3A, 3B etc.). Special routes have the name of the destination instead. Every time you come to a major intersection or a major new highway, there should be a new log.

The scenic rating is a subjective evaluation based on a scale of 4. A scenic rating of 0 is as dull as dirt and 4 is close to heaven. At the bottom right is the page number. All pages are numbered sequentially.

DIVIDERS — OR ROUTE DECISIONS

Since there is sometimes more than one way you could go, we've included alternate routes. Just before you come to an important junction there will be a yellow divider page. Please read this. It will tell you what choices you need to make. **Skip to the next yellow page for another route.**

ACCURACY

Folks, I drive 20,000 or more miles a year to try to update all of Mexico. It's a little like the Dutch boy and the dike. As Carl Franz, author of *The People's guide to Mexico* and a hero of mine, put it: "Compared to updating a guidebook of this size, painting the Golden Gate Bridge is an easy project." By putting the date travelled on top of the log, you'll have an idea of the recency of the info. No other guidebook has as fast a turnaround as we do, but we don't do the whole country every year. Still, things change and I do make mistakes, so in general, if there is a big green sign telling you to do something that disagrees with my directions, it's usually right — unless I've told you that it's a bum steer. You comments and help are appreciated. I get hundreds of letters a year from folks who've told me about their trip, or given me some new info on roads, hotels, restaurants or RV parks. I do read them and sometimes use the hints (giving credit unless you ask me not to). Sadly, postage costs preclude me from thanking you personally, sadly.

Just so you'll know how I do update, here's a glimpse. No, I don't talk into a tape recorder. It seems like a good idea until you do it a few times. My companion takes notes of changes. Next year, we'll try a lap-top. By the way, if you'd like to try Traveloging, write me. It's an unpaid position, but all expenses are taken care of and you get to see places most folks don't. I go to more places that don't get written up because the road isn't up to our standards or facilities are too humble even for me.

MAYA LEGEND

1992-93

The Traveloger takes notes while I drive. I have a special mileage computer that converts the revolutions of my truck's drive-shaft to miles. When we return, my assistant types the notes into a desk-top publishing program. Believe me, it's a chore! We then print the *Travelog* right here in McAllen and distribute it. I try to personally visit each hotel and restaurant, though I can't sleep and eat at every one. Sometimes a closed one will slip by me, but I've learned, it's better than deleting an open one. When inspecting, I don't identify myself, so I get the same treatment you would. I peek into the kitchens, too. Places change, though. When several customers write me to say a place has gone downhill, I may put a note in the log. I keep all your comments in a database and when I redo that route, I make certain to check the place out. I'm sorry I can't respond to them all. Thanks.

GAS

Unleaded gas "Magna Sin" is readily available, though not at all gas stations. Look for the green pump or a white triangle on the roof of the gas station. We tell you where we found it by the symbol "Mgas".

EAT AND STRAY LEGEND

Our stars are a subjective combination of quality + price and are different than the Mexican Tourism Commission's star system. The more stars, the more it will cost. ** or *** can be a bargain. B is budget: cheap & basic — not for everyone: they may be very spartan. AE = American Express, MC = Mastercard, VI = Visa. SATV = satellite TV SMC = Sanborn's Mexico Club. RR = reader recommendation, not rated.

PRICES — please don't take these as gospel — prices change when a hotel adds services, but we give you a fighting chance to hold on to your bucks. Always look at the room first and ask for the best price. Prices are in US dollars. ECON — under $25, MOD — $25-$60, UPPER $60 & above. Restaurants are rated for quality and service. Prices are approximate, for two folks to eat dinner there. ECON — under $10, MOD — $10-$25, UPPER — $25 & above.

Drinks, tips & appetizers are not included. If breakfast is the specialty, cut prices in half.

For RV parks, we list approximate rates when known. ECON — under $8.00, MOD — $8-10, UPPER — $10 & above.

If a hotel has a disco and you want to sleep, ask for a room far, far, away — in another galaxy, perhaps. If the room's too noisy, think nothing of asking to change. Be sure to ask for the "sub-gerente" since the "gerente" will be home asleep.

LEGEND OF SYMBOLS

Mgas UNLEADED, MAGNA GAS.

R REGULAR GAS

Pre-Colombian or native peoples' site of interest.

A checkpoint or government post. Be ready to stop.

The Dreaded Topes. Speed bumps, vibradores. Slow down.

Mission or Spanish era historic site nearby.

H A hotel or motel nearby.

Rv Rv Park nearby.

Beach nearby.

Toll house. Stop and pay toll.

Railroad crossing. LOOK & LISTEN!

A forest or scenic spot. Not necesarily in the woods.

Mountains or scenery nearby.

Market or local crafts for sale nearby.

Tourist routes. Specially marked routes for tourists.

A restaurant nearby.

Sr. Fish means fishing (or at least a body of water nearby).

(Please turn page!)

12 STEP PROGRAMS IN ENGLISH

NOVEMBER 1992 — GENERAL INFO

We've included this because so many customers wanted to be able to plan their trip based on a routine they're used to back home. Your help in getting new info is appreciated. You'll see a circle with a triangle and "AA" at Spanish-speaking meetings everywhere. You are always welcome, even if you don't speak Spanish. Spanish for "meeting" is "reunión" or "sesión". The phone numbers below were either provided by the contact person or from newspapers.

BAJA

CABO SAN LUCAS, BC — Hotel Hacienda, around back, second floor — 7 days a week, 6 PM. Ph: Barbara (684) 3-2726.

MULEGE, BC — 1 block east of bank — Fri. 3 PM. (may not be operating)

MANEADERO, BC — Cultural Social Salón (on Hwy #1), 10.6 MI south of Ensenada at Jct. with paved roads to Bufadora. Sun, 10 AM. Ask for Albert.

TODOS LOS SANTOS, BC — There are a couple of loners here. Ask around.

ROSARITO BEACH, BC — Calle Escondido #110 Baja Tradewinds. Thurs, 7 PM.

WEST COAST

ACAPULCO — "Grupo Universidad" on Universidad. Turn NW (away from water) off Costera at intersection with Big Boy and Acapulco Plaza Hotel. Ahead 1 block to dead end. Turn left and go 1 long block. Go to end of street. AA Club on left. On beach-side of street. Mon, 6 PM; Wed, Fri, 7PM. Ph: Richard (74) 84-1022 or 84-6854 Fax: 84-8559.
Cristo Del Rey Catholic Church at Calle del Caracol #73, has ALANON — Mon, Wed 6PM Call Linda: (748) 84-7196. ACOA/CODA — Mon, 7PM Call Gail: (748) 84-2087. French-speaking AA — Tues, Fri 6:30 PM.
Acapulco Children's Home, on Gran Vía Tropical, Mon 6 PM (tenative). At University, Mon 6 PM and Wed Fri 7 PM.

KINO BAY, SON — Club deportivo — Wed & Sat, 7 PM. El Saguaro T.P., rec room. Chuck or Gloria (624) 2-0141.

MAZATLÁN, SIN — El Cid Country Club in clubhouse (across from the El Cid Hotel). M W F, 8 PM.

PTO VALLARTA, JAL — meets at Edificio Cine Bahia (in older section of town, across the Río Cuale at 181 Insurgentes (near Madero), second floor at end of hall, RM #208. Daily, 6:30 PM. Mon, Sat, 9 AM; Sun, 11:30 AM. Most meetings are non-smoking. There's an 8:00 smoking meeting some nights. NA, Tues, Thurs, Sat, 5:00 PM. OA, Tues, 8:00 PM. ALANON, Mon, 5:00 PM. CODA 8:00 PM, Fri. Ph: Helen (322) 5-5919; Paul (322) 2-6060 ext. 204; Angelo (322) 2-3906.

SAN BLAS, NAY — Check at McDonald's restaurant for times. 6 PM, M W F. 9:30 Sun. Calle Sinaloa #19 (sort of). Little shopping center across from police station. All the way in back. Go thru gate to back patio.

YELAPA, JAL. — Wed, Sat, 5:30 PM. Ask at Mike's house on the beach.

ZIHUATANEJO/IXTAPA, GRO — go on the canal road towards Playa Madero. Pass la Boquita bakery. Turn right towards Hotel Solimar. On one side of the plaza is the Spanish LALA. Across the plaza is the English speaking group. Meet at 6 PM on Thurs. Call Alanon # Ph: (743) 4-3767.

COLONIAL MEXICO

CHAPALA, JAL — AJIIC AREA — Sun, Jocotepec, call Bill (376) 5-2575. Mon — Little Chapel, 4 PM. Tues — Río Zula #1, Wed — ACOA, Hidalgo #63, Ajiic, ALANON, Río Zula #1, 4PM. Thurs — Río Zula #1, 4 PM. Sat — ALANON, Río Zula #1, 9:30 AM.

CUERNAVACA, MOR — Ph: (73) 13-4327 (Francis) or (73) 13-7831 (Minerva).

GUADALAJARA, JAL. — Clubhouse, Filadelfia #2015 (off Lopez Mateos & Las Américas, near Brazz Restaurant) — Mon, Wed, 7:30 PM. Call Bill (36) 63-1417 or Vick (36) 625-2613 for info.

MEXICO CITY, DF — Río Danubio #39 (upstairs), M W F 2 PM. Tues Thurs, 8 PM. Sat, 4 PM. Sun, 6 PM. Union Church, Reforma 1870 — M W F, 8 PM. Ladies Meeting, Nuestra Señora de Guadalupe, Corner Prado Sur y Virreyes (Basement) — Wed, 4 PM. Ph: (5) 568-5104, 525-9090.

OAXACA, OAX — Sun 12 Noon. Ph: (951) 5-1989 (Enrique).

SAN MIGUEL ALLENDE, GTO — Alanon Club, Terraplen #17; AA M—F, Sat, Sun, 12 noon. ALANON, Mon, 4:30 PM. ACOA, Wed, 7 PM. Sat, 4:30 PM. OA, M W F, 4 PM (Spanish). Tues, 7:30 PM. CODA, Fri, 6 PM (women). Sat, 7 PM. ARTA, Sun, 6 PM. Ph: (465) 2-0667 or (465) 2-2218.

YUCATAN

CANCUN, QR — AA English-speaking meetings at the Cancun International Group, 6:15 PM every day. Call Jim (98) 84-2608 (has answering machine) or Vicki (98) 84-2445. They meet at the Plaza América shopping center, on Av. Kukulkán (near corner with Av. Tulum). They are on the 2nd floor, room #33. You enter at the back of the building, walk up one flight of stairs and turn right to the end of the hall. The shopping center is near the glorietta where you would turn to go to Pto. Juarez (see map). It's down from Hotel América, across from the original Super Deli. There are also SLAA & ALANON meetings. If you go in a taxi, tell him "cerca del Hotel América". Then, when he gets there, point down the road to the shopping center ahead of you. Make sure it is the Plaza América and you are home free.

COZUMEL, QR — Tabla de Salvación, 632 20th Av. South, between 7th & 9th streets. Su M W F, 6 PM.

PUERTO MORELOS, QR — AA (English), 1 Km. beyond Villas Shanti on left just before dead end (it's a sand road). It's a 2-story house and may have "AA" sign. There's a large dog in yard.

RUTA MAYA TABLE OF CONTENTS

HIGHWAY ROUTES

FROM — TO	PAGES
Acayucan — Villahermosa	1-6
Campeche — Merida (direct)	35-37
Campeche — Uxmal — Merida (secenic)	39-44
Campeche — Isla Aguada — Villahermosa (scenic)	83, 29-30
Cancun — Valladolid	73-74
Cancun — Playa del Carmen — Cozumel — Chetumal	87-101
Chetumal — Cozumel — Playa del Carmen — Cancun	107-112
Chetumal (Jct. Hwy #307 & #186) — Escarcega	113-114
Escarcega — Chetumal	25-26
Escarcega — Isla Aguada	27-30
Escarcega — Campeche	27-32
Escarcega — Palenque Jct.	115-116
Guatemala border — San Cristobal — Palenque	125-131
Merida — Uxmal (scenic)	51-52
Merida — Chichen Itza — Valladolid (toll)	55-56
" " (free)	55 & 59
Merida — Escarcega	79-85
Palenque — San Cristobal & Guatemala border	119-121
Palenque Jct.—Escarcega	23-24
Palenque Jct. — Villahermosa	133-135
Valladolid — Cancun	61-62
Valladolid — Merida (toll)	75
" " (free)	77
Villahermosa — Palenque Jct — Escarcega	11-25
Villahermosa — Isla Aguada — Campeche (scenic)	13-14, 31-32
Villahermosa — Acayucan	137-142

EAT & STRAYS (MAPS, GEN INFO, HOTELS, RESTAURANTS, RV PARKS)

Bacalar (Lago)	99, 107
Cancun	63-72
Campeche	33
Chichen-Itza	57-58
Chetumal	103-106
Coatzacoalcos	34-35
Cozumel	91-95
Isla Mujeres	72a-72c
Majahual	99, 108
Merida	45-50
Palenque	19-22, 120-123
Playa del Carmen	89-90
Pto. Morelos, Punta Bete	87-88, 111-112
San Cristobal de Las Casas	123
Tulum	97, 109

JULY 1992   180-S-5A
ACAYUCAN — COATZACOALCOS

MEXICO TRAVELOG
Puts over 40 years of experience at your side! Copyright © Sanborn's TGP Inc.

ACAYUCAN JUNCTION (HWY #185) PAST MINATITLAN TO COATZACOALCOS JUNCTION — 42.5 MI OR 68.0 KM — DRIVE TIME 1 HOUR

SCENIC RATING — 0

MI.	KM.	
0.0	0.0	Veer right, then over bridge on Hwy #180 here at **Acayucan** Junction with Tehuantepec Isthmus Hwy #185. Gas at left.
0.7	1.1	Mandatory immigration stop. *Psychiatry...*
5.1	8.2	Pass side road (right) to **Texistepec**. Lots of nice straight stretches on this log.
11.6	18.6	Curve right and over railroad underpass. Note sulphur mine up tracks to left. Thru edge of sulphur mining town of Jaltipan (population 60,000), mostly at left. Sports center at right. Careful for "vibradores" on road.
12.3	19.7	Secretary of Mines and Minerals office at left. *Is the care...*
14.2	22.7	Pass turnoff (left) to **Oteapán**.
14.5	23.2	Pass **Rancho Tomito Restaurant** and Mgas station (very clean restrooms at our visit). KM 34.
16.5	26.4	Now curve left and up thru little town of **Cosoleacaque**, slow for "topes".
18.5	29.6	Begin nice divided toll road bypass around Minatitlan and Coatzacoalcos (follow COATZACOALCOS-VILLAHERMOSA signs).
24.5	39.2	Ahead here at junction - exit (right) is to airport. *Of the...*
25.0	40.0	Straight ahead here - exit (right) is to **Minatitlan**.
25.3	40.5	Past exit (right) to Coatzacoalcos (but there's a better one ahead).
26.5	42.4	Another exit (right) to Coatzacoalcos (better one's still ahead).
28.0	44.8	Over bridge over San Francisco Canal. *ID by the...*
30.5	48.8	Up over Rio Coatzacoalcos on spectacular suspension bridge.
31.0	49.6	Military camp, left. Note "despacio" sign with armed guard. They really mean it!
34.7	55.5	Stop and pay toll. Emergency medical service here.
36.3	58.1	Straight ahead here at junction (right) to **Ixhuatlan**. *Odd.* — Anonymous
42.5	68.0	Veer right to **Villahermosa**. Left is to **Coatzacoalcos** at sign. End of log.

Villahermosa, STRAIGHT AHEAD and start Log 180-South-5(b).

Coatzacoalcos, turn left and follow stub log below, although we must warn you that driving is slow and tedious due to the heavy commercial truck and bus traffic in this hub of the industrial section of Mexico. Needless to say, the new bypass is a terrific improvement!

Stub log to Coatzacoalcos

MI.	KM.	
0.0	0.0	Having turned left headed into **Coatzacoalcos**, proceed ahead.
3.2	5.1	Note big petro-chemical complex of La Cangregera over to right. Past Instituto Mexicano del Petroleo (Mexico Institute of Petroleum) at right.
4.5	7.2	Pass turnoff (left) to **Minatitlán**.

(Over, please)

180-S-5A
ACAYUCAN — COATZACOALCOS

	MI.	KM.	
Mgas	5.0	8.0	Pass gas at right and then side road (left) to **Nanchital**. You are now going thru a major industrial zone; this general area is often called the "Houston of Mexico".
EAT	5.5	8.8	Gas, no Mgas, **Carnitas El Tigre**, good carnitas (chopped pork treats, eaten with a taco). You know it's fresh 'cuz the slaughter house is behind restaurant.
$	7.0	11.2	Toll booth. Pay toll; second lane from right for cars and pickups.
	8.0	12.8	Up and onto big left bridge over Rio Coatzacoalcos with railroad alongside. This nice "singing" steel bridge is built so that its center span can be raised to allow ocean-bound freighters carrying oil and sulphur to proceed upriver to Minatitlan which can be seen 'way off to right.
	8.8	14.1	Killer "topes".
H	9.2	14.7	Come to congested junction - right is to downtown (follow map) and left is to **Acayucan** and Hotels **Travelodge** and **Valgrande**. Restaurant **Le Jardin** was delightful for gulfside Malecon (Thanks to John and Dorothy Hammond, McAllen, TX).

» The port of COATZACOALCOS (pronounced "kwat-zah-kwahl-koz") is a busy and growing industrial center with a population of over 500,000 (hence the aforementioned heavy commercial traffic). The city has extensive sulphur and petroleum-related operations-refineries, petro-chemical plants, etc., and is an important railhead serving as the Gulf of Mexico terminus for the Isthmus of Tehuantepec Rail Service.

End of Log.

(Next Page, Please)

COATZACOALCOS

AREA CODE — 921   Copyright © Sanborn's TGP Inc.

SLEEPING AROUND COATZACOALCOS

**** **BRISA** —UPPER— 50-room a/c hotel at Zaragoza #2001. Restaurant. Bar. Pool. Tobacco shop. Travel agency. Car rentals. Enclosed parking. AE, MC, VI. Phone 2-0490.

** **LOSSANDES** —MOD— 60-room a/c hotel on Hwy #180 ("Carretera Transisturica") just before gas station on right at west entrance to town. Restaurant. Bar. Pool. TV. Parking. MC, VI. Phone 2-9673 or 2-9285. (Folks, we heard this may have closed recently, so let us know, please).

** **MARGON** —MOD— Good 65-room, 3-story a/c hotel at Zaragoza #302 a block from plaza. Restaurant. Bar. Some servibars. On-street parking. AE, MC, VI. Phone 2-0572. Best downtown hotel.

**** **TERRANOVA TRAVELODGE** —UPPER— Very good a/c 200-unit, 2-story motor inn alongside river west of town off Hwy #180 (take side road adjacent to gas station). Restaurant. Bar. Disco. Pool. Servibars. Water skiing. Boats. SATV. Secure Parking. AE, CB, MC, VI. Ph: 4-5100 or 2-5046 FAX: 4-5482. USA — 1-800-255-3050

** **PLAYA VARDERO** —MOD— Blvd. de John Spark #411. 75 rooms. A/C. Restaurant. Disco. MC, VI. Ph: 2-6256 or 2-6258 Fax: 2-6434

TOLUSCO —ECON— Good hotel at mile 65.5 of Log 180-S-5A. Good restaurant. MC, VI, AE.

** **RIVER PALACE** —MOD— Av. Camacho #311. 2-story. 14 rooms. A/C. CATV. OK place. Humble. Ph: 2-8769 (also fax).

** **VALGRANDE** —MOD— 4-story, 62-room a/c hotel downtown at corner of Hidalgo and Morelos. Restaurant. Bar. Cafeteria. CATV. Servibars. Parking a block away. AE, MC, VI. Phone 2-1476 or 2-1624 Fax: 2-3139.

EATING COATZACOALCOS

CARNITAS "EL TIGRE" — 2.5 miles on road into town. For the adventurous they have great "Borrego" (lamb) and pork.

END OF EAT AND STRAY

(More Goodies on other side)

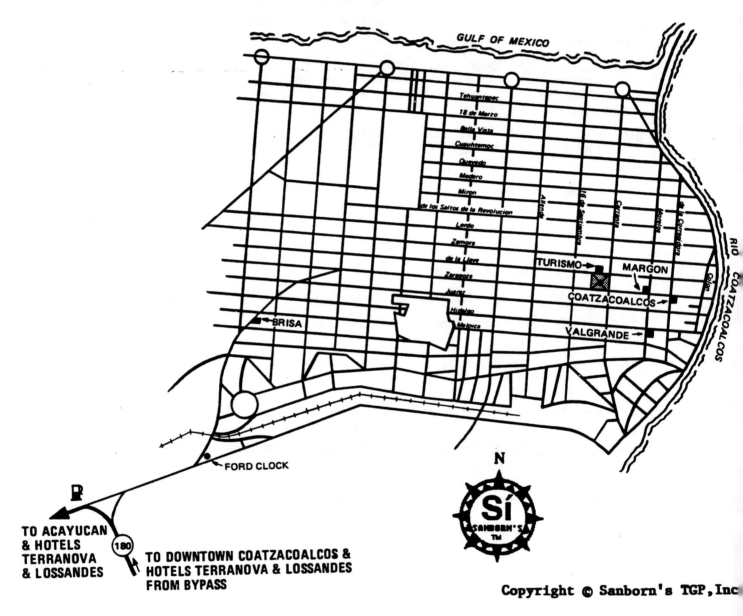

JULY 1992   COATZACOALCOS — VILLAHERMOSA

Sanborn's

MEXICO TRAVELOG
Puts over 40 years of experience at your side!   Copyright © Sanborn's TGP Inc.

COATZACOALCOS JUNCTION — CARDENAS — VILLAHERMOSA (JUNCTION HWY 195) 95.5 MI OR 152.8 KM — DRIVE TIME 2 — 2½ HOURS

SCENIC RATING — 1

» **KAMIKAZE** = Mayan word TO DRIVE — derived from Mayan rite of passage in which young men in VW's are tested for their valor in competition dedicated to god Kamikaze. ED. NOTE — as of yet unverified by any reputable source (maybe the road logger has logged one too many roads).

MI.	KM.	
0.0	0.0	Here at final junction into **Coatzacoalcos**, continue ahead on divided. (Highway is in the process of being widened to four lanes all the way to Villahermosa.)
3.2	5.1	Note chimney rock, left and orange Bird of Paradise flowers blooming at right.
5.5	8.8	Nice **Rancho San Cristobal** at left. The first 15 minutes of a rain storm are the most dangerous for drivers. Park and wait it out.
6.9	11.0	Big silicon glass plant at right
7.3	11.6	Cement plant at right.
10.0	16.0	Jog left and come to end of divided.
12.5	20.0	Pass side road (left) to **Agua Dulce** ("Sweet Water")
13.5	21.6	Livestock inspection station at right. Then pass side road (right) to **Las Choapas**. Gas at left, and a little farther down road pass Pemex pumping station and microwave tower at left.
16.3	26.1	**Rancho Hermanos** ("brothers") **Graham RV Park** at left (200 spaces, 100 with electrical and water hookups; showers; toilets; pool; dump station; tennis; fishing lake; restaurant; very nice accommodating management. They also offer Folkloric Ballet and lunch and dinner. Calle Salamanca #126, Col. 4 Caminos, Agua Dulce, Ver. Ph: (923) 3-0666 or 3-0120).
17.0	27.2	Bend right and up and over Rio Tonala. Come to state line - leave Veracruz and enter Tabasco. After bridge pass **Ejido La Ceiba** at right and monument at left to Presidente Adolfo Ruiz Cortinez (1952-58) commemorating the building of this highway. Then a new 1992 immigration inspection station — have paprers ready.
19.3	30.9	Pass side road (left) to Pemex camp of **La Venta**.

» It was in the swamps of La Venta area where the huge Olmecan heads which were carved from single solid chunks of stone were discovered - and how the dickens it was managed to get 'em into the middle of these swamps miles and miles from the nearest known stone deposits, is one of the world's great mysteries. The entire site has been relocated to Villahermosa and reconstructed at La Venta Museum because of the oil discoveries in this immediate area.

24.3	39.9	Pass side road (right) to Pemex camp of **Ogarrio**.
31.5	50.4	Come now to crossroads community of **Entronque** (Spanish for "junction") **Sanchez Magallanes** at left. Sanchez Magallanes is a gulf beach layout 23 miles away, more for locals, but just off its shore is beautiful **Santa Ana** sandbar. No hotel evident.
39.0	62.4	Thru big **Ejido Palo Mulato** with little blue Pentecostal church at left.
42.2	67.5	Bright pink Presbyterian church at right.
43.0	68.8	Bamboo houses with palm roofs and dirt floors often seen.

(Over, please)

180-S-5B
COATZACOALCOS — VILLAHERMOSA

MI.	KM.	
48.0	76.8	Thru settlement of **Pico de Oro**. The Aztecs believed in the four cardinal points and the central direction (or upwards). All beings were grouped according to this. They assigned white to the west, red to east, black to north, blue to south. This may account for their acceptance of the Christian symbol of the cross, which points in all four directions.
50.3	80.5	Past **Ejido Benito Juárez** at right.
53.0	84.8	Colegio Superior de Agricultura at left (ag college).
59.0	94.4	Pemex oil wells "**Pozos Cardenas**" at left. — A lost motorist slowed down to ask his way to the nearest town. The surly old man, whom he nearly knocked down, replied: "dunno." The motorist drove on slowly, but was soon recalled by shouts behind him. He put the car in reverse and backed until he was alongside the old man who had just been joined by another. "Well?" said the motorist. "This is m' buddy," said the old man, "an' 'e dunno either."
61.0	97.6	Military campo over at left.
64.5	103.2	Bridge under construction at left.
65.0	104.0	Mom and Pop alert: **Los Pilares** is not a trailer park and not for you. KM 119
65.5	104.8	LP gas at left. VW agency at right and skirt edge of town of **Cardenas**, (population 61,017) famous for its chocolate industry. Then gas at left. Pass **Hotel Tlauashco** —Mod— 92 nice a/c rooms, good restaurant, pool; AE, MC, VI. Ph: (937) 2-1940 or 2-1533. KM 120. Pass crossroads with side road (right) to downtown and to **Huimanguillo** and side road (left) to **Comalcalco** and to scenic **Paraiso** and **Limon**, popular week-end spots for locals. Then under overpass and past gas at right. Begin divided highway. Pass cacao processing plant at left and Ford agency over at right. Note road widening project at left.
69.1	110.6	Gas at right. Also **Hotel Tolusco** at right, looks ok.
72.3	115.7	Community of **La Barca de Oro** ("The Golden Boat").
73.3	117.3	Up over long bridge over Rio Samaria.
74.5	119.2	Pass side road (right) to **Cucuyulapa**.
77.3	123.7	Pass Pemex pumping station at left.
83.0	132.8	Thru settlement of **Paso de Cunduacan**.
85.3	136.5	Pass side road (right) to huge Reforma oil field.
89.3	142.9	Thru community of **Lázaro Cárdenas**.
91.3	146.8	Thru community of **Loma de Caballo** with **Motor Plaza Tabasco** (Motel de paso, not for you) at right.
92.3	147.7	**Auto Hotel La Loma** at right (rents by the hour). Traffic picks up intensity. Stay in left 2 lanes on divided parkeway thru town.
93.6	148.2	Pass **Motel Costa del Sol**, on left.
94.0	150.4	Up and over Carrizal II Bridge. Gas at right and come to "glorieta" (traffic circle) and proceed ahead. Statue in center is of ex-Presidente Lazaro Cardenas (1934-40), one of Mexico's most popular leaders.
94.1	150.6	LP gas at right.
94.3	150.9	Commercial center at left.
95.5	152.8	Come now to another circle or "glorieta" with imposing monument to Sanchez Magallanes, and junction (right) with HWY #195. End of log.

Palenque, Francisco Escarcega, Champoton, Campeche, etc. via nice inland Highway #186, proceed ahead past circle and start Log 186-East-1 or Isla Aguada Special-South on old Gulf Hwy #180 which takes you thru Isla Aguada and on to Champoton.

Teapa, Tuxtla Gutierrez, etc. on Highway #195, turn right here at circle and start Log 195-South-1. — NOTE: We don't recommend this road. You really should go on to Palenque and take Hwy #199 instead. Use Log 199-South. If you have a big rig over 30 feet long, turn around and go back to Acayucan and cross on Hwy #185. During rainy season (May—July & late Nov.—Jan.) even Hwy #199 may be difficult. Inquire at a highway patrol station or ask a Green Angel or call the Green Angel Phone # in front of travelog.

(Next Page, Please)

End of Log.

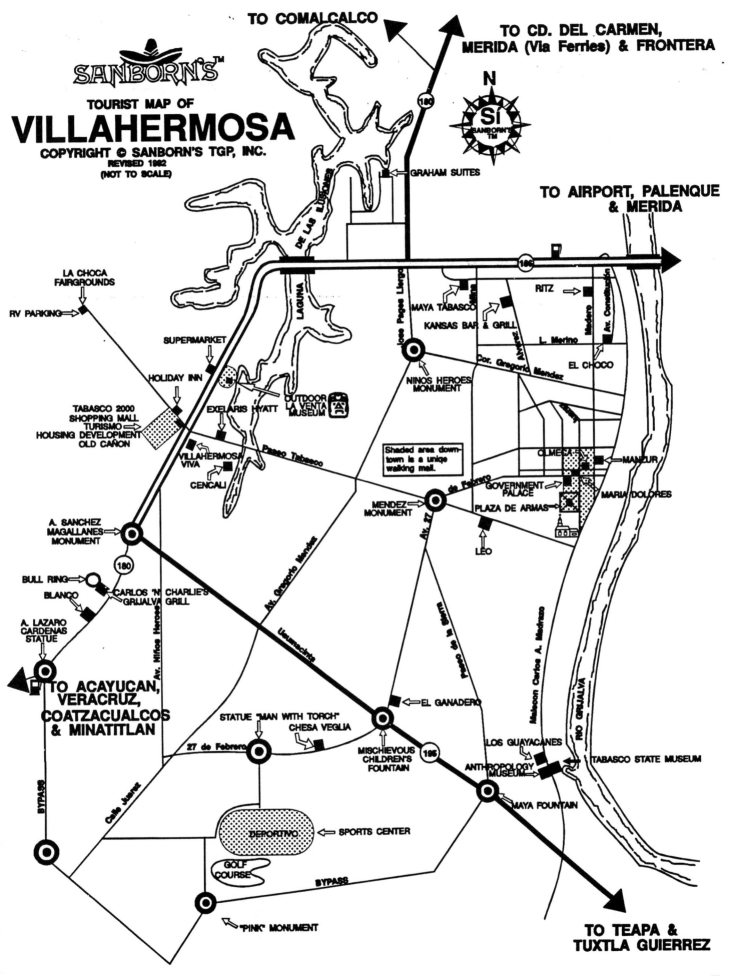

General Info
VILLAHERMOSA, TAB

VILLAHERMOSA, founded in 1596 as "Villa de San Juan Bautista", is the capital of the state of Tabasco, Mexico's main producer of oil and gas. The state has 165 operating wells which extract more than 50% of the national output. The daily production is 1,094,000 barrels of petroleum and 1.885 billion cubic feet of gas. Most of the wells are situated in the Villahermosa area and the town is growing like crazy with a population of 250,000.

Villahermosa, the crossroads of the "Sureste" (Southeast), is an important ranching and agricultural center as well as the gateway to the Yucatan. In the olden days paddle steamers, brought down from the Mississippi, would make their way up and down the Rio Grijalva using Villahermosa as their principal port.

The main attraction in Villahermosa is the outdoor Museum of La Venta, At the entrance is a huge carved head resembling a football player with a helmet from the days of Jim Thorpe. The original site of La Venta, an Olmecan Indian capital which flourished around 1200-600 B.C., is some 80 miles to the west near the coast. It had the misfortune, however, to rest atop some of the richest oil fields in this hemisphere, so the Mexican government packed up what remained of the old capital and relocated it here at this unusual museum — 20-ton head and all. This replica of the original is laid out at the edge of beautiful Laguna de las Ilusiones ("Lake of the Illusions") and should be a must stop on your trip, if only to puzzle over how these massive monumental heads were transported to La Venta, theoretically from the stone quarries clear over near Acapulco in Guerrero state. The Olmec civilization is considered the mother culture of Mexico, predating even the Mayans and most of the questions regarding their civilization still remain unanswered.

On the south side of the waterfront boulevard is the indoor Museum of Tabasco. It has a fine collection of artifacts representing Olmec, Maya, and other pre-Columbian Indian cultures which inhabited the area at one time or another. The town also features a unique walking mali, where the streets were raised to sidewalk level and converted to pleasant walkways (see shaded area of map).

Another interesting and worthwhile attraction is an excursion aboard the restaurant-boat "CAPITÁN BEULO", named in honor of a Tabascan coastal captain. Operated by Tabasco's tourist department, it travels the Grijalva River, still busy and the main means of transportation to and from the interior. The boat departs at 1:30, 3:30, and 9:00 PM daily except Monday. Its restaurant offers good regional and international dishes. Reservations can be made at the tourist department (see address and phone below).

So, don't hesitate to spend some time in this up-and-coming "boom town" on your way to (or from) the Yucatan or other parts of the "Sureste". You'll find excellent facilities.

If you need assistance here in Villahermosa, your best friends are the folks at the Secretaria de Turismo (Department of Tourism) located at the Tabasco 2000 complex, east of Hwy #180 on Paseo Tabasco #104 (Ph: 2-3171 or 3-5762). If you are driving an RV, they can arrange for an overnight spot at the fairgrounds.

JULY 1992

VILLAHERMOSA

AREA CODE — 931   Copyright © Sanborn's TGP Inc.

SLEEPING AROUND

*** **CENCALI** — MOD — Paseo Tabasco #1200 — Nice 120 room, 3 story hotel west of Villahermosa Viva on the edge of the Laguna de las Ilusiones. Restaurant. Disco. Pool. Boutique. Small parking area. Travel agency. AE, MC, VI. **SMC.** Ph: 5-1994, 2-6000, 5-1999, 5-1997 or 5-1996. Fax: 5-6600

EL CHOCO — MOD — L. Merino #100 & Constitucion — 72 room a/c hotel right in downtown Villahermosa. Restaurant. Bar. Club. Parking. AE, MC, VI. Ph: 2-9444 or 2-9649.

**** **EXELARIS HYATT VILLAHERMOSA** — MOD-UPPER — Av. Paseo Tabasco — Terrific 9 story, 215 room a/c hotel between Hotels Cencali and Villahermosa Viva. Dining room. Cafeteria. 3 bars. Pool. Tobacco shop. Tennis. Parking. AE, MC, VI. Ph: 3-4444, 5-1234, 5-1623 or 5-1624. Fax: 5-1235 or 5-5808. Mex. toll free #: 91-800-5-0777; US 800-228-9000.

** **GRAHAM SUITES** — MOD — Take University exit (Maya Tabasco), past signal light one block, take next right. Go one block and another right. Follow signs. Go one block then left. It's at end of street. Rosendo Taracena Encarnación B. de Madrazo s/n Colonia Magisterial — 46 room a/c hotel. All rooms with a view of the lake. Restaurant. Bar. Pool. Parking. Pier. Ph: 2-7602 or 2-7744. *Thanks to Jim Baker for this hotel.*

**** **HOLIDAY INN TABASCO PLAZA** — MOD-UPPER — Paseo Tabasco #1407 — Very nice 271 room, 11 story a/c hotel connected to Tabasco Plaza shopping center. 2 restaurants. 2 bars. Large, nicely landscaped pool. Parking. AE, MC, VI. **SMC.** Ph: 6-4400, 3-5567 or 3-4407.

** **MANZUR** — MOD — Av. F. I. Madero #422 — 116 room, 5 story hotel. Downtown's largest. Restaurant. Bar. Parking across street. Travel agency. AE, MC, VI. Ph: 2-2499.

* **MARIA DOLORES** — MOD — Aldama #404 — Old 76 room, 5 story a/c downtown hotel. Restaurant. Bar. Parking. AE, MC, VI. Ph: 2-2211.

** **MAYA TABASCO** — MOD — Av. Grijalva (Hwy #186) — 5 story, 160 room a/c hotel. 2 restaurants. Piano bar. Disco (10 PM — 2 AM, closed Sunday). Lobby bar. Pool. Car rental agency. Tobacco shop. Beauty shop. Barber shop. Parking. AE, MC, VI. **SMC.** Ph: 2-1111, 2-1599 or 2-1025. Fax: 2-1097.

* **OLMECA** — MOD — Reforma #304 — 70 room, 5 story a/c downtown hotel. Tidy coffee shop. Bar. Travel agency. MC, VI. Ph: 2-0022.

RITZ — ECON — F. I. Madero #1013 — 39 room, 2 story hotel just off Hwy #186. The best of the lack-lustre second-rate hotels. No restaurant.

*** **VILLAHERMOSA VIVA** — MOD — Paseo Tabasco #1201 — Very nice 3 story, 260 room a/c motor inn. Restaurant. Bar. Disco. Pool. Tennis. Boutique. Parking. AE, MC, VI. Ph: 2-5555, 2-4088 or 5-0000.

EATING VILLAHERMOSA

CAPITÁN BUELO — MOD — Carlos A. Madrazo Pier — Ship leaves dock at 1:30, 5:00, & 9:00 PM. Traditional food of Tabasco and international food. Tues thru Sun. Ph: 3-5767 for reservations.

(More Goodies on other side)

EAT & STRAY
VILLAHERMOSA, TAB

*** **CARLOS 'N' CHARLIE'S GRIJALVA GRILL** — MOD — Another of the familiar Anderson chain at bullring complex. Same type menu (international cuisine), same ambiance, and always crowded (never quiet). AE, MC, VI.

*** **CHESA VEGLIA** — MOD — 27 de Febrero #703. Nice restaurant. International menu with good seafood steaks, and even crepes suzette. Open 1 PM till 2 AM daily. AE, MC, VI. Ph: 2-2273.

** **EL GANADERO** — MOD — Av. 27 de Febrero #1706 — Good steak house across from Mischievous Children's Fountain. Specializes in American cuts of meat (New York, T-Bone, rib-eye, etc.) Open 1 PM till midnight. AE, MC, VI. Ph: 3-2303 or 3-4551.

** **KANSAS BAR & GRILL** — MOD — Juan Alvarez #803 — Nice "Old West" steak house. "Filete Kansas" (filet) and "Camarones Kansas" (shrimp) are specialties. Street parking. Open daily 11 AM till 1 AM. MC, VI.

* **LEO** — MOD — Paseo Tabasco #429 (plus a smaller branch at Juarez #504) — Beef-and-cheese ("carnes y queso") restaurant. Open 1 PM daily. MC, VI.

** **LOS GUAYACANES** — MOD — Malecon C. Medrazo at Pellicer #511 — Good regional food restaurant next to anthropology museum complex. Open noon till midnight. MC, VI. Ph: 4-0505.

* **OLD CAÑON** — MOD — Tabasco Plaza shopping mall — Steak-house that also features regional foods. Open 1:30 PM till 1 AM daily. AE, MC, VI. Ph: 3-4001

CAMPING, PARKING & PLUGGIN' IN.

There are presently no RV parks in Villahermosa. Caravan's park at the fairgrounds (Parque La Choca), 0.4 MI beyond Holiday Inn for a nominal fee. Proceed on the divided Paseo Tabasco 2.5 miles thru Tabasco 2000 and past the Holiday Inn on right. Follow it past the Parque and return via the little glorieta just beyond the parque. Don't take 1st. right, take 2nd. Enter the park from the 2nd entrance; parking lot at right. Attendant will be around in evening to collect money. No need to inquire. From north, take exit to lateral after statue, stay in left lane and take the next left crossing over freeway.

12 STEP PROGRAMS

AA — Calle Constitución #605. Ph: 4-0318

End of Eat & Stray.

(Please turn page!)

JULY 1992   186-E-1
                             VILLAHERMOSA – PALENQUE JCT

MEXICO TRAVELOG
Puts over 40 years of experience at your side! Copyright © Sanborn's TGP Inc.

VILLAHERMOSA (JUNCTION HIGHWAY 195) — PALENQUE JUNCTION — 72.3 MI OR 115.7 KM — DRIVE TIME 1½ - 2 HOURS

SCENIC RATING — 3

» This is a fine inland route thru nice green ranching country, and a good alternate to the older Gulf Coast route (Hwy #180). And an added attraction to this route are the Mayan archaeological ruins at Palenque, 22 miles south of this road at end of log.

» If you want to take the "ferry route" to Campeche, go ahead. We did. Take "Universidad, Comalco" exit. There is only 1 ferry, but the last one leaves at 6:30 PM & it is a 3.5 hour drive, so get an early start. There are accommodations at La Cabaña Cabins & an RV park at Isla Aguada, but there's not always someone around, particularly in summer. Next accommodations are at Champotón, 91 miles away, at the funky and really neat Si-Ho Playa.

	MI.	KM.	
	0.0	0.0	Starting at Hwy #195 junction (right) and monument circle ("glorieta") to Sanchez Magallanes at west end of Villahermosa, with John Deere at right, ahead. Be ready for hotel exit, otherwise stay in left 2 lanes on divided Blvd Ruiz Cortines and down under overpass.
H	0.3	0.5	Pass Exit for Holiday Inn, Viva Villa hermosa and Hyatt Hotels (Paseo Tabasco). RV — La Choca is about 0.25 miles west Holiday Inn. No hookups, but ok.
	0.8	1.3	Villahermosa's pride at right, the famous La Venta Museum where 27 Olmec archaeological cultures, including the huge altar with the face of a monkey, are exhibited. Park is open daily from 8:30 AM till 5 PM (admission charged). Be ready for scenic Hwy. #180 exit, otherwise keep going straight.
	1.0	1.6	Centro de Convivencia Infantil (kiddy park) at right. Then bend right and over bridge over Laguna de las Ilusiones. Green signs for Jose Llergo or Tierra Colorada and Hotel Graham Suites.
	1.3	2.1	Straight ahead for you, UNLESS TO:

Frontera, Cd. del Carmen and Isla Aguada on the gulf on Hwy #180, exit right and under overpass onto Universidad and go toward Comalcaco and Cd. Industrial. Go this way also for Tierra Colorado and Hotel Graham. Start Isla Aguada Special-South on page 13.

	MI.	KM.	
	1.4	2.2	Over bridge.
H	1.8	2.9	Hotel Maya Tabasco at right on access road.
	2.0	3.2	Under pedestrian overpass. Ford agency at right.
Mgas	2.1	3.4	Mgas on left, exit right after Ford, go under overpass and it's on your right, otherwise straight ahead.
	2.3	3.7	Under another pedestrian overpass and up on big bridge over Río Grijalva.
🏠$	2.8	4.5	Slow and stop at toll house and pay toll. Ahead on divided.
	3.1	5.0	Come now to fancy glorieta (circle) with monument to Tabscoob-Nuestro Tata ("founding father" or "our forefather").
	6.0	9.6	Over Zapote II bridge.
	7.0	11.2	Now over Zapote I bridge and careful at end for sharp rise.
	8.5	13.6	Settlement of Dos Montes at right. Then pass side road (left) to airport and under another overpass.

(Over, please)

186-E-1
VILLAHERMOSA — PALENQUE JCT

MI.	KM.	
9.0	14.4	Divided boulevard ends. Pass abandoned motel construction site at left (must have run out of funds??). Km 13.
10.2	16.3	LP Gas, Left
12.2	19.5	Topes. Toll Booth.
14.4	23.0	Pass side road (left) to Ismate.
15.5	24.8	Community of Zapotillo at right. Then side road (left) to Tequila.
19.0	30.4	Chop suey Restaurant!! How'd dat get dere?
21.5	34.4	Pass crossroads (left) to Ciudad Pemex, an oil area community, and (right) to Cacao.
22.5	36.0	Fancy church at right as you pass thru settlement of San Juan el Alto.
23.5	37.6	7th-Day Adventist Church, left.
25.8	41.3	Come to another crossroads (left) to Belen ("Bethlehem") and (right) to Jalapa.
30.0	48.0	Mgas at left. (next gas at Palenque Junction 42.3 miles) and pass side road (left) to Macuspana (a dangerous crossroad). Note nice stadium, also at left, and Monument to Lazaro Cardenas. Although only 200 feet above sea level, Macuspana is a town in the "mountain region" situated on the banks of the river of the same name.
30.8	49.3	Up and over Río Puxcatán and past community of Puxcatán.
34.5	55.2	Pass side road (right) to Estacion Macuspana and E. Zopo on railroad, 4.3 miles away.
35.8	57.3	At our passing, observed road crew making potholes. KM 55.
38.8	62.1	Thru community of Manatinero. Watch for school crossing.
41.8	66.9	Side road to Agua Blanca, right.

☛ + **SANBORN'S EXTRA** —To AGUA BLANCA, turn off at Km 65. It's 3 Mi to railroad and 1.4 Mi farther to Agua Blanca. Take this gravel road (good - but not for RV's, it has rock "topes"). Heliconia flowers in bloom - orange blossoms. Pass Plaza of Las Palomas on left (green benches), Public Library, church on right. Continue straight thru past plaza, over pipe bridge, past Telesecundaria, over narrow bridge and past Heliconia Restaurant. Electric light in restaurant. Cross railroad. Then come to Agua Blanca. Nice with water falls, pools, grutas (caves). dry camping, night watchman. It's an unspoiled area: clean, simple restaurant with rest rooms and changing rooms. picnic table, BBQ pit. Natural spring water. Bring insect repellant. Orchids in trees. Small fee charged. (Thanks to A. Corelis, Pto. Vallarta, Jal.)

MI.	KM.	
43.8	70.1	Cemento Apaseo (cement factory), right.
44.3	70.8	Pass side road (right) to Salto de Agua, not worth visiting (we didn't).
45.5	72.8	Pass side road (right) to Estacion Zopo. Then over bridge over Río Tulija.
47.7	75.8	Truck inspection on left. Do not stop.
47.9	76.6	Enter Chiadas. Km 78.
50.0	80.0	Past abandoned customs station at left. Then cross state line - leave state of Tabasco and enter state of Chiapas. Note Heliconia flowers at roadside - orange bracts (blooms) like multi-birds of paradise
51.5	82.6	"Topes" and Puente de Calzada bridge. KM 84
53.8	86.1	Thru little village of Bajadas Grandes.
54.3	86.9	Side road to Monte Grande, left.
58.6	93.8	Restaurant Ranch on left.
60.3	96.5	Thru stretched-out village of Nueva Esperanza ("New Hope"). KM 95
62.2	99.5	Pass side road (left) to Jonuta.
64.3	102.9	Cross Cataza county line.
64.7	103.5	Pass town of Cuauhtemoc.

» **Cuauhtemoc (1502-1525) was the 11th & last Aztec Emperor. The son of Emperor Ahuizotl & princess Tilalcaptl, he was educated in the Calmecac school for nobles. Cortes made him a prisoner on Aug. 13, 1521 & had him killed by hanging him by his feet like a common criminal, on Feb. 28, 1525. He was 23. He was betrayed by Malinche, who acted as interpreter. To this day, a "Malinche" is a woman who cannot be trusted — that's the polite version.**

68.3	109.3	Pass "Programa Hule" — Rubber tree program station.

(Next Page, Please)

JULY 1992   1 of 1   **ISLA AGUADA SPECIAL-SOUTH**
VILLAHERMOSA — ISLA AGUADA — CHAMPOTON

MEXICO TRAVELOG
Puts over 40 years of experience at your side!   Copyright © Sanborn's TGP Inc.

VILLAHERMOSA THRU ISLA AGUADA AND ON TO CHAMPOTON — 191.0 MI OR 305.6 KM — DRIVE TIME 4 — 5 HOURS

SCENIC RATING — 4

» NOTE: This route is for naturalists and slowpokes. If you are going only to ISLA AGUADA RV PARK a more direct route is the Isla Aguada-North route (page 29). Often a 20 to 40 mile stretch of bad road, but great fun. (RV's, it'll bounce your kitchen). Bring mosquito repellant for ferry — no foolin' Allow 3½ hours to ferry. The last one leaves at 7 PM. The best accommodations are at Isla Aguada. After that, the next place to lay your head is the Si-Ho Playa Hotel, 24 miles before Campeche.

	MI.	KM.	
	0.0	0.0	Starting on Av. Universidad at junction with freeway, you are heading to Comalcalco, Cd. Industrial and Tierra Colorada.
H	0.3	0.5	Graham Suites Hotel, left. *People who...*
	0.5	0.8	Curve right on divided parkway and under pedestrian crossing.
	0.6	1.0	Framboyante Subdivision Cristal bottlers at left.
	0.8	1.3	Pass side road (left) to **Comalcalco**. Straight for you. Cross Av. Mendoza.
	1.7	2.7	Pass bus station and **Colonia Casa Blanca**, right. Then over bumpy bridge.
	2.7	4.3	Generator station, right. Prison, left.
	2.9	4.6	Road narrows to 2 lanes. KM 4.
	5.3	8.5	Pass side road (left) to **Cardenas**. *Drink and drive...*
🚗	6.6	10.6	Pass side road (right) to **Jolochero**.
	11.0	17.6	Thru village of **Ocultzapotlan**. Slow for "vibradores", at least 4.
⛽	12.9	20.6	Gas at right.
	16.0	25.6	Over Nuevo Gonzales Bridge.
	19.1	30.6	Road narrows thru marshlands
	20.0	32.0	Parador Turístico (tourist stop) "El Espino".
	24.0	38.4	El Guad Bridge. KM 39.
⛽	25.1	40.2	Dangerous curve.
	31.0	49.6	Pass side road (left) to **El Bellote**. Straight for you. Gas (regular only) at left.
🚗	36.0	57.6	Get ready for "topes" ahead.
	37.5	44.	"Topes". Side road (left) to **Miramar**.
	38.0	60.8	"Topes".
	38.5	61.6	"Topes", at least 7. Village of **Madero** off to right.
	41.0	65.6	Thru settlement of **Carrillo Puerto**.
	45.8	73.3	**San Roman**, off to right. Cross very bumpy bridge. Slow down. Then over high rise Frontera Bridge. In the old days, we used to have to ferry across this river. Bumps at beginning and end of bridge.
Mgas	48.5	77.6	Mgas.
EAT	48.7	77.9	An okie-dokie-piano-bar-restaurant, no-foolin' "La Chiquita".
	49.1	78.6	At "T" turn right. Left is to **Frontera**. (There may be a hotel in Frontera, we saw a sign, but didn't check.) School at left. You're now heading due east.
	50.0	80.0	Radio tower at left. KM 71.
	50.3	80.5	Then thru windmills. Where is Sancho Panza?
⊖	52.0	83.2	Agriculture inspection station, left. Curve right at "Y".

(Over, please)

ISLA AGUADA SPECIAL-SOUTH
VILLAHERMOSA — ISLA AGUADA — CHAMPOTON

JULY 1992

MI.	KM	
62.0	99.2	Cross state line — leave Tabasco and enter Campeche. Over San Pedro bridge.
66.0	105.6	This is Egret country — both snowy and caky.
66.5	106.4	Road may get bad in here from time to time to time.
72.5	116.0	Agricultural inspection station, right.
73.7	117.9	Thru village of **Nuevo Progreso**.
74.2	118.7	"Topes".
74.8	119.7	Unmarked "topes".
77.9	124.6	Thru settlement of **San Antonio Cardenas**, "topes", at least 4.
80.7	129.1	Two "topes" at curve left.
83.6	133.8	Pass side road (left) to village of **Atasta**.
84.0	134.4	"Topes", at least 2. KM 33.
85.6	137.0	Atasta — deja vu (all over again).
86.3	138.1	"Topes".
87.2	139.5	More "topes". Misplaced body of water at right. (Lagoon?)
87.4	139.8	Church at left and more "topes".
88.3	141.3	"Topes".
89.0	142.4	Several more "topes".
96.8	154.9	Curves.
97.0	155.2	Thru settlement of **Puerto Rico**. Slow for "topes".
98.0	156.8	More "topes". Turkey in road.
100.0	160.0	Psychedelic light house, left.
101.0	161.6	Gulf of Campeche at left.
103.0	164.8	Thru village of **Zacatal**. Sharp curve right. KM 163.
104.0	166.4	Ferry across Campeche Bay. Ferry leaves at the following hours: 4:30, 7, 8, 9, 11 AM and 1, 3, 5, and 7 PM. Pay toll on other side according to size of vehicle. Cost of car:16,000; with trailer 30,000 pesos (prices and schedule subject to change). Turn right after ferry landing, heading south thru **Cd. Del Carmen**.
104.4	167.0	Veer left.
104.6	167.4	Hotel Estrella del Norte at right. Curve left at **Bay Bend Hotel** and out. KM 5.
105.0	168.0	Faschas Motel, left and Mgas also at left.
117.0	187.2	Pass balneario, left. KM 26.
124.0	198.4	Sharp curve, right and into **Puerto Real**.
125.0	200.0	Cross La Unidad Bridge. This bridge is 3,422 meters long.
127.0	203.2	Sharp curve right.
128.0	204.8	Enter Isla Aguada. CAMPECHE, STRAIGHT AHEAD. LA CABAÑA RV PARK AND HOTEL, TURN RIGHT. It's a quiet place with spaces and cabins right on Bay. The next sleeping place is the Si-Ho Playa Hotel, 24 miles before Campeche.
128.1	205.0	You may see flights of brown pelicans accompanying you and an occasional iguana.
143.7	229.9	Electric generator Sabancuy, right.
152.5	244.0	Pass side road (right) to **Sabancuy**.
153.0	244.8	Lighthouse, left and palm forest left. Cross bridge. KM 79.
171.1	273.8	Cross Chen-Kan I and II bridges.
187.0	299.2	Thru "boom-town" of **Concordia**. Slow for "topes".
188.5	301.6	Pass naval base, right.
191.0	305.6	Come to junction Hwy #261.

Often ride...

In a hearse. —MM

Escarcega, TURN RIGHT and start Log 261-South-1.

Campeche, Merida, etc., STRAIGHT AHEAD and start Log 180-South-6.

End of Log.

(Next Page, Please)

MEXICO TRAVELOG
Puts over 40 years of experience at your side! Copyright © Sanborn's TGP Inc.

MI.	KM.

R 70.3 112.5 Slow now! Come to gas station (regular only) at right with filthy restrooms, next gas at **Emiliano Zapata**, 13 miles (cleaner restrooms). Then junction (right) with road down to **Palenque** and archaeological ruins, 22 miles, where there's also a tourist information office.

Escarcega, etc., start Log 186-East-2.

Palenque (an archaeological gem) and on to San Cristobal de las Casas, Tuxtla Gutierrez, or the Guatemalan border, turn right and start "Palenque Special" log. There's

Mgas   Mgas at Palenque.

End of Log.

(Over, please)

P.O. Box 310   McAllen, Texas 78505-0310   (210) 686-0711

LET US EXPLAIN OUR SERVICES

INSURANCE —Recommended limits are: **$50,000** property damage / **$40/80,000** bodily injury liability and **$2,000/10,000** medical. These coverages, added to your Fire, Total Theft and Collision coverage give you the total cost of your policy. By special arrangement with our insurance company, a Sanborn's Mexico Club member can purchase an annual policy for almost 50% less than the regular annual policy. That's right. a **50% savings.**

MEDEX — Assists you through a 24-hour phone service in locating the right kind of medical care nearest you. Directs you to a doctor who speaks your language. Monitors your progress and coordinate communication with your family and doctor in your home country and arrange for medical air evacuation if necessary

SANBORN'S MEXICO CLUB — offers you special annual vehicle insurance rates. An annual liability policy for a little more than $100. An only Sanborn's policy includes MEDEX MEDICAL ASSISTANCE SERVICE WITH EACH INSURANCE POLICY.

MEDICAL AIR EVACUATION — If you become seriously ill in Mexico, with this coverage you will be evacuated in an air ambulance to a U.S. or Canadian hospital. Do you want coverage for yourself, or your wife and family too? The individual rate is $45.00 and the family rate is $90.00 a year.

TOWING, MECHANICAL & LEGAL SERVICES — This coverage provides towing, and mechanical service and legal service up to contract limits as well as the locating and shipping of your vehicle part to you in Mexico (cost of part excluded). Choose either 6 months or a year, high limits or lower ones!

THE CLUB — Gives you a free pocket road map, a health information book on Mexico, a Hotel/RV park directory offering discounts to Club members, and of course, our famous mile-by-mile Travelog to your destination.

ALSO OFFERED TO CLUB AND NON CLUB MEMBERS: TRAVMED — It is a $100,000.00 medical policy for sickness or accident. TRAV-MED covers physicians fees and hospital expenses, emergency dental and emergency medical evacuation. TRAVMED also includes MEDEX, making it your complete medical package. Its cost — $3.00 per day through age 70 and $5.00 per day age 71-80.

MEDICAL AIR SERVICE — For #150.00 good anywhere in Canada, U.S., Mexico, and the caribbean for you and your family.

LEGAL SERVICE BY THE DAY — The Mexico auto policy DOES NOT COVER ANY LEGAL EXPENSE AS A RESULT OF AN AUTOMOBILE ACCIDENT. This service will cover your expenses for a small daily fee up to contract limits. (Show Rate Sheet)

TRAVEL WITH HEALTH TO MEXICO BOOK — Loaded with expert information on staying healthy in Mexico.

Call for current prices, There are special rates for small groups.

MEXICO TRAVELOG
Puts over 40 years of experience at your side! Copyright © Sanborn's TGP Inc.

PALENQUE JCT (HWY #186) — PALENQUE STATION, PALENQUE TOWN, AND ON TO MAYAN RUINS - 22 MI OR 35.2 KM — DRIVE TIME 30 MIN — 1 HOUR

SCENIC RATING — 4

This side road will take you down to Palenque and the famous Palenque archaeological ruins. Prior to the construction of Hwy #186, the only way to get there to visit these magnificent Mayan ruins was either by private plane or by train - and it was indeed a chore! Don't hesitate to take this very worthwhile side-sortie.

MI	KM	
0.0	0.0	Having turned off Hwy #186 at gas station, proceed ahead south — **watch for livestock and "topes"**.
2.4	3.8	Pass Conalep de Palenque Vocational School. *If all the cars...*
4.2	6.7	Slow now for left curve.
7.5	12.0	Pass Palenque county line (63,000 population).
9.0	14.4	Curve left and pick up railroad at right. *In Mexico were in a line...*
11.5	18.4	Pass **Hotel Hacienda** at right, a motel del paso.
12.7	20.3	Slow now for sharp dangerous curve left.
13.5	21.6	Over "tope" and then pass side road (left) to **La Libertad**. Then slow, slow for very bumpy **RR XING**. Then curve right and slow for tope in front of railroad depot over at right. Pass **Hotel Santa Ursula** and **Hospedaje El Kichan** at right also. Then curve left thru community of **Paka-Na** or **Estación Palenque** and over another **tope**.
15.1	24.2	Pass Palenque's airport at left.
15.6	25.0	Pass VW agency, right and curve right.
16.0	25.6	Past LP gas at right. *Some idiot would try to pass. — MM.*
16.4	26.2	Past **Hotel Plaza Palenque** at left.
16.5	26.4	Slow for poorly banked left curve with **Hotel Maya Tucán** at right and **Mayorca** at left. Then pass **Tulija Hotel** at left. Good garage next door. Both built by enterprising fellow named "Choyote" in his 60's.
17.0	27.2	Careful now. Come to fork at white "Cabeza Maya" (Maya head). (To get to Doctor's office take left fork to Quaker State on right and Hotel Tulija. Turn left, pass market, he's on left.)

Ruins, take right fork.

Palenque, take left fork.

Los Tulipanes motel at left; La Canada also at left.

17.5	28.0	Having taken right fork, pass side road left to hotel **Nututun** and **Agua Azul State Park**. Go straight ahead over "topes". This road eventually ends at junction with old Pan American Highway #190 below San Cristobal de las Casas. It is a fine blacktop road, but a little twisty. You'll also find *deslaves* during the rainy seasons — May-July and late Nov.-Jan. (Log 199 South takes you here.) If you are over 30 feet long (or your rig is), then go to La Ventosa and cross Hwy #185. Don't even think about Hwy #187 from Villahermosa.
18.2	29.1	"Topes". Slow down.
18.7	29.9	Pass **Hotel Los Leones** at right, then **Kin-Ha Hotel & Trailer Park** at right.
19.5	31.2	Slow for sharp downgrade right curve. **Motel Chan-Kah** (Little Village) at left.

(Over, please)

PALENQUE SPECIAL
PALENQUE, CHI

MI	KM	
20.0	32.0	"Tope". Pass entrance to Palenque National Park. Then curve right.
Rv 20.8	33.3	Mayabell RV Park at left. Past Cascades Monument.
21.7	34.7	Now sharp left and wind up. Then sharp right and up some more.
22.0	35.2	Curve left and come to archaeological "zona" and stop at little toll house at right. Pay admission and parking charge and turn into parking lot at left and lock car. Then walk on up past gate into clearing which is where the action begins — better wear a hat.

You should get yourself a guide if you really want to enjoy this unusual attraction. Also, bear in mind that the "zona" is open 8 AM till 5 PM. And there's a little refreshment stand at right behind toll house. A sound and light show is planned. Let us know when it starts.

End of Log.

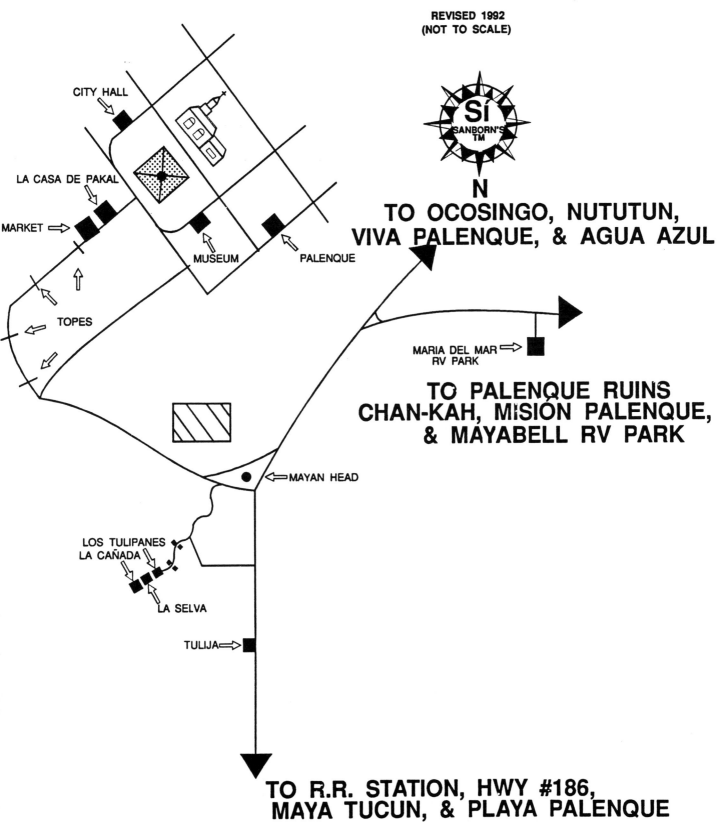

General Info
PALENQUE, CHI

PALENQUE was called by historian Dr. Franz Blom "the most beautiful, dramatic, and satisfying of the Maya masterpieces". This magnificent and mysterious Maya archaeological complex is different in a way from other Maya ruins in that it was a sort of ceremonial center, a Holy City of priests and pilgrims and not just another Maya town. It would have been created even before Christ and thrived somewhere around 600 A.D. The Spaniards discovered it in 1750. The sculptured ruins of its temples, pyramids, and palaces cover some 20 square miles, but only the central portion has been cleared and restored.

During the classic period of Mayan civilization (300-900 A.D.), Palenque flourished along with other cities and ceremonial centers. Then around 900 everything stopped! With no evidence of decline, communities, including Palenque, were abandoned for no apparent reason. Some say that war-like tribes from the North invaded, while others theorize that agricultural failure forced the exodus. It's also been suggested that the outlying city-states became more and more independent and less willing to work for and pay tribute to the priestly class in the temple cities. Perhaps it was a combination, but at any rate the destruction of most records by the Spanish and the inability, thus far, to decipher much of the existing hieroglyphics have indeed created a great deal of mystery surrounding Palenque.

Another unusual feature about Palenque is its direct trans-Pacific link between Mexico's cultures and the Orient. For example, the sacred tree (or cross) found only in the Americas here on Palenque's "Temple of the Foliated Cross" is also found at Angkor Vat in Cambodia. Likewise some lotus flower sculpturing here at Palenque is also found in distant India.

While you're here, you might also wish to take in the huge monolithic sculptured slab of rock (10 feet long and 7 wide) found at the bottom of the Temple of the Inscriptions. Discovered in 1952, it served as the cover for the royal tomb of one of the high priests.

Palenque has always been a special place, attracting special people. Now, like everywhere else, it is changing. Change brings good and bad. Our "Palenque correspondent", Ms. Sandy Hall says, "Everyone thinks hoards of tourists are about to flock there so everyone is building rooms. Little people along the road to the ruin turned their modest homes into restaurants. All this is in anticipation of a sound and light show that is supposed to be installed at the zone. Sigh, I guess it had to come. It's been promised for many years. I hope they do a good one." She's reflective, realizing that change is inevitable and the Palenque of her memories will always be intact. For today, she says, "... it continues to be the best, most interesting place to stay....." On a bright note, despite the changes a'comin', "The howler monkeys still live in the trees there and I was happy to awaken to their roars, one morning."

May you find your spot in Mexico now, and should you return someday to find it changed, may you also find the howler monkeys, or whatever touched your soul, still there. Mexico is like that. Some of us "discovered" our special place many years ago. Some of us only found our soul-spot today. Let us newcomers appreciate what we find with the newness of vision that you had when you first arrived. May you have the grace of spirit of Ms. Hall.

SPECIAL NOTE TO WOMEN TRAVELLING ALONE

Folks, we are not alarmists by any means, but we have been informed by enough trustworthy sources that you should be more cautious in and around Palenque than usual. Most women who come here have a perfectly safe time, but times being what they are, we want you to be aware. There have been a number of rapes here, and not always at night. Even two Peace Corps volunteers were assaulted while walking together on a back trail near the ruins. We suggest that you travel in groups of three or better yet, grab a guy for protection. (We do have our uses). — MM.

PALENQUE

AREA CODE — 934   Copyright © Sanborn's TGP Inc.

SLEEPING AROUND

*** **CHAN-KAH** —UPPER— 60 bungalows in jungle setting about 2 miles from ruins. Restaurant. Bar. Natural pool. No phones or TV. MC, VI. Ph: 5-1100; 5-1134 Fax: 5-0820.

** **CHAN-KA** —MOD— 16 room hotel downtown on plaza. Owned by same family as the one above. Most rooms have balconies. Restaurant. Bar. Parking. Ceiling fans 4 rooms with A/C. Ph: 5-0318.

* **KASHLAN** —ECON— Nice hotel located at 5 de Mayo #105, across from bus station. Restaurant. Bar. MC, VI. Ph: 5-0297 Fax: 5-0309.

** **LA CAÑADA** —MOD— Calle Cañada #14 near entrance to town —Favorite of ours— 13 unit inn (8 with A/C; rest with ceiling fans). Restaurant. Bar. Soon to have pool. Arts and crafts. Pets OK. Parking. MC, VI. Ph. and Fax: 5-0024. Howler monkeys still live in trees.

* **LA CASA DE PAKAL** —MOD— Av. Juárez #8 — 16 room, 3 story A/C hotel just off main plaza. Restaurant. Street parking. Ph: 5-0042.

LA CROIX —ECON— Hidalgo #18, across from church by plaza. Clean. Ph: 5-0014

* **LOS LEONES** —MOD— KM 2.5 on road to ruins. 8 rooms, good bed. TV. Restaurant. MC, VI. Ph. 5-1110 Fax: 5-1140.

** **MAYA TULIPANES** —MOD— North edge of town, before La Cañada. 36 rooms (16 new with A/C). Pool. Parking. MC. VI. Ph: 5-0201 Fax: 5-1004.

* **KIN-HA** —MOD— See "Camping" list.

*** **MAYA TUCAN** —UPPER— Between airport and Tulija on other side of street. 56 A/C rooms & 6 suites. Restaurant. Bar. CATV. Phones. Pool. Parking. Disco. MC, VI. Ph: 5-0290; 5-0287; 5-0443 Fax: 5-0337.

*** **MISION PALENQUE** —UPPER— Rancho San Martín de Porres — 160 room hotel, 3.5 miles from ruins. Restaurant. Bar. No TV. Natural pool and mud packs. Tennis. Shuttle to/from ruins. Shops. Parking. AE, MC, VI. Ph: 5-0241 Fax: 5-0333.

** **NUTUTUN** —UPPER— 45 room A/C hotel on Ocosingo road. Restaurant. Bar. Phone. CATV. Natural pool. Tent camping. AE, MC, VI. Ph: 5-0161 & Fax. 5-0620, 5-0626; 5-0640.

** **PALENQUE** —MOD— Av. 5 de Mayo & Av. Jiménez — Old-time 41 unit hotel near plaza in town. Restaurant. Bar. Pool. Travel Agency. Parking. MC, VI. Ph: 5-0188 Fax: 5-0039.

**** **PLAZA PALENQUE** —UPPER— 100 room A/C hotel between airport and Tulija on airport side of street. Apdo #58. Reasonably priced restaurant. Pool. Pool disco (apart from hotel, so quiet). Enclosed parking. Phones. AE, MC, VI. Ph: 5-0555 Fax: 5-0395.

* **TULIJA** —MOD— OK 47 unit, 3 story hotel on highway before town. Restaurant. Bar. Pool. Parking. MC, VI. Ph: 5-0104 Fax: 5-1033.

EATING PALENQUE

** **MAYA** —MOD— "The" hangout for Gringros. Across from Plaza. Typical food. AE, MC, VI.

(More Goodies on other side)

EAT & STRAY
PALENQUE, CHI

* **CHAN-KAH** —ECON-MOD— In hotel of same name on plaza. Comida corrida. MC, VI. Open 7 AM till 11 PM.
* **EL RODEO** —ECON— ½ block before plaza on Calle Juárez #10. Economical breakfast, Mexican food, burgers. Lots of ceiling fans. Comida corrida. Serves Peñafiel mineral water! (sometimes). Good coffee. MC, VI. Open 7 AM till 10 PM. Ph: 5-0233.

ARTEMIO'S —ECON— Popular backpacker restaurant. Mexican food. Open 7 AM till 11 PM.

* **MARA'S BURGERS** —ECON— Spic & span restaurant across from Chan-Kah on Av. Juárez. Hamburgers and Mexican food.
* **LA KAN-HA** —ECON— On Av. Juárez. Regional food. AE, MC, VI. Open 7 AM till 10 PM.
* **PIZZERIA PALENQUE** —MOD— Av. Juárez #168. Open 3 PM till 11 PM. Ph: 5-0332.
* **KASHLAN** —ECON-MOD— In hotel of same name. Good regional food.

MONTES AZULES —ECON— Across from bus station.

CAMPING, PARKING, & PLUGGIN' IN

AGUA AZUL NATIONAL PARK —ECON— Located 60 KM from town, on Ocosingo Hwy. Called Parque Nacional Turístico Ejidal. Camp here next to some of the most spectacular waterfalls in Mexico, formed by the Lacanja River. Rough entrance road, but passable by all vehicles. 60 spaces. No hookups. Swimming. Picnic area. Humble restaurants.

KIN-HA —MOD— 30 space park on road to ruins. 22 cabañas with thatched roofs and concrete walls with mosquito-netting. All hookups. Showers. Toilets. Palapa restaurant/bar. Pool. MC, VI. Ph: 5-0533.

MAYABELL —ECON— 30 space park 4 miles from town near ruins. All hookups. Cold showers. Toilets. Restaurant. 6 nice little rooms.

OTHER

CLINICA PALENQUE — Av. Dr. Manuel Velazco Suárez #35. Dr. Alfonso Martinez Ramos, studied in US and a USAF veteran; speaks English and will probably accept our MEDEX program. Open 9:30 AM - 1:30 PM; 4 PM - 8 PM. Ph: 5-0273. Turn off highway by Quaker State & Hotel Tulijo.

ATC — A good travel agency at Allende and Juárez #6. Ask for Victoria. Ph: 5-0210 Fax: 5-0356.

END OF EAT AND STRAY

(Please turn page!)

JUNE 1992   1 of 1   186-E-2
                                              PALENQUE JCT – ESCARCEGA

MEXICO TRAVELOG
Puts over 40 years of experience at your side! Copyright © Sanborn's TGP Inc.

PALENQUE JUNCTION – ESCARCEGA (JUNCTION HWY #261) – 113.3 MI OR 180.8 KM – DRIVE TIME 2½ HOURS

SCENIC RATING — 1

MI.	KM.	
0.0	0.0	At **Palenque** side road (right) proceed ahead on Hwy #186.
3.3	5.3	Truck stop of San Joaquin at right. Then **El Cuyo** to left.
13.0	20.8	Side road (right) to town of **Emiliano Zapata**. Gas and so-so restaurant ahead at right - fairly clean restrooms.
14.5	23.2	Slow a bit for slightly bumpy bridge - then 3 more bridges.
19.3	30.9	Come now to hamlet of **Usumacinta** at left and over bridge over famous Río Usumacinta, a very important river. Slow now on other side of bridge for toll house - pay toll. Rio Usumacinta is also the state line - leave Chiapas and enter Tabasco again.

☞ » Originating in Guatemala, **RÍO USUMACINTA** runs into the jungles and is the boundary between Guatemala and Mexico. The brown waters of the Usumacinta (meaning "place of the sacred monkeys"), along with those of the Grijalva, empty into the Gulf and together they compose one-third of the water in all rivers in Mexico. It is navigable (more than half its length is more than 20 feet in depth) and is the only means of transportation and communication for all the ranchers and lumber mills up in the wilds.

20.0	32.0	Little river town of **Chable**.
25.0	40.0	Pass side road (right) to **Balacán** (where Cuahtemoc, the last Aztec emperor, is believed to have been hanged by Cortez, his Spanish captor) and on down to railroad and lumber town of **Tenosique**, birth place of martyred statesman Pino Suárez (1869-1913), who was Madero's vice-president.
25.5	40.8	Come to state line again - leave Tabasco and enter Campeche. Then come to side road (left) to **Palizada**.

Anecdote: The truck driver stopped suddenly on the highway, and the car behind crashed into him. The truck driver was sued. "Why didn't you hold out your hand?" the judge asked the truck driver. "Well," said the truck driver, "if he couldn't see the truck, how in the world could he see my hand?"

38.0	60.8	Pass side road (right) to **San Elpidio**.
50.1	80.2	Up and over Río Chumpán and thru **Ejido Aguacatal**, mostly at left.
52.5	84.0	Gas station and so-so restaurant at left. **KM 198**

Definition: A Pedsestrian is a man who thought there were a couple of gallons left in the tank

59.8	95.7	Microwave tower La Libertad at right.
64.8	103.7	Cross bridge over Río Candelaria. Settlement of **Buenavista** at right.
73.0	116.8	Little **Ejido Ojo de Agua**.
77.1	123.4	Pass side road (right) to village of **Candelaria** and then gas at right.
80.5	128.8	Microwave tower San Jorge at right.
86.3	138.1	Pass side road (right) to **Nuevo Chontalpa**.
87.3	139.7	Careful for "topes". Then thru village of **Manantel**. Then more "topes".
94.0	150.4	**Ejido Pital** at left. Then lumber mill at right.
96.8	154.9	Slow for "tope" and then curve right thru sizeable village of **18 de Marzo**. More "topes".
102.8	164.5	**La Victoria** at right.

(Over, please)

186-E-2
PALENQUE JCT - ESCARCEGA

MI.	KM.	
		107.0 171.2 Ejido Kilometer 36. Then forestry experiment station at right (visitors welcome).
		112.0 179.2 Big microwave tower, **El Tormento** at left. Then onto older blacktop road and past lumber mill.
Mgas		113.0 180.8 Slow for "topes" and pass infantry outpost.
		113.8 182.1 Curve left and enter **Escarcega**, population 11,000. Mgas at left, watch 'em like a hawk, they got me. MM. Then come to junction Hwy #261.

Champoton and Merida, PROCEED AHEAD (highway number changes to #261) and start Log 261-North-1.

Chetumal and Belize, TURN RIGHT and start Log 186-East-3.

End of Log.

(Next Page, Please)

ROUTE SELECTION RS-MAYA-1

CHETUMAL & BELIZE, TURN TO PAGE 25, THEN SKIP TO PAGE 100, MI 84.0

CAMPECHE, MERIDA, CANCUN VIA THE DIRECT ROUTE, SKIP TO PAGE 27, SKIP PAGE 29 AND GO TO PAGE 31

THEN FOLLOW 180-S-7 (PAGE 35)

ISLA AGUADA, USE NEXT

JULY 1992   186-E-3
ESCARCEGA — JCT HWY #307

MEXICO TRAVELOG
Puts over 40 years of experience at your side!   Copyright © Sanborn's TGP Inc.

ESCARCEGA (JCT HWY #261) — JUNCTION HWY #307 — 154 MILES OR 246 KM — DRIVE TIME 3 — 3½ HOURS! GET AN EARLY START. SEE NOTE.

SCENIC RATING — 1

This is still the shortest way to Chetumal, but sometimes this road is so rough you'll be barking when you've finished it. Nov. — Apr. is usually the worst. In summer it usually gets patched. Go slow or you'll be looking for a "taller muelles" (spring shop) — especially RV's. If it's bad, the worst is from here to the Quintana Roo state line. Going up to Merida and down will take you 2 days of hard driving, or 3 normal days, if you want to avoid this route. Ask a Green Angel what it's like lately. Scenery is low scrub jungle and flat nothing. It's little travelled, so if you break down, you'll have a long wait. The Green Angels do patrol it, twice a day.

All along this route you'll be driving through villages whose names are preceded by an "x", which in Mayan, is pronounced "sh". For example, a village named "X-Moo" would be pronounced "schmoo" or one named "X-Nuk" would be pronounced "schnook". Thanks to Sanborn's regulars, George & Dot Young. They spend every winter on the Yucatan and suggest everybody learn a few words of Maya. They say local folks really appreciate it.

Mgas   » **NOTE: We recommend a very early start. Hwy #186 is a lonely road with few services. Please be off it well before dusk. There's MAGNA SIN here, at the junction, but watch 'em like a hawk! The next gas on this route is at X-Pujil (regular only), 93 miles. Next MAGNA is outside Chetumal and at mile 9, log 307-N-1. There's also a station at mile 160.8 that will most likely have it.**

MI.	KM.	
0.0	0.0	Having turned at junction at **Escarcega** (population 17,000), bend left a trifle and into town proper. Incidentally, Escarcega is a chicle town — for many years it was headquarters for chicle hunters (The place ought to be called "Wrigleys" instead of Escarcega.)
0.6	1.0	Pass Hotel Escarcega at right. Also pass **María Isabel Hotel & Restaurant,** not exactly like the Maria Isabel (Sheraton) in Mexico City, but there's nothing finer in Escarcega and the rates aren't quite as high as those of its counterpart in Mexico City and it's A/C, clean and comfy. VI only.
1.0	1.6	LOOK-&-LISTEN as you cross railroad — trains do run on this Merida main line. Then pass bus station at left.
1.8	2.9	Immigration check station at right — you might be waved on.
6.5	10.4	Curve left and thru village of **Matamoros** and then curve right.
15.5	24.8	Slow for "tope" and pass village of **La Libertad.** Then another "tope".
21.8	34.9	Pass settlement of El Lechugal, mostly at left.
25.1	40.2	Thru community of **Justicia Social.**
31.1	49.8	Curve wide left past village of **Lopez Mateos,** mostly at right.
32.3	51.7	Thru lumber mill village of **Centenario.** Note **Lake Nah** off to right.
33.8	54.1	Pass side road (right) to **Silvituc.**
39.5	63.2	**Ejido Santa Lucía** at right. "The secret of staying young is to live honestly, eat slowly and lie about your age." — Lucille Ball.
40.5	64.8	Slow for "tope" and thru village of **Ixbonil.** Then another "tope" at far end and straight.
42.5	68.0	Thru settlement of **Constitución** - and slow for "topes".

(Over, please)

186-E-3
ESCARCEGA — JCT HWY #307

JULY 1992

49.3	78.9	Microwave relay tower up at right. Then down on straight.	*Try to drive...*
71.8	114.9	Another microwave tower at left and down thru cuts and then a long, straight stretch.	
76.8	122.9	Over little bridge - there are very few bridges on this route and no rivers.	
87.8	140.5	Mayan ruins of CHICANNA down trail at right about a ½-mile.	*So your license...*

» CHICANNA has several structures of the late Classic Río Bec style which are pretty well preserved. One exhibits a complex facade that has been restored by the Middle American Research Institute of Tulane University. This facade was built in the "Chene" style similar to the one at Hochob (and reproduced in the national museum in Mexico City).

MI.   KM.

88.8   142.1   Now thru lumber mill settlement of Becán with ruins of BECAN over to left.

» BECAN, a good-size Mayan city, was discovered in 1934 by a Carnegie Institute expedition under the guidance of Karl Ruppert. The city was constructed around 800 A.D. and its most prominent structure is "Temple B" measuring 55 feet in height and 58 feet in length. It has excellent carved stonework and six rooms. Archaeologists rank it in importance with Uxmal's "Governor's Palace" and Palenque's "Temple of the Sun".

92.5   148.0   Trail (right) is to ruins of RIO BEC.

» RIO BEC, so named because they were once a large ceremonial center mostly around the Río Bec, is unique in that it is surrounded by a moat and contains over 20 temples, several of which are still standing including a large palatial structure. Jungle-like trails lead to all the major structures of this lost city.

Then pass side road (left) to settlement of Zoh Laguna. Gas at left (regular only) (next gas at Chetumal, 72 miles). Down into X-Pujil.

101.0	161.6	Thru La Tierra Prometida "The Promised Land".	*Expires before...*
105.5	168.8	Now curve left and up past ranger tower at right. Then right and down thru village of La Mosa, then another long, straight stretch.	
111.1	177.8	Come to state line — leave Campeche and enter Quintana Roo.	**Road should improve.**
112.5	180.0	Pass side road (right) to San Antonio.	
113.0	180.8	Slow past customs check at left. Then side road (right) to Caobas.	
123.0	196.8	Thru little town of Nicolás Bravo and ahead, still on straight stretch.	
129.0	206.4	Thru village of Francisco Villa, better known as "Pancho" Villa.	
129.8	207.7	Pass side road (right) to ruins of KOHUNLICH, 5 miles.	*You do. — MM.*

KOHUNLICH was first discovered in 1968 by looters of pre-Hispanic treasures and was rediscovered in 1970 by archaeologist Victor Segovia Pinto. This site is a huge Mayan city, possibly the largest find yet made in the Americas, with over 200 buildings uncovered thus far. Among them is a ball court, oldest among all known Mayan cities, and the "Piramide de los Mascarones" ("Pyramid of the Masks"). The eight Mayan stucco masks flanking the pyramid's central stairway are the only ones of their kind, some still having their original colors. Also uncovered was the ingenious hydraulic system for collecting and conserving rain water. Sr. Segovia has done a superb job of restoration and landscaping.

135.3	216.5	Down thru village of Nachi Cocom.
140.5	224.8	Thru village of González Ortega. 50% of men like sex better than money. Women? 26%.
150.1	240.2	Pass side road (right) to Alvaro Obregón. Thru village of Ucúm and slow for "topes".
152.5	244.0	Pass side road (right) to Juan Sarabia.
154.1	246.6	Curve right and come now to junction (left) with Hwy #307. Water plant at right.

Felipe Carrillo Puerto and Cancun, go north following Log 307-North-1 starting at mile 11.8.

Chetumal, TURN RIGHT and start Log 307-South-2 at mile 81.5.

End of log

(Next Page, Please)

MEXICO TRAVELOG
Puts over 40 years of experience at your side! Copyright © Sanborn's TGP Inc.

ESCARCEGA (JUNCTION HWY #186) TO CHAMPOTON (JUNCTION HWY #180) 51.0 MI OR 81.6 KM – DRIVE TIME 1 – 1½ HOURS

SCENIC RATING — 1

» NOTE: The highway numbering is a bit confusing thru here. Hwy #186, on which you were just traveling, curved right at the junction in Escarcega and took off to Chetumal over on the caribbean coast. And the 51 mile stretch of highway from Escarcega to Champoton only is Hwy #261; at Champoton you again pick up Hwy #180 you left in Villahermosa. Incidentally, you'll see some village names that have an X in front of them. In Maya this is pronounced "sh". For example, a village named X-Moo would be pronounced "Shmoo"; one named X-Nuk would be pronounced "Schnook".

MI.	KM.	
0.0	0.0	After junction, bend left and head north on Hwy #261. (It'll seem like you should be going south, but technically Campeche and Merida are north of here.)
0.5	0.8	Past school at left. *I never met...*
3.0	4.8	Now up and down thru several miles of rock cuts.
6.3	10.1	K-10 and bend right thru rock cut.
9.0	14.4	Thru community of **La Esperanza**. Then easy winding and thru **Villa Carranza** at right.
14.0	22.4	Thru community of **Cantemo**.
18.5	29.6	Pass side trail (right) to microwave tower. Then straight. *A flan...*
21.0	33.6	Thru **Ejido Revolución**. Then past lumber mill over to left.
23.5	37.6	Pass side road (right) to Pixoyal. Thru village of **X-Bacab**. Bend left and start straight stretch.
24.7	39.5	Pass side road (right) to railroad village of **Aquiles Serdan**, a revolutionary hero (1876-1910) and forerunner of the Mexican Revolution.
32.7	52.3	Thru stretched-out village of **José María Morelos y Pavón**, named for one of Mexico's greatest revolutionary heroes (1765-1815), the man with the terrible headaches.
37.0	59.2	Thru big **Ejido Pixtun**. Then curve left.
42.5	68.0	Thru village of **Vicente Guerrero**, also named for a revolutionary hero, general, and president (1829-1831).
47.5	76.0	Pass side road (right) to **Ulumal** and **Pustunch**.
49.5	79.2	Lienzo de Charro (rodeo arena) at left. *I didn't like. —MM*
50.0	80.0	Rice processing plant at right.
50.3	80.5	Careful for sign saying Campeche at left. Turn left and ahead toward Malecón (waterfront Blvd.). Straight ahead is to downtown **Champoton** (population 12,000).
51.0	81.6	Slow as you approach junction Hwy #180. Gulf is straight ahead. End of log.

R Campeche, TURN RIGHT onto Hwy #180 and start Log 180-south-6. Next gas just ahead; next worthwhile accommodations at Si-Ho Playa, 15 MI, and at Campeche, 39 MI.

H Isla Aguada and on to Villa hermosa via ferry on old Gulf Hwy #180, TURN LEFT and start Isla Aguada Special-North. There's a nice RV park, hotel, cabin layout at Isla Aguada.

End of Log.

(Next page, please)

☐ **MEXICO:** On the Road

Punta Vista RV Park offers new look at life

By MIKE NELSON

MIKE NELSON

I met Edgar Osuna three years ago, and this year I met Ana, his wife. They own the Punta Vista (PH: 632-4-0769), an RV park in Santa Ana, Sonora. That's on the west coast, near the junction of Hwy #2 from Sonoyta and Hwy #15, between Nogales and Hermosillo.

I didn't intend to stop. As usual, I was running late (something to do with a water pump or sleeping late). I make sure that the RV parks I write about still exist, but the Punta Vista is pretty small (12 spaces), so driving through was enough.

As I turned around, a couple came out of the little house in front. I identified myself. Edgar smiled.

"Yes, I remember you! Welcome back!" he said. "Please come in for a cup of coffee. Meet Ana."

I've never turned down a free drink. It was nice to be remembered. Most folks don't remember me from one day to the next (thank God), much less one year to the next.

Ana was from Mississippi, but doesn't claim it. She'd moved to California. She's a middle-sized woman who's comfortable with herself and kind of bubbles around. Just being near her made me feel light. As she flowed around their simple house, she apologized for not having cleaned up. Heck, I like folks like that. I don't trust people whose houses are neat.

While the coffee water brewed, Edgar filled me in on the history of the area. He is a soft-spoken man, middle-sized, too. They were like salt and pepper shakers.

Gold mining was coming back to the area. Prospectors were wandering off into the desert and the hills around and finding decent diggings. A couple of 'em stayed there.

Ana brought me coffee and told me about their meeting. She'd come to Mexico long ago with a friend.

"I always felt my destiny was in Mexico," she said. "Then, when I met Edgar, I knew it was with him."

"This will sound weird, Mike," he told me, "but I knew I'd meet Ana long before she showed up. When I actually saw her, I knew we would be married."

Fortunately for everyone, Ana's friend was a little too fond of Mexican firewater. While he stayed put, and then got very sick, Edgar helped Ana take care of him. The Lord works in strange ways, and that man's drunkenness led to those two folks' happiness.

They knew they were for each other, and had to decide where to live.

"If we lived in California, we'd spend all our time working and trying to make a living," he said. "If we lived in Mexico, we could spend more time together."

Edgar smiled. See, the Mexican is smarter than the gringo. It's better to live to love and work than to work to live and not have time to love.

They started a motel. That didn't work out too well. Edgar wasn't a builder. The unfinished rooms proved it. Next came the RV park. That worked out OK. They'd planned to have electricity, water and drainage for every unit. Edgar had promised me it would be finished soon during my last visit.

"Then our electricity went up 1,500 percent. Then the taxes went up," he said. "It seemed that all our money went somewhere else."

He wasn't bitter, just accepting.

"We like having guests," he said. "It's like a new party every night. We never know who's going to stop in. We have friends who stop every year."

Edgar speaks at least Spanish, English, French, German, Swedish, Portuguese. He likes to learn. He's a scholar without pretensions. I knew that he knew more about everything than me. He was polite enough to listen to me, but I know when I'm in the presence of genius.

"I guess we'll never be rich," Ana said.

No, Ana, probably not — not materially. Folks like you will always have one more thing go wrong or a new tax bounce up and take our savings. You'll always have great ideas and rotten carpentry or masonry skills. You're dreamers.

As I pulled out of their driveway, I saw them, arm in arm in my mirror. They were two bookends, with a library of shared experiences between them.

Old White & I headed north. I plopped Bob Dylan into my fancy cassette player to make me feel less alone. The Anas and the Edgars and the rest of us are all just doing the best we can with what we have. We try to build a material wall around us to keep us safe.

They've found each other to shore up the holes in the material world around them. They've done such a good job that the material doesn't matter anymore. Their walls will always have holes in them. Those holes let the winds of change blow through. It may blow away their plans, but it freshens their dreams.

I've stopped building. You can't build alone. I've protected myself with Big White, Bob Dylan and a career. Fame and Fortune may keep the wolf from my door, but they make me need a door. It blocks the fresh air.

We all make a choice sometime. Ana and Edgar have something that'll last forever. I have things that will rust and rot. How 'bout you?

(Mike Nelson is a travelogue writer for Sanborn's Insurance in McAllen.)

JULY 1992 1 of 1 **ISLA AGUADA SPECIAL-NORTH**
CHAMPOTON — ISLA AGUADA — VILLAHERMOSA

MEXICO TRAVELOG
Puts over 40 years of experience at your side! Copyright © Sanborn's TGP Inc.

CHAMPOTON THRU ISLA AGUADA AND ON TO VILLAHERMOSA — 191.0 MI OR 305.6 KM — DRIVE TIME 4 – 5 HOURS

SCENIC RATING — 4

» NOTE: This route is for naturalists and slowpokes. Often a 20 to 40 mile stretch of bad road, but great fun. (RV's, it'll bounce your kitchen). Bring mosquito repellant for ferry — no foolin'. The last ferry leaves at 6 PM. The best accommodations are at Isla Aguada. After that, the next sleeping place is in Villahermosa.

	MI.	KM.	
	0.0	0.0	Starting at junction Hwy #261, proceed ahead on Hwy #180 with Gulf of Campeche at right.
	2.5	4.0	Pass naval base, left.
	3.0	4.8	Thru "boom-town" of Concordia. Slow for "topes".
	18.7	29.9	Cross Chen-Kan I and II bridges.
	36.8	58.8	Cross bridge. Palm forest, right and light house, right. KM 79.
	37.5	60.0	Pass side road (left) to Sabancuy.
	46.3	74.1	Electric generator Sabancuy, left. You may see flights of brown pelicans accompanying you and an occasional iguana.
Rv	61.9	99.0	Enter Isla Aguada. CAMPECHE, STRAIGHT AHEAD. LA CABAÑA RV PARK AND HOTEL, TURN LEFT. It's a quiet place with spaces and cabins right on Bay.
	63.0	100.8	Sharp curve left and over La Unidad Bridge. This bridge is 3,422 meters long.
	66.0	105.6	Thru Puerto Real, then curve left.
Mgas	73.0	116.8	Pass balneario, right.
	85.0	136.0	Mgas at right, Faschas Motel also at right.
H	85.4	136.6	Curve right at Bay Bend Hotel. Hotel Estrella del Norte at left. KM 5.
	85.6	137.0	Thru Cd. Del Carmen to ferry landing. Pay toll according to size of vehicle. Cost of car:16,000; with trailer 30,000 pesos. Ferry across Campeche Bay. Ferry leaves at the following hours: 3:30, 6, 7, 8, 10 AM and 12, 2, 4, and 6 PM. (prices and schedule subject to change).
	87.0	139.2	Sharp left curve and thru village of Zacatel.
	89.0	142.2	Gulf of Campeche, right.
	90.0	144	Psychedelic lighthouse, right.
	92.0	147.2	Turkey in road. Slow for "topes".
	93.0	148.8	Thru settlement of Puerto Rico and more "topes", then curves.
	101.0	161.6	Several more "topes".
	102.6	164.1	More "topes" and past church.
	103.0	164.8	Misplaced body of water at left. (Lagoon?)
	104.6	167.4	Pass side road (right) to Atasta.
	105.0	168.0	"Topes", at least 2. KM 33.
	105.4	168.6	Atasta — deja vu (all over again).
	108.3	173.3	Curve right and 2 "topes".
	111.1	177.8	Thru settlement of San Antonio Cardenas, "topes", at least 4.
	114.2	182.7	Unmarked "topes".
	115.3	184.5	"Topes" and thru village of Nuevo Progreso.
	116.5	186.4	Agricultural inspection station, left. This is egret country — both snowy and caky.

(Over, please)

ISLA AGUADA SPECIAL-NORTH
CHAMPOTON — ISLA AGUADA — VILLAHERMOSA

JULY 1992

MI.	KM.	
126.5	202.4	Over San Pedro Bridge. Cross state line — leave Campeche and enter Tabasco.
137.0	219.2	Curve left at "Y". Agriculture inspection station, right.
138.7	220.8	Then thru windmills. Where is Sancho Panza?
140.0	224.0	Radio tower at right. KM 71.
140.8	225.3	School at left. At "T" TURN LEFT. Right is to **Frontera**. (There may be a hotel in Frontera, we saw a sign, but didn't check.) You're now heading due south.
141.2	225.9	An okie-dokie-piano-bar-restaurant, no-foolin' "**La Chiquita**". Mgas.
142.5	228.0	Over high rise Frontera Bridge. In the old days, we used to have to ferry across this river. Bumps at beginning and end of bridge. Then cross another very bumpy bridge. Slow down. **San Roman**, off to left.
150.0	240.0	Thru settlement of **Carrillo Puerto**.
152.5	244.0	At least 7 "topes". Village of **Madero**, off to left.
153.0	244.8	"Topes".
153.5	245.6	"Topes" Side road (right) to **Miramar**.
160.0	256.0	Pass side road (right) to **El Bellote**. Straight for you. Gas (regular only) at right.
165.9	265.4	Dangerous curve.
167.0	267.2	El Guad Bridge. KM 39.
171.0	273.6	Parador Turístico (tourist stop) "**El Espino**". Road narrows through marshlands.
175.0	280.0	Over Nuevo Gonzales Bridge.
178.1	285.0	gas at left.
180.0	288.0	Thru village of **Ocultzapotlan**. Slow for "vibradores", at least 4.
184.4	295.0	Pass side road (left) to **Jolochero**.
185.7	297.1	Pass side road (right) to **Cardenas**.
188.1	301.0	Begin four-lane divided. KM 4.
188.3	301.3	Prison, right. Generator station, left.
189.3	302.9	Over bumpy bridge. Then pass **Colonia Casa Blanca** and bus station, left.
190.2	304.3	Cross Av. Mendoza. Pass side road (right) to **Comalcalco**. Straight for you.
190.4	304.6	Framboyante Subdivision Cristal bottlers at right.
190.7	305.1	**Graham Suites Hotel**, right.
191.0	305.6	Come to junction Hwy #186.

Palenque, Escarcega etc. turn left under overpass and start Log 186-East-1.

Coatzacoalcos, Acayucan etc. turn right and start Log 180-North-4A.

End of Log.

(Next Page, Please)

MEXICO TRAVELOG
Puts over 40 years of experience at your side! Copyright © Sanborn's TGP Inc.

CHAMPOTON (JUNCTION HWY #261) — CAMPECHE AV. ESCENICA EXIT) — 38.3 MI OR 61.3 KM — DRIVE TIME 1 HOUR

SCENIC RATING — 3

» **CARSICK ALERT: You may want to take Dramamine.**

MI.	KM.	
0.0	0.0	Here at junction with Gulf Coast Hwy #180 and Bay of Campeche in front, TURN RIGHT.
0.3	0.5	Bay at left and "rastro" (slaughterhouse) at right.
0.5	0.8	**Hotel Venecia** ("Venice") at right.
0.8	1.3	Thru fishing town of **Champoton** (population, 12,000).
1.3	2.1	Past cemetery at right.
1.5	2.4	Curve right and pass social security (I.M.S.S.) hospital at right. Then bus depot at right and start divided boulevard.
2.4	3.7	Now curve left and over Champoton Bridge. Gas at right.
2.8	4.5	Curve right and out alongside gulf.
9.3	14.9	Careful for left curve and then another, this one very sharp over bridge. Then curve right and out.
10.5	16.8	Ciudad del Sol ("Sun City") subdivision at right.
12.0	19.2	Pass side road to **Edzna Ruins** (dating perhaps to the Maya Classic Period).
12.3	19.7	Pass village of **Haltunchen** over at right.
13.5	21.6	Thru **Villa Madero** and slow for "topes".
14.8	23.7	Slow for several "curvas peligrosas" (dangerous curves) and past little beachside settlement of **Acapulquito** ("Little Acapulco") at left.
16.0	25.6	More beach homes and then settlement of **Costa Blanca** ("White Coast"). Divided highway for a few miles.
16.8	26.9	Bend right and come to **Hotel Misión Si-Ho Playa** at left on beach, once an old abandoned hacienda falling to pieces, but somebody came along and did a magnificent job of fixing it up (82 a/c rooms; restaurant specializing in seafood; bar; pool; tennis; fishing and hunting; AE, CB, DI, MC, VI).
18.0	28.8	Past beachfront community of **El Pedregal** at left.
21.0	33.6	Careful now and take right fork for bypass around little town of **Seybaplaya**. Follow CAMPECHE sign and pass gas at right. Return to 2-lanes and slow for "topes".
23.0	36.8	Road from **Seybaplaya** merges at left.
29.0	30.4	SLOW for several "curvas peligrosas" (dangerous curves).
31.0	49.6	Pass side road (left) to **Playa Bonita** a public beach.
35.3	56.5	Pass side road (left) to waterfront town of **Lerma**. Straight ahead for you on short divided and start nice bypass around **Campeche**.

Uxmal, exit and start Campeche — Uxmal special.

Follow MERIDA signs.

| 38.3 | 61.3 | Slow as you come to road to **Campeche** via Av. Escenica ("Scenic Avenue") and end of log. Gas at left. |

(Over, please)

180-S-6
CHAMPOTON — CAMPECHE

JUNE 1992

Merida, straight ahead and pick up Log 180-South-7.

Campeche and to Hotels Baluartes or Ramada Inn, follow stub log below.

		STUB LOG TO CAMPECHE

MI.	KM.	
0.0	0.0	Having taken right side road at Av. Escenica exit off Hwy #180, proceed ahead.
1.0	1.6	Take left fork at this crossroads and follow PEMEX sign and wind down. Right fork is to Av. Escenica ("Scenic" Avenue).
1.5	2.4	Pemex tanks at left. TURN RIGHT on waterfront boulevard.
2.5	4.0	Come to striking magnificent "glorieta" of a man holding a torch, sort of like our own Statue of Liberty, commemorating Mexico's freedom from the rule of Spain. Now onto divided parkway and enter city of **Campeche**, population 162,000, and capital of state of Campeche. Its name is derived from the mayan words "kim" and "pech" which mean "tick of the serpent".
3.3	5.3	Come now to road fork and take left fork. Ahead to yonder "glorieta".
3.8	6.1	At "glorieta" go on around and aim for shoreline drive.
4.3	6.9	Take left fork here and continue on shoreline. (If you wish to contact the tourist department, their office is in this building in fork - but on right side.)
4.5	7.2	Note lagoon at right and fancy ultra-modern state senate building. Then highrise state capitol and farther along is another ancient fort.
4.8	7.7	Come now to Hotel Baluartes ("forts"). **Ramada Inn** (Ph: (981) 6-2233; Fax: 1-1618.) is next door. (For info on these and other accommodations in the area, see "Eat & Stray — Campeche".)
		When you're ready to return to the highway, just retrace your steps.

H

End of Log.

(Next Page, Please)

CAMPECHE

AREA CODE — 981   Copyright © Sanborn's TGP Inc.

SLEEPING AROUND

** **BALUARTES** —MOD— Good 102-room, 5-story a/c hotel on waterfront drive across from bay. Restaurant. Coffee shop. Club. Bars. Pool. Parking. No pets. AE, MC, VI. Ph: 6-3911.

*** **RAMADA INN** —MOD— Very nice 120-room, 3-story a/c hotel next door to Baluartes across from bay. Restaurant. Cafeteria. Bar. Disco. Club. Pool. Some servibars. Boutique. Playground. Parking. No pets. AE, MC, VI. Ph: 6-4611 or 6-2233 Fax: 1-1618.

LOPEZ —ECON— 39-room, 3-story downtown commercial motel on Calle 12 #189 about 4 blocks from Baluartes. Restaurant. Bar. Most rooms a/c. On-street parking. Pets OK. DI, MC, VI. Ph: 6-3344.

** **SI-HO PLAYA** —MOD— Good 70-room a/c beachside hotel 24 miles south of Campeche on Hwy #180. Restaurant. Bar. Lobby bar. Pool. Tennis. Fishing/boating arrangements. Parking. No pets. English spoken. MC, VI. Ph: (982) 6-2989. U.S. Ph: 800-633-1695

EATING CAMPECHE

303 —ECON— Restaurant-cafeteria-bar at Calle 8 #303 in front of government building. (Restaurant 303, Cafeteria Bamboo, and Bar La Escala - 3 tips in one!) International food served in relaxful atmosphere. Open for breakfast, lunch, and dinner. Closed Tuesdays.

CAMPING, PARKING & PLUGGIN' IN

CAMPECHE —ECON— 30-space park 1.5 miles off Hwy #180 in suburban Samula (follow signs). All hook-ups. Showers. Toilets.

END OF EAT AND STRAY

ROUTE SELECTION   RS-MAYA-2

CAMPECHE, MERIDA, CANCUN VIA DIRECT ROUTE, CONTINUE AHEAD, START 180-S-7 (PAGE 35)

UXMAL ARCHAEOLOGICAL SITE, MERIDA, CANCUN VIA SCENIC ROUTE, SKIP NEXT 2 PAGES, START CAMPECHE-UXMAL SPECIAL (PAGE 39)

JUNE 1992 — CAMPECHE – UMAN – MERIDA — 180-S-7

MEXICO TRAVELOG
Puts over 40 years of experience at your side! Copyright © Sanborn's TGP Inc.

CAMPECHE (AV ESCENIA EXIT) – THRU UMAN – DOWNTOWN MERIDA – 117.3 MI OR 187.7 KM – DRIVE TIME 3 HOURS

SCENIC RATING — 3

MI.	KM.	
0.0	0.0	Here on bypass with AV. ESCENIA EXIT into **Campeche** at left, proceed ahead.
3.3	5.3	Pass access road (left) to Campeche, 4 Km.
5.0	8.0	Pass another side road (left) into downtown Campeche and to Campeche's airport. Side road (right) to Uxmal and on to Merida (There's a better route to Uxmal just outside Merida). — continue ahead following MERIDA CORTO signs.
13.0	20.8	Side road (right) to **Compteon** — continue straight ahead.
15.5	24.8	Note concrete block factory at left.
16.3	26.1	State prison at right and state psychiatric hospital at left. Then thru community of **S. Francisco Kobén**.
17.5	28.0	Pig farm at left (for all that "Poc-Chuc" and "Cochinita Pibil" served in these parts).
21.0	33.6	Past rock crusher — Careful for trucks crossing highway.
32.0	51.2	Side road (left) to **Tenabo** — straight ahead for you.
34.5	55.2	Careful for traffic merging from road from Tenabo (left), and ahead past baseball stadium at left. (Baseball is quite popular throughout Yucatan, perhaps more than soccer.)
39.0	62.4	Veer right, (straight is to **Pomuch**).
41.5	66.4	Curve right at junction with road from Pomuch.
42.5	68.0	Notice ruins of old hacienda at right. Then take right fork for **Hecelchakan** bypass.
44.0	70.4	Gas station at left.
45.5	72.8	Road from Hecelchakan blends at left. Straight ahead for Merida.
47.5	76.0	Past ruins of antique church at left and deserted old henequen community of Hacienda Blanca Flor ("White Flower") at right. As henequen was formerly Yucatan's number one crop, let us tell you a little about it.

HENEQUEN, once big business in the Yucatan, has experienced a severe decline in recent decades due to nylon and other synthetic fibers. In the olden days just about all Yucatan's economy was based on henequen, and hardly a day passed without a freighter sailing from Puerto Progreso, north of Merida, with rope and twine made from the henequen plant. Each wealthy henequen grower had a magnificent hacienda with his factory workers' homes also on the home place, and his acres and acres of henequen surrounding it all. You will still see an occasional henequen field as you travel through this area.

MI.	KM.	
54.0	86.4	Side road (right) to nearby **Bacabchen**.
55.3	88.5	Take right fork and curve right for bypass around **Dzitbalche**. Coca-Cola bottling plant at right.
60.3	96.5	Side road (left) to **Calkini**.
63.0	100.8	Take right fork for Merida. (Sign says it's 80 km or about 50 miles away) Left is to village of **Tepakan**.
64.3	102.9	Take left fork for bypass around **Becal**.
65.3	104.5	Careful now! LOOK-&-LISTEN for mainline railroad crossing. Then Becal's arts-and-crafts center at left. Becal is the "Jiji" or Panama Hat capital of Yucatan.
67.0	107.2	Come now to state line – leave state of Campeche and enter state of Yucatan.
68.5	109.6	Slow past truck inspection at left. Slow for "topes" and take right fork for bypass around **Halacho**.
69.3	110.9	Note handicrafts stands thru here. Then gas at right.

(Over, please)

180-S-7
CAMPECHE – UMAN – MERIDA
JUNE 1992

MI.	KM.	
78.3	125.3	Curve left (take left fork) for bypass around **Maxcanu**.
78.5	125.6	Gas Station at right.
80.5	128.8	Over mainline railroad crossing (LOOK-&-LISTEN). Then side road (right) to Muna.
81.0	129.6	Power substation at right.
85.5	136.8	Concrete block factory at left.
86.3	138.1	Take left fork (curve left) for bypass around **Kopoma**.
94.5	151.2	Take right fork (curve right) for bypass around **Chochola**.
98.3	157.3	Note all the cattle ranches through this area was formerly aforementioned henequen fields. Come to narrow-gauge railroad, called a "tranvía", the transportation system used for hauling sisal (henequen) from the fields to the factories. Thru village of Hacienda Poxila and slow for "topes". Cross another "tranvía" and out.
		The motive power behind the **TRANVIA** is the "Mexican jeep" or burro. In the olden days the field workers cut the spike leaves off the henequen plant and loaded them onto a little rail flatcar which was pulled to the sisal factory by burro. Most "tranvías" have been pulled up, now that trucks tote what small amount of henequen is now harvested to the mills, but now and then you'll still see one in operation.
102.3	163.7	Co-op pig farm at left ("Centro Porcino Ejidal")
105.5	168.8	Now into town of **Umán** (population 25,500). Turn right and follow MERIDA signs.
106.3	170.1	Slow for "topes" and past church, and then plaza, both at left. Mayan tradition holds that souls who do not go to *Metnal* (Hell) have a weeks vacation on earth beginning Oct. 31. There are feasts and fiestas to welcome them.
107.0	171.2	Now turn right (still following MERIDA signs).
107.3	171.7	Mgas at left. Road divides.
110.7	17.1	Pemex office, left. This is the Periférico (loop).

Cancun, TURN RIGHT and begin Log 180-S-8A at mile 4.8.

Merida, proceed ahead.

Progreso, left.

111.7	178.7	Electric plant, left. Now on tree lined divided Blvd, Calle 21
112.7	180.3	Flashing light. Merida's airport over to right.
113.5	181.6	Topes. Flashing light.
113.7	181.9	Enter Merida under welcome arch. Coca Cola, left.
113.9	182.2	**Hotel Posada Maya** at left. Gas, left.
114.2	182.7	LP gas, left.
114.3	182.9	Topes. Highway Patrol, left.
114.5	183.2	**Hotel Hacienda Inn**, left.
114.7	183.5	Ford and VW agencies at right. And another gas station at left.
116.0	185.6	Look alive now! Parque del Centenario, Zoological garden at right and at far end, TURN RIGHT beyond fountain onto Calle 59 which is one-way, with University of Yucatan at left. Be careful for busses congested at corner. Mgas left. De Asis Shopping Center at right.
117.0	187.2	**Ambassador Hotel** at right and **Hotel Gobernador** at left.
117.3	187.7	Come to big church at left and plaza at right and end of this log. Left a block will take you to **Hotels Merida Misión** and **Casa de Balám**.

Progreso, north Merida hotels, Rainbow RV Park, turn left and follow map.

Chichen-Itza, Puerto Juárez (Punta Sam), Puerto Morales, Cancun, etc., continue ahead and start Log 180-S-8a. There's gas at far end of town.

(Next Page, Please)

MEXICO TRAVELOG
Puts over 40 years of experience at your side! Copyright © Sanborn's TGP Inc.

☞ » MERIDA is a fabulous city hopefully you plan to spend some time her. There are several travel agencies in the area: MERIDA TRAVEL SERVICE (in front of Hotel Casa de Balám a short block left at calle 60 #488; Ph:1-9219); VIAJES BOJORQUEZ (Calle 58 #483-Bis; Ph: 3-5127); VIAJES BARBOSO (Hotel Paseo Montejo, Paseo de Montejo #56-A; Ph: 3-9033); and RUTAS DEL MAYAB (lobby of Hotel Merida Misión, Calle 60 #491; Ph: 1-9984 or 3-9500).

End of Log.

(Over, please)

P.O Box 310
McAllen, TX 78505-0310

PH: (210) 686-3601
FAX: (210) 686-0732

SANBORN'S COMPANY BIOGRAPHY

Sanborn's Mexico Insurance traces its roots to **1948** when Dan Sanborn, an **ex-newspaperman** from **Kankakee, Ill.**, began writing a unique highway guide to Mexico for his friends. He's retired now.

In the early 1950's, he opened a roadside stand to sell citrus juice, curios, Mexico insurance and "horned toads" (lizards that shoot blood from their eyes).

With the insurance, each customer got a *"Travelog"*, **Dan's mile-by-mile highway guide of Mexico**, custom-made for the customer's itinerary (see sample of newest edition on back).

Tourists need Mexican insurance because **U.S.** and **Canadian** insurance is **not recognized in Mexico**. It's sold on a daily or inexpensive yearly group basis. Claims are settled in the U.S. We have adjusters throughout Mexico.

Today, the *"Travelog"* is **a guidebook to all Mexico** and **Central America**. It is 1,000 pages of incredibly detailed **directions, history, customs** and folksy **humor** which gets people where they're going **safely** and help them **enjoy** the historic routes they drive. Many marriages have been saved because of the diversion it offers and its factual authority which settles many disputes. It is provided, free, to customers and tailored for their personal route.

Detailed maps of most tourist towns are included, as are hotels, restaurants and RV parks. **All price ranges** are covered, unlike most guidebooks. We'll soon publish a series of "for sale" guidebooks to regions of Mexico.

It lists the names of the small towns, including many *"ejidos"*. It also explains why the *"ejido"* system was one of the cornerstones of the Revolution, what *"topes"* are (& why to avoid them) and why a stop sign is sometimes a "slow down" sign.

The *"Travelog"* is written by "Mexico" Mike Nelson, who drives 20,000 miles a year to try to keep it up to date. He'll also help individuals with route planning and info from the home office in McAllen, TX. He promotes driving in Mexico through his weekly newspaper column, publishing magazine and newspaper articles, and contributing to other guidebooks.

Sanborn's has offices at major US-Mexico border crossing, and in Guatemala. Customers can get insurance by **mail, phone** or **in person**. We also sell **Central American Insurance**. It's a "family-style" business with old-fashioned values and courtesy. Each customer is "one of the family."

Our **newsletter** is distributed free to about 800 newspapers in the US, Canada, & Europe. It contains "filler" sized info of interesting facts. Anybody can get one free by asking. Our **MEXICO CLUB** offers discounts on hotels & books. Medical air rescue & auto parts delivery are other services.

Another free service is **"TRIPSHARE"**, a ride-sharing service like a college ride-board. Simply send your name, address etc. & where & when you want to go. We'll put it in a database & mail to prospective travelers.

TRAVMED/MEDEX — $100,000.00 COVERAGE FOR $3 A DAY! — This combination provides the most attractive Travelers Medical Coverage available anywhere! TravMed takes over where your regular hospitalization & medical plan rarely go ... into a foreign country. An exclusive service for Sanborn's clients traveling Overland to Mexico & Central America.

We also publish a schedule of 12 step meetings (in English) throughout Mexico.

— END —

MEXICO TRAVELOG
Puts over 40 years of experience at your side! Copyright © Sanborn's TGP Inc.

CAMPECHE — UXMAL ARCHAEOLOGICAL "ZONE" — 111 MI OR 177.6 KM — DRIVE TIME 2½ HOURS.

SCENIC RATING — 3

MI.	KM.	
0.0	0.0	At bypass heading into downtown **Campeche** at left, proceed N.E.
3.0	4.8	Under overpass of new highway.
4.8	7.7	Past side road (right) to **China**. Straight ahead for you. Campeche to left.
4.9	7.8	Over bumpy railroad crossing.
9.6	15.4	Take right fork to Uxmal on Hwy #261.
10.0	16.0	Sharp curves.
12.6	20.2	Thru **Castamay**. Slow for "topes", 4 in all.
12.9	20.6	AA at right.
24.0	38.4	Side road (left) to **Becal** and **Tenabo**.
28.0	44.8	Thru village of **Tukinmul**, "topes".
32.0	51.2	Side road to **Cayal Edzna** ruins, after second "tope".
34.6	55.4	Papaya plantation at left.
36.0	57.6	Thru **Pueblo Nuevo**, five "topes".
42.5	68.0	Thru village of **Suctul**. "topes".
45.8	73.3	Crucero San Luis. 4 "topes".
58.0	92.8	**Hopelchén**. Begin divided, "topes", around plaza to left and straight ahead, following Merida signs.
58.9	94.2	Gas at right.
78.1	125.0	Caves at left.
79.7	127.5	"Topes" in mystery town (**Bolorchén de Rejón?**), kitty cat crossing and more "topes".
80.4	128.6	(Does that make 6 "topes"?)
80.5	128.8	No, 7!
94.5	151.2	Leaving state of Campeche and entering Yucatan. Pass thru the Arch into Yucatan.
96.0	153.6	"Topes" and side road (right) to **Xlapak** (ruins there)
99.0	158.4	Beautiful ruins at right.
103.0	164.8	**SACBE Trailer Park** owned by really nice folks. Nine spaces only. **Santa Elena**, to your right, noted for its 17th century Franciscan church. Curve left and ahead.
104.0	166.4	Santa Elena road joins highway from right.
111.0	177.6	Enter **Uxmal**, with **Hotel Villa Arqueológica** at left. Hwy #261 continues to left. **Hotel Hacienda** at right.
111.2	177.9	Restaurant Nichte-Ha at right.

» UXMAL ("Oxmal" in Mayan for "Built 3 times") was constructed during the late Classic Period (A.D. 600-900). Its most impressive building, which has 5 superimpositions, is the oval-shaped "House of the Magician" (or soothsayer) standing 93 feet high (120 steps to top). There are outstanding buildings including the 88-room "Nun's quadrangle", the 322-foot-long governor's palace, the "House of Turtles", the ball court, and the great pyramid.

(Over, please)

- » Admission is charged to enter the "zona" and there are guides available at the gate. If you do elect to use this service, be sure to set the price and hours in advance. Also on the site is a little cafeteria selling snacks and refreshments, and a gift shop with cards and guidebooks. The zone is open from 6 AM to 6 PM.
- » Nightly at the ruins is an eerie and dramatic light-&-sound show, at 7 PM in Spanish and at 9 PM in English. Its duration is about an hour and it explains much about Mayan legend and culture.

Merida, continue on Hwy #261 north and follow Log Uxmal- Merida Special.

End of Log.

(Next Page, Please)

UXMAL

AREA CODE — 983   Copyright © Sanborn's TGP Inc.

Our stars are a subjective combination of quality + price and are different than the Mexican Tourism Commission's star system. The more stars, the more it will cost. ** or *** can be a bargain. B is budget: cheap & basic — not for everyone: they may be very spartan. AE = American Express, MC = Mastercard, VI = Visa. SATV = satellite TV SMC = Sanborn's Mexico Club. RR = reader recommendation, not rated.

PRICES — please don't take these as gospel — prices change when a hotel adds services, but we give you a fighting chance to hold on to your bucks. Always look at the room first and ask for the best price. Prices are in US dollars. ECON — under $25, MOD — $25-$60, UPPER $60 & above. Restaurants are rated for quality and service. Prices are approximate, for two folks to eat dinner there. ECON — under $10, MOD — $10-$25, UPPER — $25 & above. Drinks, tips & appetizers are not included. If breakfast is the specialty, cut prices in half. For RV parks, we list approximate rates when known. ECON — under $8.00, MOD — $8-10, UPPER — $10 & above.

SLEEPING AROUND

*** **HACIENDA UXMAL** —UPPER— Colonial-style, 82 big rooms, A/C, tubs, cable-TV. Restaurant, Bar, Pool, Gift Shop, Tropical Gardens, Tickets for light-&-sound show, Parking, No pets, AE, MC, VI, Phone: (99) 24-7142; reservations: (Cancun) (98) 87-7405 & 84-3414 Fax 82-2062; (Merida) (99) 25-2122 & 25-2133 Fax (99) 25-2397.

*** **MISION INN UXMAL** —UPPER— 49-Room Hilltop hotel with commanding view of the ruins a mile away, cieling fans, Restaurant, Bar, Pool, Parking, No pets, AE, MC, VI, Phone: 23-9500 or 24-7038 & Fax.

*** **VILLA ARQUEOLOGICA** —UPPER— Spanish-colonial-style 40-room, A/C hotel accross from ruins. Small rooms, Restaurant (note: many dishes on the menus are prepared with booze), Bar, Pool Tennis, Botique, Art Exposition, Parking, No pets. AE, MC, VI, Phone: (99) 24-7053 & Fax.. (This is one of Mikey's favorites, a quiet, romantic spot, bring your sweetie.)

EATING UXMAL

RESTAURANT NICHTE-HA — MOD — (name is Mayan, not German, for type of flower) in front of Hotel Hacienda, open 1 PM to 8:30 PM. Comida Corrida, Enchiladas, Vegitarian Pizza, speak English, nice. Showers.

CANA-HA RESTAURANT — ECON — 5 spaces next door. No hook-ups.

CAMPING, PARKING & PLUGGING IN!

RANCHO UXMAL — ECON — Couple of miles before entrance of ruins, 30 spaces, maybe hook-ups and Pool. 14-room hotel.

SACBE TRAILER PARK — ECON — Located 9 Mi. south of Uxmal on west side (just past Sta. Elena) Apdo. Postal #5, Tikul, C.P. 97860 Yucatán, Mex. Managed by a nice French/Mexican couple.

END OF EAT AND STRAY

(More Goodies on other side)

42

$8.95
$11.90 (Mail Order)

SANBORN'S™ book

To order (or request review copy)
Call 1-800-222-0158
(Order blanks on reverse)

Mexico from the Driver's Seat

Tales of the Road from Baja to the Yucatán

By
"Mexico" Mike Nelson

Essential reading for automobile adventurers by an author who really knows Mexico's roads

Scrivener Pr

ISBN 1-878166-04-2

Mexico from the Driver's Seat

"You know those little gravel roads leading from the highways, headed nowhere in particular? That's where Mike Nelson turns off to bring home Mexico from the inside looking out. Nobody can lay bare the soul of a country as complex and misunderstood as Mexico, but *Mexico from the Driver's Seat* comes far closer than many books dedicated to Holiday Inn wannabes, cheap straw hats and hamburgers like back home. Take one of those books along. But read *Mexico from the Driver's Seat* before you go. It is sometimes funny, sometimes bittersweet and always a valuable perspective."

Joseph B. Frazier
Associated Press News Editor for Mexico & Central America

"Mr. 'Mexico' Mike makes all of Mexico accessible for U.S. and Canadian tourists in an easy to read, enjoyable way. His stories tell them what they have been asking about my country better than anyone I know."

Rolando Garcia
General Director for Mexican Surface Tourism for the U.S. & Canada

"Those who know the real spirit of Mexico are enchanted by it continually. Mike Nelson is more than enchanted: he is moved to experience it. Thankfully he has shared his travels with us. *Mexico from the Driver's Seat* is must reading for those who seek to experience Mexico for themselves."

Ibarro Torres
Mexico Tourist Board

Nelson

"Mexico" Mike has driven Mexico's roads for over 20 years. Unlike a "travel" writer, he tells of both known and little-known places, everyday people, and oddballs. He writes the only guide for drivers, *Sanborn's Travelog*, a weekly column for the McAllen, TX *Monitor*, the *Mexico City News*. He's written for Frommer's *Mexico On $35 A Day*, the *Dallas Morning News* and others. His factual observations have been printed in the *New York Times*, *Wall Street Journal* and others. His ramblings were chronicled in *Texas Monthly*.

Shortcuts often aren't. A pickup truck overtook us. Desperate for somebody to talk to, I motioned for it to stop.

"How far to Zacatecas?"

"Lejos, muy lejos," was the reply. (Man, it's so far you don't want to know!) The driver saw my face fall.

"But I know a shortcut" he said. "It is only three ranches to the highway."

Aha, I thought. How far can three ranches be?

JUNE 1992   1 of 1   UXMAL — MERIDA SPECIAL

MEXICO TRAVELOG
Puts over 40 years of experience at your side! Copyright © Sanborn's TGP Inc.

UXMAL — MERIDA — 2 LANE — 50.6 MI OR 80.0 KM — DRIVE TIME 1 HOUR

SCENIC RATING — 3

	MI.	KM.	
H	0.0	0.0	Pass entrance to ruins and **Villas Arqueológicas**, left. At right is **Hacienda Hotel** and **Nitche-Ha Restaurant**.
EAT	0.9	1.4	**Misión Park Inn Hotel**, left.
	2.5	4.0	Pass **Restaurant Cana**, left.
Rv	2.6	4.2	Pass **Restaurant and Trailer Park Rancho Uxmal** (so-so), left.
	3.1	5.0	Pass **Tourist Restaurant**, left.
	3.6	5.8	Experimental Agricultural campo, right.
OOPS	8.2	13.1	Dangerous curves and beautiful view. Km 155. Begin major roller coaster stretch.
	9.4	15.0	Enter town of **Muna** (population 17,000) to left, topes (at least 4).

Merida, STRAIGHT, right for plaza and Franciscan cathedral.

	11.4	18.2	Handicrafts, right.
	13.6	21.8	Village of **Choyab**, ½ mile off to right.
	21.6	34.6	Pass side trail (right) to **Abala**.
	25.6	41.0	Pass side trail (left) to **Cacao**, 2½ miles away.
	27.9	44.6	Village of **Yaxacopoil** with topes.
	33.0	52.8	Topes, twice as you pass thru handful of houses forming settlement of **Xtepen**.
	34.5	55.2	Note farms on right and left.
🏘	37.0	59.2	**Enter town of Uman** (population 25,500) 3 topes. Left to **Campeche** (the short way).
	37.8	60.5	Pass church, left. Mayan tradition holds that souls who do not go to *Metnal* (Hell) have a weeks vacation on earth beginning Oct. 31. There are feasts and fiestas to welcome them.
	38.2	61.1	Topes.
Mgas	38.6	61.8	Mgas, left. Road divides.
	42.0	67.2	Pemex office, left. This is the Periférico (loop).

Cancun, TURN RIGHT and begin Log 180-S-8A at mile 4.8.

Merida, PROCEED AHEAD.

Progreso, TURN LEFT.

	43.0	68.8	Electric plant to left. Now on tree lined divided Blvd, Calle 21.
OOPS	44.0	70.4	Flashing light. Airport to right.
	44.8	71.7	Topes, flashing light.
H	45.0	72.0	Enter **Merida** under welcome arch. Coca Cola, left.
R	45.2	72.3	Pass **Hotel Maya**, left. Reg. gas, also left.
	45.5	72.8	LP gas, left.
	45.6	73.0	Topes, Highway Patrol, left.
	45.8	73.3	Pass **Hotel Hacienda Inn**, left.
	45.9	73.4	Go Straight at light. Coca Cola, right.
	46.0	73.6	VW dealer, right. Entering automobile row.

(Over, please)

UXMAL — MERIDA SPECIAL JUNE 1992

	MI.	KM.	
	47.0	75.2	Topes.
	49.4	79.0	Parque del Centenario, Zoological gardens, left. Traffic light, then turn right onto Calle 59, with University of Yucatán at left. Be careful for busses congested at corner. Mgas left. De Asís Shopping Center at right.
	50.0	80.0	**Hotel Residencial**, left.
H	50.2	80.3	Cross Calle 72, at left is park and right is school, Escuela Nicolás Bravo.
	50.4	80.6	Cross Calle 68, There is a Cinema, right.
	50.5	80.8	**Ambassador Hotel**, right. At left, **Hotel Gobernador**.
Mgas	50.6	81.0	Mgas at left, **Hotel Reforma**, come to Calle 60. Left 1 block ahead will take you to Hotels **Merida** and **Casa Del Balam**. Come to plaza with big church at left and end of log.

☞ » **MERIDA is a fabulous city** hopefully you plan to spend some time her. There are several travel agencies in the area: MERIDA TRAVEL SERVICE (infront of Hotel Casa de Balam a short block left at calle 60 #488; Ph:1-9219); VIAJES BOJORQUEZ (Calle 58 #483-Bis; Ph: 3-5127); VIAJES BARBOSO (Hotel Paseo Momtejo, Paseo de Mantejo #56A; Ph: 3-9033); and RUTAS DEL MAYAB (loppy of Hotel Merida Misión, Calle 60 #491; Ph: 1-9984 or 3-9500).

Chichen-Itza, Puerto Juárez (Punta Sam), Puerto Morelos, Cancun, etc., continue ahead and start Log 180-S-8a. There's gas at far end of town.

Progreso, north Merida hotels, Rainbow RV Park, turn left and follow map. There's gas ahead in north part of town.

End of log.

(Next Page, Please)

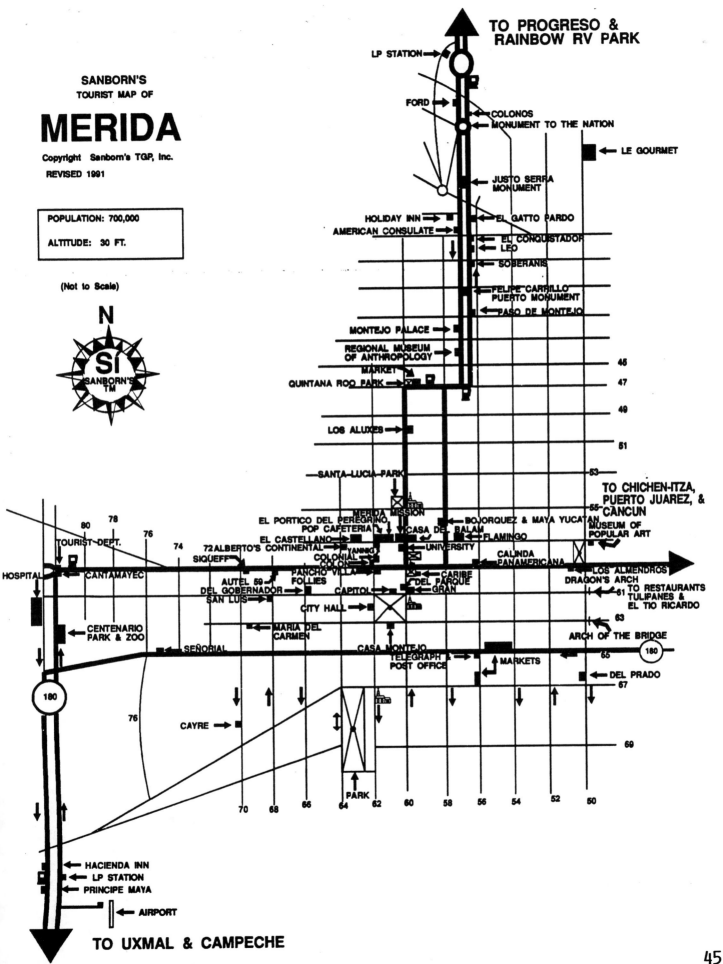

General Info
MERIDA, YUC

OCT. 1991

MERIDA (population 700,000, elevation 30 ft), also known as the "White City", is the capital of the state of Yucatan. It is located in the midst of several Archeological zones. Mayan ruins abound throughout this region. Chichen Itza, Uxmal, Kabah, Sayel, Chacmultan, Oxkintok, Dzibichaltan, Lol Tun, and Balankanche ruins are close by.

REGULAR WEEKLY EVENTS (Most begin at 9 P.M.)

Monday — Folk dances (Composer's Garden, a park behind city hall) at 9 PM.

Tuesday — Musical Remembrances; a program of popular and nostalgic music. (Santiago Park at corner of Calles 72 and 59) at 9 PM. Ballet Folkloric of the Univerisity of Yucatan — music and dance of Mayan legends at 10 AM in Theater Peon Contreras on Calle 60 at 57.

Wednesday — Orchestral performances; operettas and other works by Yucatecan authors (Santa Lucia Park). Re-encirentro con lo nuestro Indig art work, music, poetry, dance on display at 8 PM. Also watchh various crafts being made — training of young to keep crafts alive.

Thursday — Traditional Yucatecan serenade with folkloric dances (Santa Lucia Park) 9 PM on Calle 60 by 55.

Friday — Romantic night; marimba music, poetry, and stories of "old" Merida (garden of Ermita de Santa Isabel); and performances of Yucatecan music, dance, and song (university's central patio, Calles 60 & 57).

Saturady — Theater works (Composer's Plaza).

Sunday — Antiques bazzar; coins, books, furniture, ceramics, food, and drink (9 AM, Santa Lucia Park) and Children's festival; clowns, musical groups, and prizes (11 AM, Centenario Zoo).

CASA DE LAS ARTENISAS — Calle 63 #503. La Dicrecion de Disarrollo Artesanal of the State of Yucatan. M-Sat. 8 AM till 8 PM. Sales de Essado de Yucatan.

SPECIAL BUYS — Guayaberas (embroidered men's button shirt); woven hammocks ("hamacas"); and the Panama Hat, (actually made in caves near Merida).

LA CEIBA GOLF COURSE — 18-hole facility with golf carts and caddies as well as tennis courts, pool, restaurant-bar overlooking pool and course, open noon till 9 PM daily, and pro shop; located 8.5 miles north of downtown Merida on road to Progresso; phone 27-0035.

AMERICAN CONSULATE — Paseo de Montejo #453 next to Holiday Inn. Open 8:30 AM till 1 PM and 2 PM till 5:30 PM (Monday-Friday); Ph: 25-5011 or 5-5409. Emergency after hours Ph: 25-5039.

TOURIST DEPARTMENT — Calle 86 #499 Ph: 24-5726. Fax: 24-9781. Calle 60 near 57. Open 9 AM till 9 PM. Ph: 24-9290.

POST OFFICE — Located on main market at Calle 65 & 56.

AA — English. Contact Dolores Blaser, Ph: 24-0357.

End of General Info.

JUNE 1992

MERIDA

AREA CODE — 99   Copyright © Sanborn's TGP Inc.

SLEEPING AROUND MERIDA

** **AMBASSADOR** —MOD— Good 106-room, 6-story A/C motor hotel on corner at Calle 59 (& Calle 68) #546. New section very nice. Restaurant. Bar. Laundry. Pool. Servibars. TV. Travel Agency. Curio shop. Enclosed parking. AE, MC, VI. Ph: 24-2100. Fax: 24-2701 Reservations (MX) 91-800-20-011.

** **BOJORQUEZ** —MOD— 6 story, 78-room A/C downtown hotel between Calles 55 and 57 at Calle 58 #483. Restaurant. Disco. Pool. Parking nearby. AE, MC, VI. Ph: 21-1616.

*** **CALINDA PANAMERICANA** —MOD— 110-room A/C hotel on calle 59 #455. Restaurant. Bar. Shops. Pool. Parking. AE, MC, VI. Ph: 23-9111. Fax: 24-8090. Reservations in US: 1-800-228-5151.

* **CARIBE** —ECON-MOD— VALUE 56-room, 3 story downtown hotel at Calle 59 #500 on corner of Plaza Hidalgo, formerly a colonial convent. 30 rooms A/C. Patio restaurant. Restaurant. Cafeteria. Bar. Pool. Billiards. Bowling. Steam baths. Massage. Golf. Tennis. Gym. Volleyball. Video room. Child care. AE, MC, VI. Ph: 24-9022.

*** **CASA DEL BALAM** —MOD— Charming 7-story, 56-room A/C posada-type colonial-style inn built from an old mansion, opposite Hotel Merida Mision at Calle 60 #488. Restaurant. Bar. Pool. SATV. Shops. Servibar. Travel agency. Car rental. Gift shop. Laundry. Parking nearby. AE, MC, VI. Ph:24-8844 or 24-8130. Fax: 24-5011. USA PH: 1-800-624-8451. (Victor - English speaking bellboy, helpful)

** **CAYRE** —MOD— 100-room A/C hotel at calle 70 #533, 8 blocks from downtown. Restaurant. Bar. Pool. Parking. AE, MC, VI. Ph:24-8655.

* **COLON** —MOD— Worthwhile older colonial 44-room, 3-story A/C downtown hotel at Calle 62 #483. Restaurant. Bar. Pool. Travel agency. Car rental. Steam baths. Parking around corner. Ph: 23-4255 or 23-4253. Fax:24-4919.

COLONIAL —MOD— 5-story, 73-room A/C hotel on Calle 62 #476. Restaurant. Bar. Pool. Laundry. Parking. Travel agency. Car rental. Ph: 23-6444 or 24-2120. Fax: 28-3961.

** **DEL GOBERNADOR** —MOD— Nice intimate 61-room, 3-story Hotel on Calle 59 #535. Nice staff. Restaurant. Small pool. CATV Parking. Ph: 23-7133 Fax: 28-1590; USA Ph:1-800-423-1004 Fax: 407-834-3337.

* **DEL PARQUE** —ECON-MOD— 20-room A/C hotel at Calle 60 #497 between Calles 57 & 59. Parking. Travel agency. Car rental. Ph: 24-7844 or 24-7989.

DEL PRADO —MOD— Fair 32-room, 3-story hotel east of downtown area on Calle 50 between Calles 67 & 69. No restaurant. Pool. 14 rooms A/C. AE, MC, VI. Ph: 24-9433.

*** **EL CASTELLANO** —UPPER— 12-story highrise, 170-room A/C hotel on Calle 57 #513, Almost across from Alberto's Continental. Restaurant (breakfast and dinner only). Pool. Bar. Disco. Travel agency. Parking across street. MC, VI. Ph: 23-0100. Fax: 23-0110.

** **EL CONQUISTADOR** —MOD— 90-room hotel on Calle 56-A and Paseo Montejo #458. Restaurant. Bar. Pool. SATV. Parking. Tobacco shop. Boutique. Travel agency. AE, MC, VI. Ph: 26-2155, 26-2110, or 26-2610. Fax: 26-8829.

(More Goodies on other side)

EAT & STRAY
MERIDA

FLAMINGO —MOD— 3-story 38-room downtown economy hotel on Calle 57 #485, a short way from Casa del Balam. Restaurant. Pool. On-street parking. AE, MC, VI. Ph: 24-7755 or 24-7070.

GRAN HOTEL —UPPER— 50-room, 3-story A/C hotel on Calle 60 #496 in front of Cepeda Peraza Park (Hidalgo). Delightful courtyard. Colonial charm. Woodwork. Tile. Restaurant. Bar. Travel agency. Parking. Laundry. Ph: 24-7730. Fax: 24-7622.

** **HACIENDA INN** —UPPER— Colonial-style 70-room A/C motel at south end of town on Hwy #180 near airport at Calle 63 #550. Restaurant. Bar. Pool. Servibars. Parking. AE, MC, VI. Ph: 23-9133

**** **HOLIDAY INN** —UPPER— Very nice 214-room multi-story A/C motel on Colon #498 & Calle 60 just behind American Consulate. Restaurant. Bar. Pool. Servibar. Shops. Tennis. Parking. SATV. AE, MC, VI. Ph: 25-6877. Fax: 25-7755. Reservations in US: 1-800-466-4328.

*** **LOS ALUXES** —MOD— Good 109-room-and-suite A/C hotel at Calle 60 #444. Restaurant. Coffee shop. Lobby bar. Pool side bar. Pool. Travel agency. Car rental. Boutique. Parking. AE, MC, VI. Ph: 24-2199. Fax: 23-3858. (Named after magic/religious idols, protectors of the ancient Mayans.)

** **MARIA DEL CARMEN** —MOD— Modern 94-room, 6-story A/C hotel at west edge of business district at Calle 63 #550 Dining room. Pool. Servibars. Parking. AE, MC, VI. Ph: 23-9133 Fax: 23-9290. Best Western.

MAYA YUCATAN —MOD— 72-room A/C hotel on Calle 58 #483 between Calles 55 & 57. Restaurant. Bar. Disco. Pool. Parking. Travel agency. Car rental. Ph: 23-5395, 23-5215, or 23-5146. Fax: 23-4642.

*** **MERIDA MISION** —MOD— Colonial 150-room, 11-story A/C hotel a couple of blocks north of main plaza at Calle 60 #491. Nice dining room. Bar. Night club (live entertainment). Pool. Solarium. Parking across street. AE, MC, VU. Ph: 23-9500.

MONTEJO —ECON— Colonial 22-room, 2-story downtown economy hotel on Calle 57 #507 near Hotel El Castellano, converted from old mansion. 18 rooms A/C; 4 with ceiling fans. No restaurant. Parking. AE, MC, VI. Ph: 21-4590.

*** **MONTEJO PALACE** —UPPER— Modern 7-story, 90-room A/C hotel at Paseo de Montejo #483 in north part of town. Restaurant. Coffee shop. Rooftop club. Bar. Pool. Gift shop. Enclosed parking. AE, MC, VI. Ph: 24-7644 or 24-7678.

** **PASEO DE MONTEJO** —UPPER— 5-story, 92-room A/C hotel at Paseo de Montejo #482 on north side of town. Dining room. Bar. Club. Pool. Gift shop. Parking. AE, MC, VI. Ph: 23-9033 or 23-9550.

POSADA MAYA —MOD— 47-room A/C hotel on Av. Internacional #841. 14 Cottages. Restaurant. Cafeteria. Disco-bar. Travel agency. Boutique. Pool. Parking. Ph: 24-0411 or 24-0675.

* **PRINCIPE MAYA** —MOD— GOOD VALUE. 40-unit, 2-story A/C tropical decor motel on Hwy #180 southwest of town near airport. Restaurant. Bar. Small pool. Parking. AE, MC, VI. Ph: 24-0341.

* **REFORMA** —ECON— Nice 45-room (30 A/C, 15 vents) hotel on Calle 59 #508 Pizzeria. Bar. Pool. Parking across street. MC, VI. Ph: 24-7922. Fax: 24-7223.

SAN LUIS —MOD— 40-room, 2-story hotel on west edge of business district at Calles 61 and 68 #534. Some A/C rooms; others with ceiling fans. Restaurant. Pool. Parking. AE, MC, VI. Ph: 24-7629.

TRINIDAD —MOD— A/C hotel on Calle 62 #464. Parking. Can arrange for parking in Hotel Colonial parking (across street). AE, MC, VI. Ph: 21-3029 or 23-2033.

(Please turn page!)

EATING MERIDA

**** **ALBERTO'S CONTINENTAL** —MOD-UPPER— Outdoor patio-restaurant in beautiful colonial mansion at corner of Calles 64 #482 and 57. International, regional and Lebanese cuisine. "Fillet Mignon Maya Especial" specialty. Open 11 AM till 11 PM. AE, MC, VI. Ph: 21-2298.

** **ANADA MAYA GYNZA** —MOD— Vegetarian restaurant at 59 #507. Exhibits works of Mario Trejo Castro - famous local artist and environmentalist. He used genre of plastic arts, oil paintings, drawings, ceramic bas reliefs and laquerwork to exalt the beauty and culture of Yucatán. (Acknowledgements to Rodolfo Ruiz Menenoez).

AMARANTAUS —UPPER— Restaurant-video bar located on Prolongación de Montejo #250 and Calle 1-C. International menu. Nice ambiance. Live music. Open for breakfast. Open 7 AM till 3 AM. AE, MC, VI. Ph: 26-8752.

BUFALOS —MOD— Good restaurant located at Calle 27 #178. Good giant hamburgers. Large burger can feed 2. They make their own bread.

* **CANTAMAYEC** —MOD— Open air restaurant in Mayan decor in west end at Calle 59 #630 (couple of blocks from zoo. Yucatecan dishes. Open 11 AM till 11 PM. Ph: 23-2843.

CARLOS & CHARLIE —MOD— Restaurant on Prolongación de Montejo. Ph: 26-0274.

CEDRO DEL LIBANO —MOD— Tidy restaurant at Calle 59 #529. Lebanese food. Open 11:30 AM till 11:30 PM. Ph:23-7531.

CHICKEN EXPRESS —MOD— A la KFC type restaurant at Calle 62 #493. Very clean. Serve hamburgers also. Eat there or to go.

*** **COLONOS** —MOD— Very good restaurant at Calle 29 #290. Claiming to serve "the best of the best". Specialties include Yucatan dishes such as "Tacos de Cochinita" "Escabeche" (pickled fish), "Relleno Negro", Chicharra (locust), venison, papazules, etc. Open 11 AM till 4:30 PM 6 days; 11 AM till 3:30 PM Sundays. Nice playground. Mc, VI. Ph: 27-0834.

** **EL COMENDATOR** —MOD— In lobby of Hotel Del Gobernador (Calle 59 #535 (Corner of Calle 66) Nice Breakfast, liquados. Open 7:15 AM till 11 PM. Ph: 23-7133.

EL GATTO PARDO —MOD— A pizza and pasta restaurant at Calle 56-A #471 and Calle 35. Ph: 27-3244.

*** **EL PORTICO DEL PEREGRINO** —UPPER— "Simply the best", intimate "indoor" patio restaurant behind Merida Hotel at Calle 57 #501. Zazuela de Mariscos - seafood platter. Excellent regional and international cuisine. Very good service. No smoking section, but don't count on it. Open noon till 3 PM and from 6 PM till 11 PM. Ph: 28-6163. Reservations suggested.

** **EL TIO RICARDO** —MOD— Very popular restaurant at Calle 8 #207. Excellent meat including steak and "cabrito" cooked Northern Mexico style. Open noon till 10:30 PM.

EXPRESS —MOD— Popular restaurant on Corner Calle 59 & 60 #502 in front of Plaza Hidalgo. Good food. Comida. Open 7 AM till 11 PM. Ph: 21-2728.

LA BELLA EPOCA —UPPER— Good restaurant on Calle 60 #493. Turn of the century atmosphere. Yucatecan and health food menu. Ph: 28-1928.

*** **LE GOURMET** —MOD— Chic restaurant in a restored home at Pérez Ponce #109-A. Creole cuisine featuring the best domestic and imported products as well as international food served in several intimate dining rooms. AE, MC, VI. Ph: 27-1970.

* **LEO** —ECON— Grilled beef and cheese ("carne y queso al carbón") restaurant on north end on Paseo de Montejo #458-A. Open-air sidewalk service. Also mini LEO at Calle 58 #496. Open 12:30 PM till 1 AM. Closed wed. Ph: 27-6514.

(More Goodies on other side)

EAT & STRAY
MERIDA

*** **LOS ALMENDROS** —MOD— Exclusively regional restaurant on Calle 50-A #493 at Mejorada Park. Has pictures of dishes to help educate and piano player who plays "As Time Goes By. Specializes in regional Poc-chuc (pork), handmade tortillas, and wild games (including Soc-kol de Jabal). Open all day. Others in Ticul and Cancún. Open 11 AM till 11 PM. Ph: 21-2851.

** **PANCHO'S** —MOD— Good restaurant-bar, club and disco on Calle 69 #509 between Calles 60 & 62 with lots of antiques and nick-knacks. Parking. Good shish-kebab, seafood, steaks and flaming Spanish coffee. Dine in garden patio from 6 PM till 2 AM. Disco open from 6:30 PM in outdoor garden lounge. Ph: 23-0942

POP CAFETERIA —MOD— Restaurant at Calle 57 #50. Yucatecan and international cuisine. American breakfast and lunch. Open 7 AM till Midnight. Ph: 28-6163

* **SIQUEFF** —MOD— Patio restaurant at Calle 59 #553. Specialties include Yucatecan, International, and Lebanese dishes as well as "lima" (lime) soup and lobster and venison in season. Open 7:30 AM till 7 PM. Ph: 24-7465 or 24-9287. More than 50 years of service.

* **SOBERANIS** —MOD— Famous restaurant with 4 locations (Paseo de Montejo #468; Calle 60 #483; Calle 60 #503 and Calle 1-A; Calle 72 #400). Seafood specialties and excellent oyster cocktails. Open 10 AM till 9:45 PM. Ph:21-1971.

TIKAI —MOD— Arabic restaurant at Hotel Flamingo. White table cloth.

** **TULIPANES** —MOD— Unique restaurant with natural scenery at Calle 42 #462-A. Good regional and international cuisine. Famous for its 8:30 PM show, a ritual of Mayan offerings plus a dance dedicated to the sun and a Mestizo "vaquería" dance. Live music. Disco-show restaurant "Las Guitarras" (The Guitars) upstairs with typical Mexican atmosphere. Open for lunch and dinner. AE, MC, VI. Ph: 27-2009 or 27-0967.

YANNIG —MOD— Elegant French restaurant at Av. Pérez Ponce #105. Excellent. Open for dinner only, M-T, F 5 PM till 11:30 PM. TH, S, Sun 1 PM till 10:30 PM. Close Wed. Ph: 27-0339 or 21-8468.

YULIANGS —MOD-UPPER— 2-story oriental style building located at Prolongación de Montejo #453. Typical Chinese decor. Very popular. Good food. Open noon till midnight. Ph: 27-4176.

CAMPING, PARKING & PLUGGING IN!

RAINBOW — 100-space park north of town on Hwy #261 to Progreso (just beyond huge Cordemex plant). All hookups. Showers. Toilets. Small pool. Rec. hall. Laundry. Pets OK. (Watch for very bumpy crossing.) Ph: 23-2643.

OASIS RV CAMPGROUNDS — 50 spaces (30 E) and pool. (Folks, this opened in Oct. 1992; they offer a discount to Sanborn's Mexican Club members.) KM 10

OTHER

LAVANDERIAS AUTOMATICAS DE MERIDA — Laundramat at Calle 59 # 580-B (between Calles 72 & 74). Ph: 25-0631.

AUTO REPUESTOS — Auto Parts place at Calle 59 #560 (Corner of Calle 70) Open 8 AM till 6:30 PM; 8 AM till 2 PM Sat. Ph:23-1155 Fax: 23-1128.

GUAYAVERAS JACK — A good place to buy guayaveras at Calle 59 #507-A. Ph: 21-1344.

"SIN NOMBRE" — Public Fax and long distande on corner of 59 & 64. Open Mon-Sat, 8 AM till 8 PM; Sun, 9 Am till 1 PM.

END OF EAT & STRAY

(Please turn page!)

JUNE 1992   1 of 1   **MERIDA — UXMAL SPECIAL**

MEXICO TRAVELOG
Puts over 40 years of experience at your side! Copyright © Sanborn's TGP Inc.

MERIDA (CALLES 50 & 60) — MUNA — UXMAL ARCHAEOLOGICAL "ZONA" 48.5 MI OR 77.6 KM — DRIVE TIME 1 HOUR

SCENIC RATING — 3

» It's a breeze to reach the Uxmal archaeological "zona", approximately 49 miles from down town Merida, so don't hesitate to run over, and take a look-see at these famous ruins.

» Here are a few Mayan words: Bish Acabo = Como se llama, Malokim = Morning, Malo Yesamonta = Afternoon, Mala Ahbee (or something like that) = night.

MI.	KM.	
0.0	0.0	Here in middle of downtown **Merida** at corner of calles 59 and 60 with church at left and plaza at right, proceed ahead (eastward) on one-way Calle 59 for a block up to calle 58. At calle 58, turn right and ahead for 3 blocks up to Calle 65. Careful, as there's usually a lot of traffic as well as pedestrians.
0.5	0.8	Now turn right onto Calle 65 and ahead all the way.
1.5	2.4	Zoological garden at right. Then come to stoplight and turn left onto busy, divided Itzaes Blvd.
2.3	3.7	Gas, right. Ford and VW agencies, left, Coca-Cola, left too.
3.0	4.8	Sign says MEXICO, UMAN, & AEROPUERTO (airport) straight ahead. **Hacienda Inn**, right.
3.3	5.3	Federal Highway Patrol station, right. Then LP gas, right.
3.5	5.6	Gas, right. Pass **Hotel Principe Maya**, right.
4.0	6.4	Slow for "topes" and pass big cement plant "Maya", right.
4.5	7.2	Pass entrance (left) to Merida airport. Ahead for you.
6.0	9.6	"Periférico" (loop), left to **Cancun/Progreso**.
6.3	10.1	Mgas, right. Mayan tradition holds that the souls who do not go to *Metnal* (Hell), have a weeks vacation beginning Oct. 31. There are feasts and fiestas to welcome them.
9.0	14.4	Mosaic plant, right.
10.0	16.0	Enter town of **Uman** (and follow CAMPECHE VIA RUINAS sign) Gas at left. Turn right, slow for "topes", and ahead on one way street.
10.5	16.8	Slow for bad left curve and for "topes". Plaza, left and city hall, right.
11.0	17.6	Careful and follow "261/UXMAL VIA RUINAS" sign (261 is the Hwy number).
11.5	18.4	Thru Umán and come to stop sign and turn left (still following CAMPECHE VIA RUINAS and CHETUMAL signs). At end of block is another stop sign. TURN RIGHT here, follow VIA RUINAS signs, and take leave of Umán.
13.5	21.6	Note farms on right and left.
15.0	24.0	Thru handful of houses forming settlement of **Xtepen** and curve left and out.
20.5	32.8	Village of **Yaxcopoil**, mostly at right. Slow for "topes".
23.5	37.6	Pass side trail (right) to **Cacao**. 2½ miles away.
27.5	44.0	Pass side trail (left) to **Abala**.
35.5	56.8	Village of **Choyab**, ½ mile off to left.
38.0	60.8	Enter town of **Muna**. Church, left and slow for "topes", school at right, and more "topes". Another church at left al lat 17th century Franciscan church, once part of a convent. Straight ahead (follow CAMPECHE signs) at junction (left) Hwy #184 to Carrillo Puerto and (right) to **Opichen**.

(Over, please)

MERIDA - UXMAL SPECIAL　　　　　　　　JUNE 1992

	MI.	KM.	
⛽	38.8	62.1	Gas, right.
	39.0	62.4	Sign says that **Campeche** is 190 Km. or 119 Mi. away.
🍽	39.3	62.9	Curve left then right and out. Then roller coaster stretch followed by straight.
	45.0	72.0	Experimental agricultural campo, left.
H	46.0	73.6	Pass **Restaurant Rancho Uxmal**, right (a so-so RV park, a better one ahead) and curve left.
	47.5	76.0	**Hotel Misión Inn Uxmal** at right on hill, with beautiful view of ruins just ahead.
	48.5	77.6	Pass entrance (left) to **Hotel Hacienda Uxmal** and **Restaurant Niche-Ha** (English spoken). Then come to fork. Take right fork.

Campeche, **TURN LEFT.**

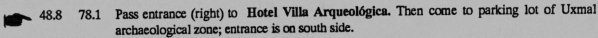

☞　48.8　78.1　Pass entrance (right) to **Hotel Villa Arqueológica**. Then come to parking lot of Uxmal archaeological zone; entrance is on south side.

» **UXMAL** ("Oxmal" in Mayan for "Built 3 times") was constructed during the late Classic Period (A.D. 600-900). Its most impressive building, which has 5 superimpositions, is the oval-shaped "House of the Magician" (or soothsayer) standing 93 feet high (120 steps to top). There are outstanding buildings including the 88-room "Nun's quadrangle", the 322-foot-long governor's palace, the "House of Turtles", the ball court, and the great pyramid.

» Admission is charged to enter the "zona" and there are guides available at the gate. If you do elect to use this service, be sure to set the price and hours in advance. Also on the site is a little cafeteria selling snacks and refreshments, and a gift shop selling cards and guidebooks. The zone is open from 6 AM to 6 PM.

» Nightly at the ruins is an eerie and dramatic light-&-sound show, at 7 PM in Spanish ans at 9 PM in English. Its duration is about an hour and it explains much about Mayan legend and culture.

RETURN ROUTE TO MERIDA TURN TO PAGE 43.

End of Log.

(Next Page, Please)

MAY 1990   PROGRESO SPECIAL

MEXICO TRAVELOG
Puts over 40 years of experience at your side!   Copyright © Sanborn's TGP Inc.

MERIDA (MAIN CORNER CALLES 59 & 60) TO PROGRESO (GULF SHORELINE DRIVE) — 23.5 MI OR 37.6 KM — DRIVE TIME ½ HOUR

	MI.	KM.	
H	0.0	0.0	Starting in Merida at main corner of Calles 59 and 60, head up Calle 60. Pass church at right, **Del Parque Hotel** and University at left, tall **Hotel Merida**, left and **Hotel Casa del Balam** on Corner at right. Then past small church on next corner at right and famous Park of Santa Lucía at left. Watch for lights ahead.
	0.3	0.5	Pass **Hotel Los Aluxes** at right, near corner of Calles 49 and 60. Come to Calle 49 and move to right lane.
	0.5	0.8	Then TURN RIGHT at next corner at San Gabriel Pharmacy with Pepsi sign on top (at left) and onto Calle 47. Then two blocks ahead (past couple of gas stations; better one a mile ahead). Then TURN LEFT at Banco del Sureste onto nice wide divided Paseo Montejo.
H	1.0	1.6	Worthwhile museum (Instituto Yucateco de Antropología e Historia) at left in huge 2-story mansion of late General Canton; open weekdays from 8 AM till 2 PM, and Sundays from 9 AM till 1 PM; (admission charged). Then pass **Hotel Paseo de Montejo** on corner at right. **Montejo Palacio**, left. Then past monument to Felipe Carrillo Puerto. **Hotel El Conquistador del Paseo de Montejo** at Calle 35.
	1.3	2.8	U.S. Consulate (green building), left and **Holiday Inn** just beyond. Then Monument to Justo Sierra (1848-1912), Mexico's most famous philosopher, historian, essayist, sociologist and Secretary of Education.
	1.8	2.9	Come to magnificent semi-circular Monument to the Nation, with history of Mexico engraved on its stones. Go halfway around and ahead, past Ford garage at left and then over standard- and-narrow-gauge railroad. Then gas at right.
	2.5	4.0	Go halfway around fountain circle and continue on Paseo Montejo.
	2.8	4.5	Slow for topes. San Francisco de Asís Supermarket with underground parking at right and then Blanco, another supermarket and discount store at right in next block.
	3.5	5.6	Bend left and past pretty modern country club on right.
	4.5	7.2	Bend right and alongside railroad. Divided highway ends and pass huge Cordemex plant at left on other side of track, a most interesting place —stop by if you like; tours are conducted Monday- Friday, 8 AM - 1 PM. This is where the tough "sisal" fibers from the henequen plant are taken where they are woven into beautiful indoor-outdoor carpets.
Rv	5.8	9.3	**Rainbow RV Park** over to left across very bumpy railroad tracks. Then pass Periférico (right) around Merida.

Progreso, straight ahead.

Valladolid, Cancun, etc, right.

	6.0	9.6	Now start four-lane highway.
	9.1	14.6	Pass side road to La Ceiba golf course - tourists welcome.
	10.3	16.5	Come now to side road (right) to DZIBILCHALTUN Mayan archaeological ruins, 4 miles. Go over and have a quick look-see if you wish (admission charged).

» **DZIBILCHALTUN means "writing on the great flat stones". This ancient Mayan center (2000-1500 B.C.) is the largest of its kind covering near 31 square miles. It is famous for its "Temple of the Seven Dolls" which is the only Mayan structure with windows.**

(Over, please)

PROGRESO SPECIAL MAY 1990

MI.	KM.	
10.8	17.3	Nice four-lane highway comes to an end.
11.3	18.1	Planta de Cal (lime plant), left
14.3	22.9	Now come to port and resort town of Progreso and slow for "topes" at water tower. Into town on divided past gas station at right. Then stop street and go halfway 'round plaza and proceed ahead on divided. Pass light house at left and then railroad. Municipal market over at left.
23.5	37.6	Come to Gulf of Mexico and to monument to Juan Miguel Castro (1871-1930), founder of city of Progreso. End of Log.

» Progreso is a resort town where Merida folks come to enjoy their vacations, although it gets pretty hot in July and August. And there are several hotels and restaurants on the ocean front drive. An absolute "must" while you're in the vicinity is the mile-long pier and ocean-going freighters tied up at the far end - it's quite an engineering feat and there's plenty of room at the end of the pier for turning around.

» Hopefully, you had fun here in Progreso. Just reverse this log to return to Merida.

End of Log.

(Next Page, Please)

JUNE 1992   180-S-8A TOLL
MERIDA – CHICHEN-ITZA – VALLADOLID

MEXICO TRAVELOG
Puts over 40 years of experience at your side! Copyright © Sanborn's TGP Inc.

MERIDA (MAIN CORNER CALLES 59 & 60) – CHICHEN-ITZA – VALLADOLID – MOSTLY DIVIDED, SOME TOLL – 102.7 MI. OR 164.3 KM.

SCENIC RATING — 3

» NOTE: This log will take you from downtown Merida to the famous Mayan archaeological ruins at Chichen-Itza where there are several good hotels. Likewise, if your going to Puerto Juarez (and taking a ferry to Isla Mujeres) or to Puerto Morales or Playa del Carmen (and taking a ferry to Cozumel), use this log. There's gas at edge of Merida.

MI.	KM.	
0.0	0.0	Here in middle of downtown **Merida**. proceed ahead (eastward) on one-way Calle 59. Pass "Palacio del Poder Legislativo" (state house), left.
0.2	0.3	San Francisco de Asís Store, right. Banamex, left.
0.3	0.5	**Calinda Panamericana of Merida**, left.
0.5	0.8	Come to little plaza, left and STOP for stop sign (cross traffic has right of way). Then continue straight ahead past church, left.
1.5	2.4	School, right. and over couple of "topes". Then come to a stoplight and ahead.
2.0	3.2	Over bumpy railroad crossing (LOOK-&-LISTEN). Then straight out on divided. Topes.
2.3	3.7	School, left.
2.7	4.3	Topes.
3.1	5.0	Topes.
3.7	5.9	Careful now as you come to junction with Periférico. Follow CANCUN sign and TURN RIGHT.
3.8	6.1	Topes.
4.5	7.2	Over "topes" and come to ALTO (stop) sign at junction (often a cop here, so stop.)

Cancun (Hwy #180). TURN LEFT here and follow CANCUN-VALLADOLID sign.

		Straight is to Chetumal and Campeche on 184. Right is back to Merida.
4.8	7.6	Take right fork (follow CANCUN sign). Straight is to village of **San Pedro**.
6.0	9.6	**Oasis RV Campgrounds** with 50 spaces (30 E) and pool. (Folks, this opened in Oct. 1992; they offer a discount to Sanborn's Mexican Club members.) KM 10
7.3	11.6	Bend right past bypass around village of **Teya**.
13.5	21.6	Veer left. Right fork to **Tepic**. KM 20
15.0	24.0	Take left fork. Right goes to **San Bernardino**.
21.0	38.4	Curve left around **Holactun**.
26.0	41.6	Curve left around **Tahmek** (gas in town). KM 40
29.5	47.2	Straight and bypass little town of **Hoctun**. Hospital, left.
32.5	52.0	Take left fork to bypass **Xocehel**.
41.0	65.6	Cancun free road, right. Cancun toll road left.

Chichen-Itza Stub Log (180-S-8-Stub) will take you to Chichen-Itza with lots of topes. Otherwise take toll road to Mi. 72 and exit unless more is finished when you arrive.

| 43.0 | 68.8 | Pass **Kantunil** exit, right. We veer left. KM 68 |

(Over, please)

180-S-8A TOLL
MERIDA – CHICHEN-ITZA – VALLADOLID

JUNE 1992

MI.	KM.	
72.0	115.2	**Chichen-Itza and Piste** to right. To Cancun and Valladolid, left lane and go straight. Pay toll at KM 115. Scenic value is enhanced by highly colored painted rocks. Mexican NPA project?
82.0	131.2	Iguana Xing
96.0	153.6	Tourist stop, left, with restaurant, shops, rest rooms. KM 153
97.5	156.0	End of toll road for now. If it is finished when you get here, keep going to Cancun. Veer right to Valladolid
100.4	160.6	Electric generating station, right
100.5	160.8	Stop sign, topes.
100.6	161.0	Now enter old Spanish town of **Valladolid**, founded in 1543 and state's second largest city. Down 1-way divided into town. Topes. Plaza, left.
101.3	162.1	Topes. Colegio Hispano Mexicano, left.
101.4	162.2	Light. Nice Hotel San Clemente, right. Plaza and Cathedral (founded in 1552), left. Two hotels are down street to left on plaza: **María de la Luz** (28 air-con rooms; restaurant; pool; MC, VI; phone 6-2071) and **El Mesón del Marqués**, an 18th-century colonial hacienda converted to a hotel (air-con rooms; MC, VI; phone 6-2073).

Cancun, TURN LEFT. Follow Pto. Juárez sign at light.

| 101.5 | 162.4 | Pass light and head out of town. |

Good Restaurant Casa de los Arcos, Turn left after four blocks, go one block to one way, and turn left again.

| 101.7 | 162.7 | Presently you'll come to sign up at left to a "cenote" (sacred well), a worthwhile attraction. Turn left (a block before second park) and go a couple of blocks. and there it will be a big block-square walled in park called "CENOTE ZACI" ("zaci" - white hawk in English). |

» At Chichen-Itza the Mayans used to toss virgins and jewelry into their "cenote" (a terrible waste of both virgins and jewelry). The Carnegie Institute people, who originally worked the ruins, dredged up all kinds of skeletons and carved jade and gold medallions and bells, etc. Its almost-perpendicular stairway zig-zags 150 feet into the "cenote's" limestone depths where a large pool disappears beneath the overhanging rock. There's a restaurant on the grounds with a luncheon special plus a variety of sandwiches. Admission es charged to enter the park. Incidentally, Valladolid is famed throughout the Yucatan Peninsula for its "longaniza" sausage don't hesitate to stop and buy some.

102.2	163.5	After side street to "cenote" proceed ahead on Hwy #180 past plaza and church, left. Then little **Hotel María Mercedes**, right.
102.6	164.2	Slow for two topes as you pass the 33rd Infantry Battalion, right.
102.7	164.3	Stop sign. Cross Avenida Heroes del 4 de Junio.

Cancun, Straight ahead. Begin Log 180-S-8B.

End of Log.

(Next Page, Please)

JUNE 1992

EAT & STRAY
CHICHEN-ITZA

CHICHEN-ITZA

AREA CODE — 99   Copyright © Sanborn's TGP Inc.

Our stars are a subjective combination of quality + price and are different than the Mexican Tourism Commission's star system. The more stars, the more it will cost. ** or *** can be a bargain. B is budget: cheap & basic — not for everyone: they may be very spartan. AE = American Express, MC = Mastercard, VI = Visa. SATV = satellite TV SMC = Sanborn's Mexico Club. RR = reader recommendation, not rated.

PRICES — please don't take these as gospel — prices change when a hotel adds services, but we give you a fighting chance to hold on to your bucks. Always look at the room first and ask for the best price. Prices are in US dollars. ECON — under $25, MOD — $25-$60, UPPER $60 & above. Restaurants are rated for quality and service. Prices are approximate, for two folks to eat dinner there. ECON — under $10, MOD — $10-$25, UPPER — $25 & above. Drinks, tips & appetizers are not included. If breakfast is the specialty, cut prices in half. For RV parks, we list approximate rates when known. ECON — under $8.00, MOD — $8-10, UPPER — $10 & above.

CHICHEN-ITZA is one of the archaeological wonders of the world, covering 7 square miles. If you really want to do a thorough job of inspecting these great ruins, it'll take you a couple of days, but you can give 'em a quick once-over-lightly in a few hours. It's best to hire yourself a licensed guide, and also to obtain one of the official guide books fo sale at the shops in the various hotels and at the ruins' "Box office". Incidentally, Chichen-Itza means "Brim of the Well" in Mayan.

We hope you have a most enjoyable time poking around these tremendously interesting relics of the great Mayan civilization.

SLEEPING AROUND

DOLORES ALBA — ECON — 12-Room hotel 1.5 miles south of Chichen-Itza on Hwy #180. Some A/C; rest with ceiling fans. Small dining room. Pool, Parking. No pets. No credit cards. Ph: (99) 21-3745

** **HACIENDA CHICHEN** — UPPER — Nice 18-unit guest house converted from a 17th-century hacienda built by the Spaniards and said to be the oldest house in Yucatán. Dining room. Bar. Pool. Gift shops. Parking. No pets. AE, DI, MC, VI.

*** **MAYALAND** — UPPER — Very good 4-storey, 38-room inn plus 22 oval-shaped thatched bungalows in nice tropical gardens. No A/C; ceiling fans only. Pleasant dining room. Bar. Pool. Gift shops. Parking. No pets. AE, DI, MC, VI. Phone: (98) 56-2777. Reservations: (Cancun) (98) 84-3414 & 84-7405 Fax 84-2062; (Merida) (99) 25-2122 & 25-2133 Fax (99) 25-2397.

** **MISION CHICHEN-ITZA** — UPPER — (In Piste) Good 42-room 2-storey air-con colonial-style hotel 1 mile from archaeological zone (in Piste). Dining room. Bar. Pool. Botique. Children's zoo. Parking. No pets. AE, MC, VI. Phone: 23-9500.

PIRAMIDES INN — MOD — (On Hwy #180 in Piste) 45-unit, 2-storey motel type air-con inn. Restaurant, Bar. Pool. Tennis. 47-unit RV facility across highway. All hook-ups. Showers, Toilets, No pets. MC, VI. Genuine mini-pyramid just behind inn. Aptdo. Postal # 407 Merida, Yuc. 97000 Phone: 24-8844.

(More Goodies on other side)

57

EAT & STRAY
CHICHEN-ITZA

*** **VILLA ARQUEOLÓOGICA CHICHEN-ITZA** — UPPER — (East access road) Good 40-room air-con hotel just north of Hacienda Chichen. Restaurant. Bar. Pool. Tennis. Library (with many archaeological books in English, French and Spanish). Parking. No pets. No credit cards. PH: (5) 203-3833 or (98) 56-2513.

EATING CHICHEN-ITZA

TEXANO'S RESTAURANT on Hwy 180_S_8b Mile 18.25 in Vega de Alatorre. Good food, great treatment. Luckenbach replica almost. (Thanks to John and Dorothy Hammond, McAllen TX)

END OF EAT AND STRAY

(Please turn page!)

JUNE 1992　　　　　　　　1 of 1　　　　　　　　**180-S-8A LIBRE**
　　　　　　　　　　　　　　　　　　　　　CHICHEN-ITZA – VALLADOLID

MEXICO TRAVELOG
Puts over 40 years of experience at your side! Copyright © Sanborn's TGP Inc.

STUB LOG FROM MERIDA-CANCUN TOLL ROAD TO CHICHEN-ITZA AND ON TO VALLADOLID ON FREE ROAD

SCENIC RATING 3

» NOTE: This log begins at mile 41.0 of the Log 180-S-8A. Use this log if you wish to visit Chichen-Itza's famous Mayan archaeological zone where there are several good hotels. Continue this log to visit BALANKANCHE CAVES (guides available). 25 miles farther there's a an interesting "cenote" or sacred well (and fair accommodations) at Valladolid.

MI.	KM.	
0.0	0.0	Take Cancun Libre (free) road, right. Left is Cancun Toll Road.
1.8	2.9	Thru village of **Kantunil** and careful for "topes". At plaza pass side road (left) to **Izamal** (meaning "City of the Hills" according to books of Chilam Balam), 15 miles away, an ancient Itzas town of 15,000... Its archaeological zone is of interest, particularly the temple standing on Kinich Kakmo, a huge pyramid with the highest staircase of any Mayan structure. Also on site is a 1549 Franciscan convent. Four lanes end.
8.3	13.3	Straight thru village of **Holca** and again slow for "topes"
10.4	16.6	Thru village of **Libre Union** with its "topes"
21.4	34.2	Into village of **Yokdzonot** (just sneeze it!). Topes.
22.4	35.8	Now enter **Piste**. gas at left. Pass side road (left) to **Dzitas**. **Restaurant Fiesta** at left.
23.4	37.4	**Hotel Misión Chichen-Itza** at left. Then **Pirámide Inn** at right (it's called "Pirámide" Inn because of a little ancient pyramid on its grounds just behind motel. RV Park at left. (For info on these accommodations in area, see "Eat and Stray — Chichen-Itza".)
23.9	38.2	Slow now and come to fork. Left is Valladolid and Cancun and straight ahead is to Chichen-Itza archaeological zone. (For ecological reasons, the road that once went thru the archaeological zone now ends at the ruin's entrance.)
		After visiting the ruins you can continue 25 miles down the "Libre" (free) road to Valladolid where there's an interesting "cenote" or sacred well (as well as gas and fair accommodations. Also down this road at mile 27.7 is a turnoff to BALANKANCHE CAVES (guides available). OR go back to toll road to get to Valladolid and onto Cancun. Rejoin the Log 180-S-8A at mile 72.0.
25.9	41.44	Pass side road to **Hotels Mayaland, Hacienda Chichen,** and **Villa Arqueológica**.
26.7	42.72	**Hotel Dolores Alba** at left.
27.7	44.3	Side road (left) over to GRUTAS ("caves") DE BALANKANCHE.

» GRUTAS DE BALANKANCHE are really somethin'. In addition to being quite interesting, there's a pool with blind fish and shrimp at the cave's end. Part of this cave was discovered as late as 1959 by a tourist guide. Guided tours are scheduled at 8-9-10-11 in the morning and 2-3-4 in the afternoon (admission charged; no kids under 6).

28.2	45.1	Cemetery at left and curve left. Then slow for "topes" and thru village of **Xcalacoop**.
35.5	56.8	Thru village of **Kaua** and more "topes". Farther on, pass microwave station at left.
43.5	69.6	Past village of **Cuncunul** mostly at right.
46.5	74.4	Straight thru village of **Ebtun**, mostly at left with its prison at right.
48.0	76.8	Side road (right) to **"Cenote Dzitnup"**, 2.5 miles away (admission charged).
49.0	78.4	Over narrow-gauge railroad that runs all thru these parts.
49.8	79.7	Now enter old Spanish town of **Valladolid**. Rejoin Log 180_S_8a at mile 101.4.

End of log.
　　　　　　　　　　　　　　　　　　　　　　　　(Next Page, Please)

☐ **MEXICO:** On The Road

Saying and doing the 'right' thing

MIKE NELSON

Sometimes saying the right thing comes naturally. Sometimes doing the right thing is hard. All three of my fans taught me that this week.

Sometimes, we all lose track of what got us where we are.

Jim, a retired U.S. Customs officer visited me at work. He told me about how peoples' attitudes would change when he used the right words. He also told me how the right words had one time saved his life.

He'd driven to Mexico with a buddy in the 1930s and began a love affair that is still going on. He fell in love with Mexico and his Mexican wife.

Outside of Pachuca, Hidalgo, they had a flat. He left to hitchhike into town for help. A fancy touring car stopped on the deserted night highway, occupied by rough-looking men with pistols, probably bodyguards. He got in and was sandwiched between two big guys in the back. Onward the car lurched through the night.

What do you like best about Mexico, *gringo?* they demanded.

La gente (the people), *amigos, la gente.*

They laughed, slapped him on the back and got him to a gas station. When you're young things like that are an adventure.

Yes, it's the people who are important, whether in Mexico or right here. It's the people who make us return, to a country or a newspaper column.

Writers are odd ducks. I first wrote this column for the ego-jolt. Then came the money. Now it's love — to show folks how to appreciate a Mexico that not all of us are able to know.

Once, while Jim was on duty at the bridge, a new Mercedes drove up with four well-dressed Mexican businessmen. Their passports seemed in order, but his job was to make sure. He told one he'd have to be inspected.

Why me?

Your passport says you're from Ticul, Yucatan. What is your town famous for?

Poc chuc, the bewildered Mexican-Mayan answered.

Jim smiled and said in Mayan, Yes and it is very good. You may pass.

Jim managed to do his job and spread good will at the same time. So may we all. *Poc chuc*, by the way, is a pork dish, cooked in banana leaves. Many Mayan towns are famous for special dishes.

U.S. and Mexican Customs officers are people — and law enforcement officers. Their job is to protect their borders. They often get a bad rap from those of us who have been inconvenienced.

Sooner or later, everyone will be searched. Considering all the different types of people the officers put up with, you wonder how they keep such a good attitude.

An officer told me once that he didn't want his men to win awards for joviality, but they darn sure had better be polite and professional. Most of 'em are. Help 'em do their job by being polite, too. Sometimes the bad guys look like the good guys. Let 'em do their job and thank 'em for protecting us.

Another fan accosted me in church. Yes, there are churches that will even admit me, though they make me sit in the back. She said my column about love and the Ozunas touched her heart. Another said it made her sad. Heck, that a hard-hearted cuss like me could affect anybody's heart is a miracle.

JUNE 1992   180-S-8B
VALLADOLID – PUERTO JUAREZ

MEXICO TRAVELOG
Puts over 40 years of experience at your side! Copyright © Sanborn's TGP Inc.

VALLADOLID – PUERTO JUAREZ – MANY TOPES – 103.0 MI OR 164.8 KM – DRIVE TIME 2½ HOURS

SCENIC RATING — 2

» NOTE: Start on this log if you wish to visit the beautiful islands of Cozumel and Isla Mujeres. If you're heading for Cozumel, there's a car-passenger ferry service at Puerto Morales and passenger ferry service at Playa del Carmen. And car-passenger ferry service at Punta Sam if you're heading for Isla Mujeres. Departure schedules are listed in the travelog at each embarkment point, but are subject to a lot of change, so check on arrival.

MI.	KM.	
0.0	0.0	After crossing Av. Heroes del 4 de Junio exit from **Valladolid** on Hwy #180 over a short stretch of divided hwy.
0.8	1.3	Handicraft stands, left.
4.0	6.4	Take right fork (curve right) onto bypass around **Ticuch**.
8.0	12.8	Pass side road (left) to village of **Xalau**.
10.0	16.0	Note big church dead ahead in next town.
15.8	25.3	Curve left (LEFT FORK) and enter little town of **Chemax**, home of 4 "topes". Mgas, right.

Cobá and Tulúm, TURN RIGHT. This is a shortcut road that local residents have been using for the past few years. We haven't logged it yet, but its pretty straightforward until you get to Cobá. There you'll have to ask.

20.8	33.2	Slow for 4 "topes" and straight thru village of **Catzin**. Then another "tope" at far end.
23.0	36.8	Nice tourist stop, right.
37.8	60.5	Over 7 "topes" thru town of **Xcan**, Mgas, left.
43.0	68.8	Thru village of **Nuevo Xcan** and slow for "topes". Ruins of Cobá at right. Begin divided hwy.
46.0	73.6	Customs checkpoint. You may or may not have to show papers. Cross state line — leave Yucatan and enter Quintana Roo (named after Andres Quintana Roo, lawyer and writer born in Merida, Yucatán, who was president of the Chilpancingo Congress which formulated the Declaration of Independence).
48.0	76.8	Straight thru village of **Ignacio Zaragoza**, 4 "topes". KM 240
51.0	81.6	Thru settlement of **El Pocito** with its "topes".
51.8	82.9	Down thru village of **Tintel** with 3 "topes".
57.6	93.0	Thru village of **Santo Domingo** and more "topes".
60.4	96.6	Thru village of **Cristobal Colón** and its 2 "topes".
61.7	98.1	Thru village of **Valladolid Nuevo**, 3 "topes".
70.0	112.0	Straight thru village of **Leona Vicario**, a record-holding 10 "tope" town. Slow past school at far end.
86.0	137.6	**"Alice Does Live Here"** ranch. KM 300
89.0	142.4	Coca Cola, left.
92.8	148.5	Dyna agency, left.
93.0	148.8	Farmers' market, left.
93.5	148.6	Army camp, right.
94.0	150.4	Conasupo warehouse, right

(Over, please)

180-S-8B
VALLADOLID – PUERTO JUAREZ

MI.	KM.	
95.0	152.0	Begin divided highway.
95.5	152.8	"Topes" Infonavit.

☛ » **INFONAVIT (Instituto Nacional de Fomento a la Vivienda del Trabajador)** is the government housing program. The federal government build these apartment-like complexes. People qualify to buy them with no down payment and very little per month for long-term payments. To qualify, they must: fall under a certain income level, be married with 2 kids, work. They must be recommended by an employer or union. True, some people have managed to buy some units who do not qualify, then rent them out, but this is being cleaned up. On the whole, it is a very worthwhile endeavor. You'll notice, too, that the people who live here have a real pride in their surroundings, unlike our "projects."

	MI.	KM.	
	95.7	153.1	Traffic light. Housing development, left.
Mgas	96.0	153.6	Topes. Comercial Mexicana Center, right. Mgas, left.
	96.1	153.8	More "topes", two-way traffic for a while, then divided.
	96.2	153.9	Airport to right. Traffic light.

Cancun, TURN RIGHT, also for Tulúm, Playa del Carmen, Puerto Morelos, Felipe Carrillo Puerto, or Chetumal (follow ZONA HOTELERA, CANCUN, CHETUMAL signs) and start Log 307-South-1.

Puerto Juárez or Isla Mujeres, proceed ahead.

	MI.	KM.	
	97.0	155.2	Banco Atlantico, right.
	97.9	156.6	Topes. Plaza Cancun 2000, right. Goodyear, left.
	98.0	156.8	Hotel zone, left, traffic light at Av. Tulum.
	99.0	158.4	Plaza Puerto Cancun.
	99.3	158.9	Bumpy! Veer left onto pavement. Topes. Seacoast town of **Puerto Juárez**
	100.0	160.0	Passenger boat dock to **Isla Mujeres**, right. If you'd like to take a boat over to Isla Mujeres, there are daily departures from Puerto Juárez at: 6:00, 8:30, 9:30. 10:00, 10:30, 11:30 AM, 12:30, 1:30 PM; and returning from Isla Mujeres to Puerto Juárez daily departures at: 2:30, 3:30, 4:30, 5:30, 6:30, 7:30, 8:30 PM (Please check locally as schedule varies).
🚗	100.4	160.6	**Odyssey Sports Club Marine** bays, right.
	100.6	161.0	Topes, Condos and more topes.
H	101.7	162.7	Playa Milla Hotel and **Flamingo hotel**.
	102.0	163.2	**Cabañas Punta Sam**, right and past excellent **Flamingo Restaurant**, also at right (fresh seafood; select your own live lobster; bar; beachside zoo, open daily 1 PM to midnight).
	103.0	164.8	Turn right into **Punta Sam** ferry dock parking lot. You can take your car over to **Isla Mujeres** on the ferry, although there aren't many places to drive on the island, but you might prefer to take it along rather than leave it here. No RV facilities are available on the island, but there are two parking areas about halfway between town and the south end of the island for self-contained units. There are daily departures from Punta Sam at: 7:15, 9:45 AM, 12:00, 2:30, 5:15, 7:45, 10:00 PM, and from Isla Mujeres at: 6:00, 8:30, 11:00 AM, 1:15, 4:00, 6:30, and 9:00 PM. The one way trip takes about 20-30 minutes.

End of log.

(Next Page, Please)

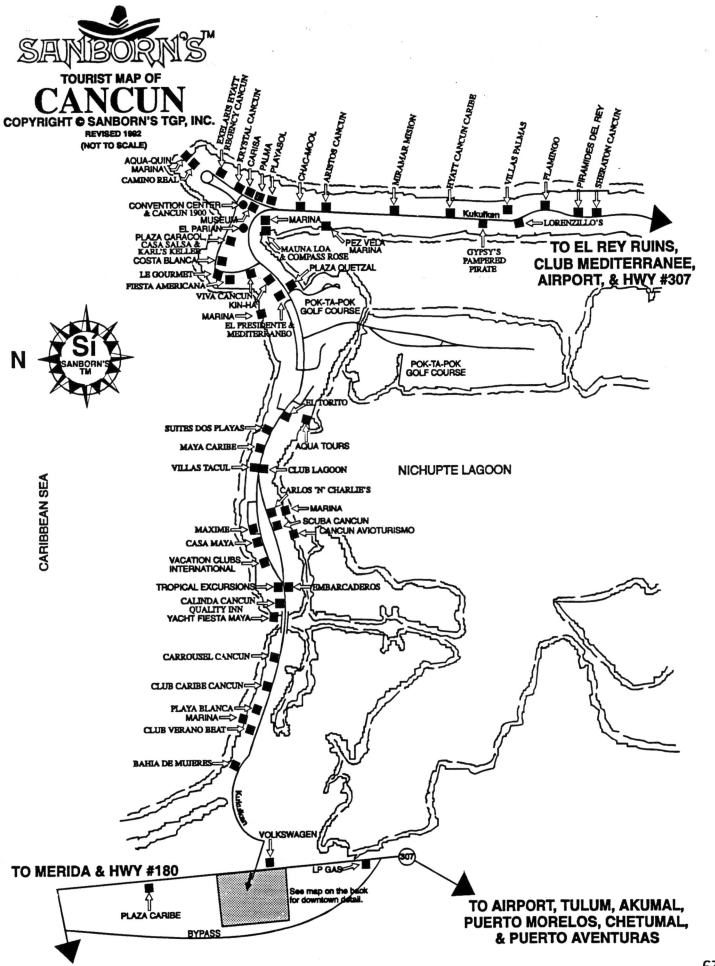

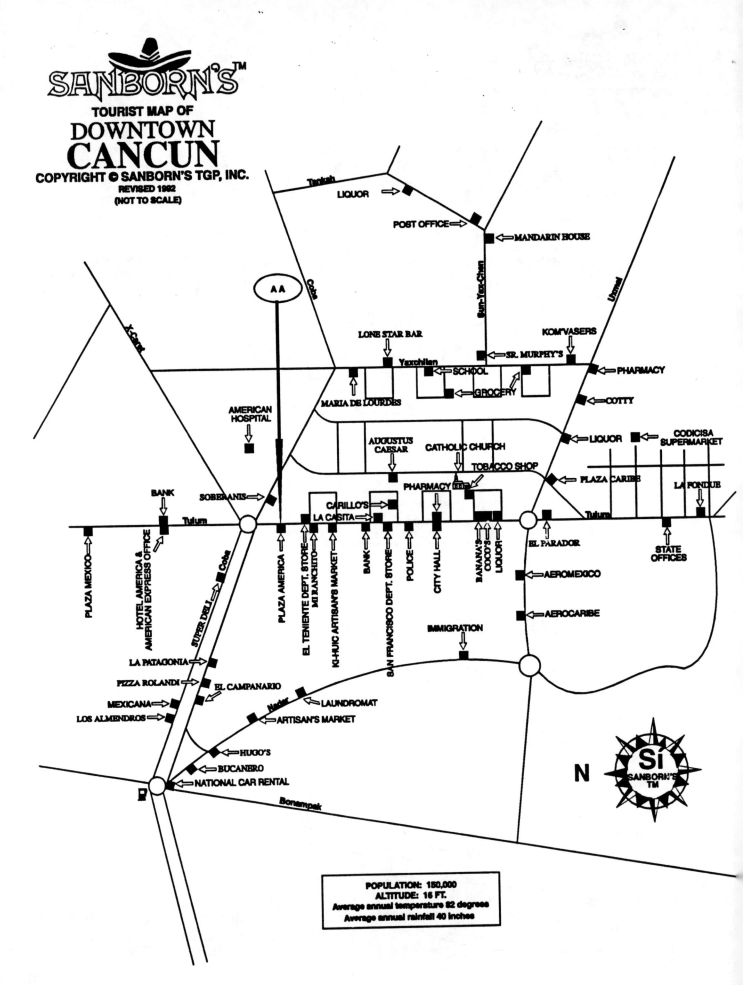

General Info
CANCUN, Q. ROO

CANCUN has come a long way since it was a fishing village in 1971. Which direction is subject to debate, but there is no denying that it is the first introduction to Mexico for many Norteamericanos. There are some ruins past Hotel Row, but mostly this is for the sun & fun group. Serious archeology buffs will head south. There are rooms in all price ranges. Ask if a hotel is a member of our Mexico Club for a discount. Some hotels will actually offer deals if the season is slow, but don't count on it. They cater to the group tourist and package buyer. The pure white sands and crystal clear waters attract many, while the extravagant night-life lures others. English is widely spoken and all water is purified. You can't shake the feeling that you are in Miami Beach, but many folks find that reassuring. If this ain't your bag, then head on south, to some of the other less-developed spots.

AA & OTHER 12 STEP PROGRAMS — Contrary to popular rumors, you don't have to get loaded in order to visit Cancun. If that's not your bag, or if you'd like to not do that anymore, check out the Alcoholics Anonymous English-speaking meetings at the Cancun International Group, 6:15 PM every day. (Non-smoking meeting 7:30 PM Sun) PH: Vicki, 842-445. They meet at the Plaza America shopping center, on Av. Kukulkán (near corner with Av. Tulum). They are on the 2nd floor, room #33. You enter at the back of the building, walk up one flight of stairs and turn right to the end of the hall. The shopping center is near the glorietta where you would turn to go to Pto. Juarez (see map). It's down from Hotel America, across from the original Super Deli. There are also SLAA & Alanon meetings. If you go in a taxi, tell him "cerca del Hotel America". Then, when he gets there, point down the road to the shopping center ahead of you. Make sure it is the Plaza America and you are home free. There is also an English-speaking group in Pto. Morelos (see Eat & Stray).

BEST SOURCE OF CURRENT INFORMATION — Get a copy of *Cancun Tips*, a large format magazine available at most hotels. They have information centers at: Plaza Caracol, Plaza Kukulcán, Playa Langosta and El Parian Hotel. It is well-nigh impossible to keep up with Cancun's changing scene, so check here for the best information, particularly phone numbers. They change as frequently as assistant managers in shoe stores. Cancun added a sixth digit to all numbers last year, so if you are calling somewhere and it doesn't work, try putting an "8" in front of it.

DISCOS — There are plenty of 'em and they are all glitzy. Admission ranges from a few dollars to $20. They tend to get going late, so don't plan to arrive before 10 PM if you want to see the in-crowd. They are loud, but that's what many folks like. See our "Clubs, Discos, Bars" listings.

CHURCHES — The following offer English-speaking services: PRESBYTERIAN:10:45 AM Sun, Ph: 84-2362. ROMAN CATHOLIC: 5 & 7 AM daily, 8 AM Sun, Ph: 84-0513. SHERATON: 9:15 AM Sun, Ph: 83-1988. CAMINO REAL: 11 AM Sun, Ph: 83-0100. KRYSTAL 7 PM Sat, Ph: 83-1133.

CRUISES — There are a bunch of them and you can find out about them from your hotel or *Cancun Tips* for current times etc. Every one that I know of is a booze-cruise. You can expect a party aboard, with lots of loud music, heavy drinking, and high-spirited gaiety. If you aren't a drinker, you probably won't like them. If you are, you will have a ball. If you want to go to Isla Mujeres, and don't want to pay big bucks for a booze-cruise, drive to the ferry terminal (see log), park and take the passenger ferry over. You can also take a couple of city busses. Once there, you'll have to take a taxi to Garrafón, the underwater park. The bus just doesn't go there. You can snorkel all day and have a laid-back afternoon, which is more than the cruisers will have.

FISHING — Many folks say the fishing here is very good. You can go bone-fishing or deep-sea fishing, grouper, barracuda, tuna, red snapper among other types. Check with your hotel or better yet, at the marina. You can fish from the shore, too. Go over to the lagoon side of **Puente Nichupte**.

SNORKELING AND DIVING — This is the best thing about Cancun. The best snorkeling is over at Isla Mujeres, on the north end. Stay on the windward side. **Garrafón** is a water park where neophytes can experience a wonderful undersea world. You can rent gear there.

Visit the **Sleeping sharks cave** if you are a diver. Dives can be arranged at your hotel. The best-known dive-master in Luis Hurtado, who is NAUI, CAMS & PADI certified. He has over 30 years experience. You can find him across from the Vacation Clubs Int. on Kukulcán Blvd. They offer resort courses, one-day dives, certification. Gear is available for rent. Other dive shops include Mundo Marina PH: 83-0554, Agua Tours, PH: 83-0207.

MEXICAN FIESTAS OR NOCHE MEXICANAS — You'll see these "folkloric shows" advertised all over the place. They are a fine glimpse into the costumes and dances of the rest of Mexico and probably worth seeing at least one. They are the same all over Mexico, so if you've seen one, you've seen them all. They do have one practice that you should be aware of, though. They have "games" where tourists are "volunteered" from the audience. They are brought on-stage and made to take part in drinking contests — like tequila guzzling. This is ok for some, but for those who don't want to take part, you should be aware of what to expect. Now you know. If you don't want to participate, be forceful from the beginning when someone tries to pull you on-stage. The hustlers who grab you can be pretty insistent. They speak English. Tell 'em you are sick and will throw up on them if they persist.

CONDO SALESMEN — Whether you want to buy a condo is your business. Be aware that time-share hustlers will accost you on the street with come-ons like. "Enjoying your vacation?", or "Are you from the

(More Goodies on other side)

United States?" If you don't relish paying for a free breakfast with a hard-sell presentation, pass their offers by.

FERRY SERVICE — There's a passenger ferry from Pto. Juárez and a car service to Isla Mujeres. The times are in Log 180-S-8B. Or check Cancun Tips. You don't really need a car there, so I recommend leaving it here.

COZUMEL — There has been talk of a boat service again, but none now. You have to go onm to Playa del Carmen. There is an air-shuttle operated by Taesa.

MEDICAL FACILITIES — HOSPITAL AMERICANO DE CANCUN is located at Viento #15, Super-Manzana 4. That's behind the Hotel America. They a top-notch facility with 24 hour service, hospitalization, emergencies, x-rays, ultrasound, pharmacy and laboratory, 48 beds and an operating theater. They accept Trav-Med, the traveller's medical insurance program we sell. They also take credit cards. They are highly recommended.Ph: 84-6133 or 84-6068. RED CROSS: Labna & Xcaret, first aid, emergency medical service, and ambulance service. Ph: 84-1616.

U.S. CONSULATE — Av. Coba #30 (corner Tulum). PH: 84-2411. They are open 9 AM — 2 PM and 3 PM — 6 PM.

TOURIST OFFICES — State tourism is at Av. Coba and Nader. Open 10 AM — 3 PM. PH: 84-3238. There is a kiosk at Tulum close to Av. Tulipanes.

ANNUAL EVENTS — The Cancun Jazz Festival is a big draw and it's held in mid-June.

My old *Checkered Flag* (Austin TX, circa 1967-8) buddy Rod Kennedy puts on a folk music festival in Oct 14-19, 1992, on nearby Isla Mujeres. If you are here, go on over. Back home, you can contact his office at 210-257-3600. or 1-800-435-8429, or write him at POB 1466, Kerrville, TX 78209-1466. Each year it's held in the 2nd or 3rd week in Oct.

The annual Wind-Surfing Championship is held on June 1.

(Next page, please)

JULY 1992

**EAT & STRAY
CANCUN. Q. ROO**

CANCUN

AREA CODE — 98   Copyright © Sanborn's TGP Inc.

NOTE: Cancun has a top-notch Hospital called Hospital Americano de Cancún with 24 hour service: Hospitalization, Emergencies, X-Rays, Ultrasound, Pharmacy and Laboratory which provide 22 Specialties, 48 beds, 4 operating rooms and a Maternity ward. They accept Trav-Med customers; English spoken. It's located at Viento # 15 SM4 Cancun, near Hotel América. Phone: 84-6133 or 84-6068 Their motto is: "We hope you never need us, but if you do, we're here."

Here are some more Emergency Numbers: Bomberos (Fire) 84-1202; Cruz Roja (Red Cross) 84-1616; Policia 84-1913; Federal de Caminos (Hwy Patrol) 84-1107; Transito (Traffic police) 84-0710 C.F.E. 84-2588; Capitania de puerto (Port Hqs.) 84-1677; Migración (Immigration) 84-1404; US Consular Representative 84-2411; Cancun Chamber of Commerce 84-1201; Cancun Hotel Association 84-5895 or 84-2853 Fax 84-7115; Turismo (Tourism) 84-3204; Aeropuerto (Airport) 84-3715.

SLEEPING AROUND

***   **AMERICA** —MOD— 180-room, a/c downtown hotel at Av. Tulum and Brisa, situated on four-acre site. Restaurant. Coffee shop. Palapa bar. Club. Pool. Boutique. Bank. Tobacco shop. American Express office. Free shuttle to its beach club. Parking. AE, MC, VI. Ph: 84-7500 Fax 84-1953. Reservations: 1-800-227-0212

***   **ARISTOS CANCUN** —MOD-UPPER— 244-room, 3-story a/c beachfront hotel at Paseo Kukulcán. Restaurant. Lobby bar. Pool bar. Pool. Tennis. Shops. Parking. AE, MC, VI. Ph: 83-0011.

**   **BAHIA DE MUJERES** —MOD— 86-room, 12-kitchenette a/c beachfront hotel. Restaurant. Disco. Pool. Sauna. Parking. AE, MC, VI. Ph: 83-0061.

***   **CALINDA CANCUN QUALITY INN** —MOD-UPPER— 280-room a/c beachfront hotel. Restaurant. Bars. Pool. Tennis. Parking. AE, MC, VI. Ph: 83-1600.

****   **CAMINO REAL** —UPPER— Deluxe 300-room, 6-story a/c beachfront hotel surrounded by water on 3 sides. Restaurant. Lobby bar. Disco. Pool with swim-up bar. Tennis. Parking. AE, MC, VI. Ph: 83-0100.

**   **CARROUSEL CANCUN** —MOD— 149-room, kitchenettes, 3-story a/c hotel next to bridge on beach. Restaurant. Snack bar. Bar. Pool. Jacuzzi in suite. Parking. AE, MC, VI. Ph: 83-0513 Fax 83-2312. Reservations: 1-800-333-1212.

***   **CASA MAYA** —MOD-UPPER— 356-room-and-suite hotel on beach overlooking Bahia de Mujeres. Several restaurants, bars, and clubs. 3 pools. Tennis. Parking. AE, MC, VI. Ph: 83-0555 Fax 83-1188. Reservations: 718-253-9400.

**   **CLUB CARIBE CANCUN** —UPPER— 94-room, 3-story a/c beachfront hotel. Restaurant. Lobby bar. Palapa bar. Pool. Parking. AE, MC, VI. Ph: 83-0811.

**   **CLUB LAGOON** —MOD— 93-room a/c bungalow-style complex on Kukulcán across from Villas Tacul. Restaurant. Club bar. Yacht club. Access to beach. Parking. AE, MC, VI. Ph: 83-1101.

****   **CLUB LAS VELAS** —MOD— All inclusive deal for those who want to relax and let themselves be taken care of. 285-room hotel at Blvd. Kukulcán in Zona Hotelera. Restaurant. Pool. Jacuzzi in room. Tennis. Golf. Ph: 83-2222 or 83-2150 Fax: 83-2118. Reservations: 1-800-223-9815.

(More Goodies on other side)

EAT & STRAY
CANCUN, Q. ROO

JULY 1992

**** **CLUB MED** —UPPER— Private 2- and 3-bungalow resort complex resembling an ancient Mayan city at end of "Zona Hotelera" on an isolated peninsula. Membership fee. Restaurant. Open-air restaurant. Bar. Theater. Pool. Tennis. Boutique. Arts-and-crafts workshop. Basketball. AE, MC, VI. Ph: 85-2900.

*** **CLUB VERANO BEAT** —MOD— 77-room-and-suite a/c hotel close to town facing bay. Restaurant. Snack bar. Disco. Tennis. Parking. AE, MC, VI. Ph: 83-0722 Fax 83-0173.

*** **COCONUT INN** —MOD— Air-con hotel on Av. Labna 39. Kitchenette. Terrace. Pool. English speaking — personable, helpful. Ph: 84-0193.

* **COTTY** —ECON-MOD— 38-room a/c downtown hotel at Uxmal #44 a few minutes from beach. No restaurant. No pool. Parking. Ph: 84-1319.

** **EL PARADOR** —ECON-MOD— 2-story, 66-room hotel on Hwy #307. Restaurant. No pool. Parking. AE, MC, VI. Ph: 84-1922.

**** **EL PRESIDENTE CANCUN** —UPPER— Deluxe 337-room, 6-story a/c beachfront hotel. Restaurants. Bar. Club. Disco. Pool. Tennis. Parking. AE, MC, VI. Ph: 83-0330.

***** **EXELARIS HYATT REGENCY CANCUN** —UPPER— Fabulous 16-story, 380-room a/c circular beachfront hotel in "Zona Hotelera" featuring an unusual 14-story lobby with gardens and waterfall spilling into a small stream which runs thru hotel. 3 restaurants (seafood, Italian, and continental). 3 bars with live music. Pool. Boutiques. Parking. AE, MC, VI. Ph: 83-0966 or 83-1520.

**** **FIESTA AMERICANA CANCUN** —UPPER— Terrific 281-room-and-suite a/c hotel resembling a mediterranean village not far from convention center on lagoon. Restaurants. Bars. Grill. Disco. Club. Ice cream parlor. In-house movies. Shops. Parking. AE, MC, VI. Ph: 83-1400 Fax 83-2502. Reservations: 1-800-345-5094

**** **FIESTA AMERICANA CORAL BEACH** —UPPER— 602-suite a/c hotel. Private balconies. SATV. Jacuzzi. Pool. Tennis. Ph: 83-2900 Fax 83-3173 Reservations: (212) 949-7520.

**** **FLAMINGO** —UPPER— Nice 162-room a/c beachfront hotel at far end of "Zona Hotelera" Blvd. Kukulcán #16. Restaurant. Lobby bar. Shops. Laundry. Cafeteria. 2 bars. Pool. Parking. AE, MC, VI. Ph: 83-1544 Fax 83-1029. Reservations: 1-800-458-6888.

**** **HYATT CANCUN CARIBE** —UPPER— Nice 226-room a/c hotel next to Miramar Mision in "Zona Hotelera" situated on 10 acres of gardens. Restaurant. Patio restaurant. Several bars. Disco. Pool. Tennis. Shops. Parking. AE, MC, VI. Ph: 83-0044 Fax 83-1514. Reservations: 1-800-228-9000.

**** **HOLIDAY INN CROWN PLAZA** —UPPER— On the beach between Nichupte Lagoon and the Caribbean sea on Kukulcán Blvd. Km 18.5 363 rooms. 4 restaurants. 4 bars. 4 pools. Gym with sauna and jacuzzi. Apdo. Postal #5-477, Cancun, Q. Roo. Reservations: US 1-800-HOLIDAY; MEX 91-800-0099.

** **JUAREZ** — Nearly brand new 3 story hotel, very clean, excellent value; not in tourist strip. (thanks to Sjoerd Bakker, Woodstock, Ontario.)

** **KOMVASER** —MOD— 36-kitchenette a/c hotel at Yaxchilan #15 just 10 minutes from beach. Restaurant. Bar. Pool. Parking. Ph: 84-1650.

**** **KRYSTAL CANCUN** —UPPER— Deluxe 330-room-and-suite hotel across from convention center on beach. Restaurant. Beach restaurant. Coffee shop. Bars. Disco. Pool. Lighted tennis. Shops. Parking. AE, MC, VI. Ph: 83-1133 Fax 83-1790. Reservations: 1-800-231-9860.

** **MARIA DE LOURDES** —MOD— 51-room, 2-story a/c hotel on Yaxchilan just 7 minutes from beach. Restaurant. Bar. Disco. Pool. Steam baths. Parking. MC, VI. Ph: 84-4744 Fax 84-1242.

**** **MAYA CARIBE** —UPPER— 3-story, 64-room a/c beachfront hotel. Restaurant. 2 pools. Tennis. Parking. AE, MC, VI. Ph: 83-2000 Fax 83-0605.

(Please turn page!)

**** **MIRAMAR MISION** —UPPER— Luxurious 189-room a/c hotel overlooking Caribbean in "Zona Hotelera". Several restaurants. Lobby bar with live mariachi music. Piano bar. Snack bar. Club. Large pool (among finest in Cancun) with swim-up bar. Mini-golf. Shops. Parking. AE, MC, VI. Ph: 83-1755 or 83-1581.

*** **OMNI CANCUN HOTEL & VILLAS** —UPPER— Blvd. Kukulcán L-48 Apdo.127 Cancun, Q.ROO 77500. 327-rooms-and-villas. Restaurant. Bar. 3 pools. Jacuzzi in suite. Tennis. Water sports. Ph: 85-0714 Fax: 85-0059. US Reservations: 1-800-THE-OMNI. In Mexico: 91-800-21512

*** **PLAYA BLANCA** —UPPER— 3-story, 161-room a/c beachfront hotel. Restaurant. Palapa bar. Club. Pool. Shops. Tennis. Parking. AE, MC, VI. Ph: 83-0344 Fax 83-0904. Reservations: 1-800-221-4726.

**** **PLAZA CARIBE** —UPPER— 112-room, 2-story a/c hotel in town just off Hwy #307 at AV. Tulum & Uxmal. Restaurant. Pool. Parking. AE, MC, VI. Ph: 83-1252.

*** **PUERTO AVENTURAS** —UPPER— 30-room a/c hotel at KM 60. South of Cancun on Hwy to Tulum. Restaurant. Bar. Pool. Parking. Marina. Spa. Watersports. Scuba & snorkeling facilities. Golf. Tennis. AE, MC, VI. Ph: 83-2266, 83-1002, 83-2144, 83-2142, or 83-1933. Fax 87-3232. Reservations: 1-800-SEA-MAYA.

**** **SHERATON CANCUN** —UPPER— Terrific 347-unit a/c pyramid-shaped hotel at end of "Zona Hotelera" overlooking lagoon and Caribbean. 3 restaurants. 2 bars. Disco. Pools (indoor and outdoor) with swim-up bar. Tennis. Shops. Parking. AE, MC, VI. Ph: 83-1988 Fax 85-0202. Reservations: 1-800-325-3535.

** **SOBERANIS** —MOD— 37-room, 4-story hotel at Coba #5 a block from Tulum. Good restaurant. Bar. Disco. Pool. Parking. AE, MC, VI. Ph: 84-3080.

** **SUITES DOS PLAYAS** —MOD— 84-room-and-suite a/c beachfront hotel. Restaurant. Bar. Pool. Tennis. Parking. AE, MC, VI. Ph: 83-0500 or 83-0722 Fax 83-2037. Reservations: 1-800-223-9815.

*** **VILLAS PALMAS** —MOD-UPPER— 100-suite a/c complex on beautiful sandy beach in "Zona Hotelera". Restaurant. Bar. Disco. Pool (plus 22 private pools). Curio shop. Parking. AE, MC, VI. Ph: 83-0032.

**** **VILLAS TACUL** —UPPER— Charming, private 25-cottage a/c beachfront complex (2-3-4-5-bedroom units). Restaurant. Bar. Pool. Tennis. Parking. AE. Ph: 83-0349.

*** **VIVA CANCUN** —UPPER— 212-room a/c hotel next to Fiesta Americana on beach. Restaurant. Piano bar. Pool. Tennis. Boutiques. Parking. AE, MC, VI. Ph: 83-0108 Fax 83-2087. Reservations: 1-800-228-5151.

EATING CANCUN

Although not listed, most hotels offer good-to-excellent restaurants with a variety of specialties, and in resort areas such as Cancun, the majority of restaurants serve beer, wine, and mixed drinks.

** **100% NATURAL** —ECON— Two locations: 1 at Av. Sunyaxchen # 6 (DT). Open 8 AM till midnight and open 24 hours at Plaza Terramar (HZ). Great salads, vegetarian food, licuados, etc. Inside or outside eating. Ph: 84-3617 (DT); 83-1180 (HZ)

**** **AILEM** —UPPER— (Melia Cancun Hotel) Gourmet French cuisine. Classical music. All major credit cards accepted. Open Mon.-Sat. 7 PM - Midnight. Ph: 85-1114 or 85-1990 Ext. 2010

*** **AUGUSTUS CAESAR** —MOD— Italian restaurant at Claveles #13 a block off Coba lending a Paris cafe ambience. Italian cuisine plus meat dishes and seafood. Open 8 AM till 12 AM daily. AE, MC, VI. Ph: 84-1265.

(More Goodies on other side)

EAT & STRAY
CANCUN, Q. ROO

JULY 1992

** **BANANAS** —MOD— Tropical sidewalk cafe at Tulum #9 downtown. Short orders, steaks, seafood. Open 7 AM till 12 AM daily. MC, VI. Ph: 84-0791.

*** **BISTRO** —MOD— Jazz club at Calle Tulipanes #26, cozy atmosphere. Original German sausage, fowl, great steaks, fresh seafood and lobster. Open Mon-Sat 6 PM till 2 AM. Ph: 84-2437

** **BUGATTI'S** —MOD— Italian restaurant in Plaza Quetzal in hotel zone. Informal indoor dining plus sidewalk cafe outdoors. Italian cuisine, steaks, seafood, and Mexican food. Open 7 AM till 11 PM daily. AE, MC, VI.

CASA DE LOS ARCOS — Av. Xelha S.M. 28, Plaza Bonita Local F3-4 (Recommended by Ruth & Dana Larson, New Brighton, MN; Thanks!)

*** **CASA SALSA** —MOD— Truly Mexican-style restaurant in Plaza Caracol in hotel zone. Lively Caribbean atmosphere with live salsa, jazz, popular, and mariachi music. All sorts of Mexican dishes. Open 11 AM till 1 AM daily. AE, MC, VI. Ph: 83-1114.

*** **CARLOS'N'CHARLIE'S** —MOD— Another restaurant of the zany Anderson chain on Kukulcán Blvd, Km 5.5. Strictly party-hearty atmosphere. Lots of loud music and drinking contests. If that's not your cup of tea, this isn't the place for you. American cuisine including BBQ ribs, chicken, beef, etc. plus seafood. Open 1 PM till 1 AM daily. AE, MC, VI. Ph: 83-0846 or 83-1107.

*** **CARLOS O' BRIAN'S** —UPPER— Restaurant-bar and grill on Av. Tulum. BBQ ribs a specialty. Open daily 11 AM till after Midnight. Ph: 84-1659 or 84-1838.

** **CENACOLA** —MOD— Located at Calle Claveles #26. The best Italian food in town — pasta and fish. Ph: 84-1591

**** **CHAC-MOOL** —UPPER— Dine with Vivaldi, Beethoven and Mahler. Next to the Aristos Hotel. Open 12 PM - 4 PM and 6 PM - 12 AM. Ph: 83-1107.

*** **CHOCKA'S & TERE** —UPPER— A legend of Cancun in fine seafood at Calle Claveles #7. Delicious lobster. Open daily 1 PM till Midnight.

* **COCO'S** —MOD— Tropical sidewalk cafe on Tulum downtown. Short orders. Open 9:30 AM till 1 AM daily. Ph: 84-0068.

** **COLORINES** —MOD— At Aristos Hotel. Try a romantic meal. BBQ Open 7 AM - 9 PM. Ph: 83-0011.

*** **COMPASS ROSE** —MOD— Nautical decor restaurant on Kukulcán in Mauna Loa complex. International cuisine. Open 12 PM till 1 AM daily. AE, MC, VI. Ph: 83-0693.

**** **EL MURAL** —UPPER— Carousal hotel. Quietly elegant. Open 7 Am - 11:30 PM. Ph: 83-0388.

* **EL TORITO** —MOD— Old-time pizza parlor on Kukulcán. Breakfast, pizza, and short orders. Open 7 AM till 12 AM daily.

** **EMBARCADEROS** —MOD— Seafood restaurant on Kukulcán in wharf-like decor overlooking bay. Seafood dishes plus steak and chicken. Open 12 PM till 2 AM seasonally daily; 6 PM till 2 AM summer daily. AE, MC, VI.

* **GUADALAJARA GRILL** —MOD— On Kukulcán Blvd. Km 9.5 opposite Girasol Hotel. Specialty BBQ and Mexican food. For the "Party Hearty" crowd. Rock and dance music. Open daily 5:30 PM - 1 AM.

** **GYPSY'S PAMPERED PIRATE** —MOD— Another seafood restaurant on lagoon in hotel zone in wharf decor. Various seafood dishes plus fowl. Open 12 PM till 1 AM daily. Ph: 83-2120 or 83-2015.

*** **JAGUARI'S** —UPPER— On Kukulcán Blvd Km 9.5 (HZ)Brazilian steak "Churrasquería" style. Soft music. Major credit cards accepted except DC. Open daily 5 PM - Midnight. Ph: 83-2880.

*** **HAPPY LOBSTER** —UPPER— Downtown at Calle Tulum #33-C Seafood cocktails and lunches along with tropical drink. Open daily 11 AM till 10:30 PM. Ph: 84-3316.

(Please turn page!)

** **HUGO'S** —MOD— Mexican restaurant on Nader and Kukulcán downtown in Mexican fiesta decor. Mexican dishes, seafood, and international cuisine. Open 10 AM till 11 PM daily. AE, MC, VI. Ph: 84-2251.

* **I CAN'T BELIEVE IT'S YOGURT** —MOD— Plaza Caracol. Imported (from US) gourmet frozen yogurt. Open daily 9 AM - 11 PM Ph: 83-3316

* **KARL'S KELLER** —MOD— German restaurant in Plaza Caracol in hotel zone. German pub ambience. German dishes. Live accordion music evenings. Open 8 AM till 11 PM daily. Ph: 83-1104.

*** **LA DOLCE VITA** —UPPER— Av. Coba #87. Continental cuisine, excellent seafood, homemade pastas. Open daily 5 PM till Midnight. Reservations required. Ph: 84-1384.

** **LA FONDUE** —MOD— French cafe at Tulum and Agua downtown. Cheese, shrimp, lobster, and steak fondues; soups; salads. Open 7:30 till 11:30 AM; 5 PM till 12 AM daily. AE, MC, VI. Ph: 84-1697.

*** **LA PATAGONIA** —MOD— Argentine steak house at Av. Coba #18 downtown. Grilled meats, empanadas, and seafood. Open 5 PM till 12 AM daily. AE, MC, VI. Ph: 84-1860.

** **LA PLACITA** —MOD— Av. Yaxchilán #12. Delicious tacos and grilled fine cuts. Ph: 84-0407.

** **LA POSTA** —MOD— Calle Crisantemos #10. Tex-Mex fajitas and seafood. Open daily 7 AM till 11 PM. Ph: 84-2105.

*** **LE GOURMET** —MOD-UPPER— Elegant French restaurant in front of Fiesta Americana on Kukulcán. Seafood, steaks, pasta, and fowl. Open 8:30 AM till 1 AM daily. AE, MC, VI. Ph: 83-1488.

*** **LORENZILLO'S** —MOD— Nautical-decor restaurant on stilts overlooking Nichupte Lagoon. Palapa. Seafood and steaks. Open 12 PM till 12 AM daily. AE, MC, VI.

*** **LOS ALMENDROS** —MOD— Yucatecan restaurant on Coba downtown at AV. Bonampak & Calle Sail. Regional dishes. Open 12 PM till 12 AM daily. Ph: 84-0807.

** **MANDARIN HOUSE** —MOD— Cantonese restaurant at Sunyaxchen #53 downtown. Cantonese dishes and seafood. Open 1 PM till 10:30 PM daily (closed Wednesday). AE, MC, VI.

**** **MAUNA LOA** —MOD-UPPER— Plush Polynesian restaurant across from convention center complex. Polynesian dishes plus continental cuisine. Hula dancers daily 8:30 & 10:30. Open 12 PM till 12 AM daily. AE, MC, VI.

**** **MAXIME** —UPPER— Deluxe French restaurant at Pez Volador #8 in hotel zone in French-countryside by-the-sea decor. French and continental cuisine including prime rib, lobster, and seafood. Intimate piano bar and lounge. Open 6 PM till 1 AM daily (plus Saturday and Sunday brunch). AE, MC, VI. Ph: 83-0438 or 83-0704. Coat required.

** **McDONALD'S** —MOD— Just like home (almost). Four different locations: Plaza Caracol, Plaza Flamingo (HZ), Cancun 2000 and Av. Tulum (DT). Open Sun-Thurs. 7 AM - 11 PM; Fri. & Sat. 7 AM - Midnight.

*** **MEDITERRANEO** —UPPER— Restaurant at Kukulcán #7 in the Hotel Presidente. Features the food of 5 different countries. Decor matches food. Open 7 PM till 1 AM. AE, MC, VI.

MI RANCHITO —MOD— List— Mexican restaurant on Tulum a block north of coba downtown. Mexican decor. Mexican food (natch!). Argentine Malambo show (7 PM; 9 PM daily). Open 12 PM till 5 PM (lunch) daily; 5 PM till 1 AM (dinner) daily. MC, VI.

** **PAPA GAYO RESTAURANT-BAR** —MOD— Calle Claveles #6. Mexican and Yucatecan specialties, seafood and steaks. Open Daily Noon till 11 PM. Ph: 84-6646.

(More Goodies on other side)

EAT & STRAY
CANCUN, Q. ROO

*** **PIZZA ROLANDI** —MOD— Italian restaurant at Coba #12 downtown, known for its originality and good old-fashioned Italian specialties, especially pizza and pastas. Open 1 PM till 12 AM daily. AE, MC, VI. Ph: 84-4047.

PUERTO AVENTURAS —MOD— In hotel of same name. Bar. Open 7 AM till 10:30 PM.

** **SR. MURPHY** —MOD— Tex-Mex restaurant at Yaxchilan #62 downtown. Steaks and seafood. Lively atmosphere. Open 1 PM till 2 AM daily. AE, MC, VI.

** **SUBWAY** —MOD— Have a change from local food. Imported from US.

*** **SUPER DELI** —MOD— Great Delicatessen, 2 locations: 1 on Hotel Row and 1 near Hotel America om Av. Tulum at "glorieta".

*** **YAMAMOTO** —UPPER— Japanese restaurant at Av. Uxmal # 31. Open Mon-Sat 1:30 PM till 8 PM. Ph: 87-3366.

CLUBS, DISCOS, BARS

The following are the most popular discos, clubs, and bars (some in conjunction with restaurants), most of which accept major credit cards. At discos, the action usually begins around 10 PM and continues until around 4 AM.

AQUARIUS DISCO — Hotel Camino Real. Ph: 83-0100.

CAMINO REAL LOBBY BAR — Open 10 AM till 1 AM daily. Happy hour 5 till 7:30 PM. Mariachi and marimba music from 7:30 PM. Ph: 83-0100.

CASA SALSA — In conjunction with restaurant.

CHRISTINE DISCO — Hotel Krystal. Ph: 83-1133.

COCAY DISCO — Hotel Hyatt Caribe. Ph: 83-0044.

FRIDAY LOPEZ RESTAURANT-BAR — Hotel Fiesta Americana. Live music. Open 7 PM till 4 AM daily. Ph: 3-1400.

KRYSTAL LOBBY BAR — Open 10 AM till 1 AM daily. Live music evenings. Ph: 83-1133.

LA CANTINA — In conjunction with Cancun 1900.

LONE STAR BAR — Yaxchilan & Orquideas downtown. Country-Western bar & dance hall. Open 8 PM till 2 AM daily (closed Tuesday). Happy hour 9 till 10 PM.

MAUNA LOA — In conjunction with restaurant.

MAYIC VIDEO BAR — Hotel Casa Maya. Sporting events, shows, and dancing to music TV (3 giant screens). Open 12 PM till 4 AM daily. Ph: 83-0555.

TABANO'S DISCO — Hotel Sheraton. Ph: 83-1988.

YAIMA CAAN BAR — Hotel Sheraton lobby bar. Open 10 AM till 1 AM daily. Ph: 83-1988.

OTHER

YOGA CANCUN-PUERTO MORELOS — Jean & Jack Loew. 60 Downing Ave. Sea Cliff, NY 11579. (516) 676-5128. Box 789, Cancun QR. They do Yoga workshops and rent apartments. 8 of them. If in town, ask for John Mastro Marino Jr.

12 STEPS PROGRAMS

CANCUN INTERNATIONAL GROUP — meets at 6:15 PM every day at the shopping center Plaza America, 2nd Floor Room #33. You enter around the back. It's near restaurant Henry's, by the glorietta where you turn to go to Pto. Juarez. (See map). Alanon and SLAA also meet, check here for times.

END OF EAT AND STRAY

(Please turn page!)

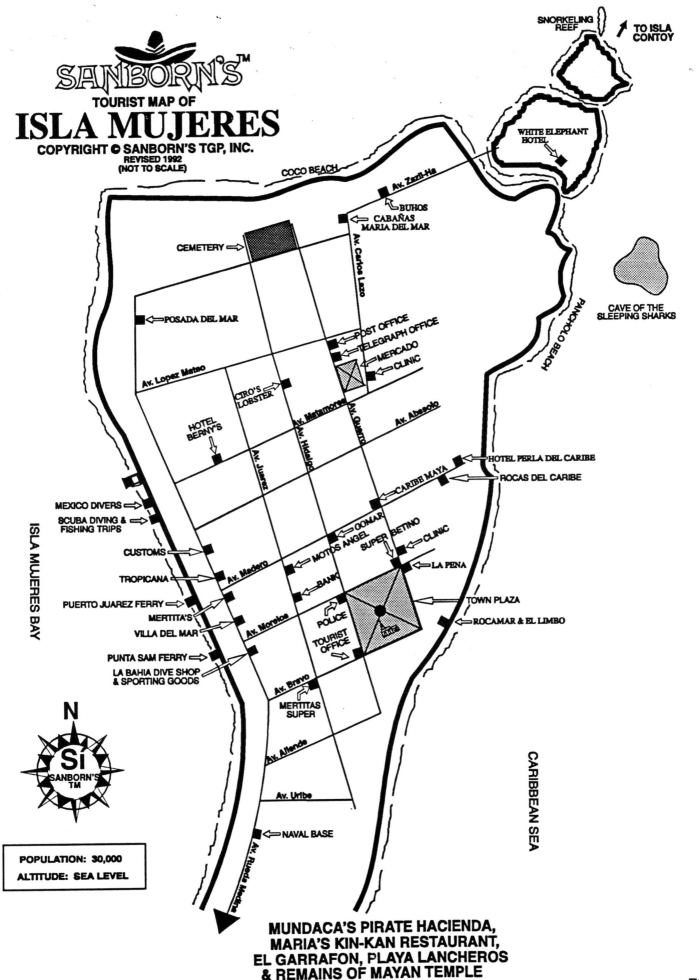

General Info
ISLA MUJERES

ISLA MUJERES (Isle of Women) was so named for the numerous statues of Mayan goddesses found by the Spaniards when they discovered the island in 1517. The island is approximately 2 miles long and a half-mile wide and is surrounded by crystal-clear Caribbean waters. Isla Mujeres is a fishing village newly discovered by tourism, but has maintained the authentic Yucatecan flavor and quaintness. It's a perfect destination for a relaxing and enjoyable vacation, with fine restaurants, sidewalk cafes, banks, grocery store, market, and souvenir shops. Many full-day excursions are available for excellent sport fishing, diving, snorkeling, and exploring the ruins of the mainland. It is truly a Mexican Caribbean paradise!

Visit the ancient ruins of a small Mayan temple up on the "hill" at the southeast tip of the island; the view is really something and there's always a cool breeze. See the ruins of an old hacienda built by the Spanish pirate Fermin Mundaca, it's picturesque. Take an all-day boat ride to Contoy Island or take the glass-bottom boat to Garrafón Reef to see the coral formations and tropical fish, or scuba dive the many coral reefs around, sun bathe, swim, etc. Stop by the turtle pens. Contact the Posada del Mar Hotel for further information.

You'll find Isla Mujeres is not for everyone. The folks who come here are not the day-trippers from Cancun. If that's your bag, then stay on Cancun and enjoy yourself. You'd be bored silly on Isla. There's not a lot of night-life, except for Tequila's Disco and they don't have smoke and glitzy sound and light shows. This is the place to come if you want to see what the Yucatan was like before Cancun and enjoy a sleepy time of it. It's one of my favorite places.

You won't be able to ride turtles anymore. President Salinas de Gortari said, "Anyone who is caught with a turtle in a pen will be put in prison for life." By the way, it is illegal to own, possess or sell turtle products. Yes, I know you see 'em for sale, but that doesn't mean you should buy any. Jojoba creme does wonders for the skin and the jojoba isn't endangered.

The old Mayan temple blew away with Hurricane Gilbert, but the folks on Isla are trying to restore it. It's still a pretty impressive place to go.

The town can be very crowded during Carnival (variable dates, the week before Ash Wednesday), so be aware. I have enjoyed the celebration on the square and so will you.

The ferries leave on a pretty regular schedule and the last people ferry is about 11:00. For a bit more money, the water taxis will shoot you back to Cancun as soon as it gets enough people. The ferry from Pto. Juarez got a new boat this year.

(Next page, please)

ISLA MUJERES

AREA CODE — 987   Copyright © Sanborn's TGP Inc.

Folks, the area code and first digit of all phones changed this year (1992) as we went to press (Dec. 1992) it is official. The above area code (clave) is correct. All numbers changed,. Old numbers started with a "2". That changed to "7". Thus, if you have an old number that doesn't work, like (988) 2-0000, try (987) 7-000. The only thing permanent in Mexico is change. — MM. We wish to express a deep debt of gratitude to Frank "Pancho" Schiell, of New York City, for his valuable last minute help in verifying info on this special place. Pancho is the PR rep for the Ixtapa Zihuatenejo Tourism Trust and others.

SLEEPING AROUND

* **BERNY'S** —ECON— Juarez and Abasolo. 40 rooms. Neat, clean, good value. PH: 7-0025. MC. VI.

*** **CABAÑAS MARIA DEL MAR** —MOD— 25-room, 2-story hotel overlooking popular north beach with original thatched-roof cabañas situated under palm trees. Restaurant next door. Pool. Ph: 7-0044 FAX: 7-0213.

*** **POSADA DEL MAR** —MOD— Good 3-story, 40-unit beachfront hotel 4 blocks north of ferry dock at Rueda Medina 15. Restaurant. Bar. Pool. MC, VI. Ph: 7-0044. FAX: 7-0266. Great island atmosphere!

** **ROCAMAR**—MOD— 30-room, 3-story hotel overlooking rocky, picturesque beach. Restaurant. Bar. MC, VI. Ph: 7-0101.

*** **PERLA DEL CARIBE**—MOD— 3-story, 60-room hotel on east beach at AV. Madero 2. Restaurant. Snack bar. Pool. MC, VI. Ph: 7-0444 or 7-0120. FAX: 7-0011.

WHITE ELEPHANT HOTEL — At the north end of the island, there is a modern structure that should be a hotel. In fact, it **has been** a hotel and probably will be again. It was first known as Zazil-Ha, then Bojorquez, then El Presidente, and lastly the Del Prado. Many guidebooks mention it, but you won't find it working ... or maybe you will. The only thing that's consistent in Mexico is change. I've had some very pleasant experiences there, but that was before they built the new addition and destroyed the lagoon.

EATING ISLA MUJERES

El CONGREJITO — for daytime eating snack off the back of a converted car. Ceviche and shrimp cocktail and oyster cocktails.

on main street just south of ferry. On the curb on the beach side.

** **EL LIMBO** —MOD— Cozy restaurant on ground floor of Rocamar serving breakfast and dinner. Reasonably priced entrees with large portions. Good bar. Ph: 7-0101.

* **GOMAR** —ECON— Fair restaurant two blocks from waterfront at Av. Hidalgo. Seafood specialty. AE, MC, VI. Ph: 7-0142.

*** **MARIA'S KIN-KAN** —MOD— Good French restaurant near Garrafón Beach at southern end of island. Specialties include king crab, Lobster Parisienne, and grouper cheeks. AE, MC, VI.

MERTITIA'S — Owned by Sra. Mertita whose family owns supermarket. Popular. Clean as a pin, with seafood and mexican dishes. no credit cards.

(More Goodies on other side)

EAT & STRAY
ISLA MUJERES, QR

TROPICANA — Simple with hearty seafood specialties. Fishermen often there to eat their own catch.

VILLA DEL MAR — Very popular with tablecloths indoor outdoor dining. Good for people and ferry-watching. Fresh seafood and Yucatan cuisine VI MC.

DISCOS

TEQUILA'S DISCO — Simple disco, open late.

ANNUAL EVENTS

My old *Checkered Flag* (Austin TX, circa 1967-8) buddy Rod Kennedy puts on a folk music festival in Oct 14-19, 1992, on Isla Mujeres. If you are here, go on over. Back home, you can contact his office at 210-257-3600. or 1-800-435-8429, or write him at POB 1466, Kerrville, TX 78209-1466. Each year it's held in the 2nd or 3rd week in Oct. and it is part of the Isla Mujeres International Music Festival.

END OF EAT & STRAY.

(Please turn page!)

ROUTE SELECTION RS-MAYA-3

CHICHEN-ITZA — MERIDA — UXMAL, START NEXT PAGE (73)

PLAYA DEL CARMEN — CHETUMAL, SKIP TO PAGE 79

JUNE 1992   180-W-1A
PUERTO JUAREZ – VALLADOLID

MEXICO TRAVELOG
Puts over 40 years of experience at your side!   Copyright © Sanborn's TGP Inc.

PUERTO JUAREZ – VALLADOLID – MANY TOPES – 103.0 MI OR 164.8 KM – DRIVE TIME 2 HOURS

SCENIC RATING — 2

NOTE: Start on this log if you wish to visit BALANKANCHE CAVES (guides available) at Valladolid where there is also an interesting "cenote" or sacred well.

MI.	KM.	
0.0	0.0	Turn left onto highway from **Punta Sam** ferry dock parking lot.
1.0	1.6	Past excellent **Flamingo Restaurant** (fresh seafood; select your own live lobster; bar; beachside zoo, open daily 1 PM till midnight) at left, **Cabañas Punta Sam** also at left.
H 1.3	2.1	**Flamingo Hotel** and **Playa Milla Hotel.**
2.2	3.5	Topes, Condos and more topes.
2.4	3.8	**Odyssey Sports Club Marine** bays, left.
2.8	4.5	Passenger boat dock to **Isla Mujeres**, left.
3.5	5.6	Pass seacoast town of **Puerto Juárez**. Topes and bumpy section of highway.
3.8	6.1	Plaza Puerto Cancun.
4.8	7.7	Traffic light at Av. Tulum, hotel zone, right.

Cancun, turn left, also to Tulúm, Playa del Carmen, Puerto Morelos, Felipe Carrillo Puerto, or Chetumal, start Log 307-S-1.

4.9	7.8	Goodyear, right. Plaza Cancun 2000, left. Topes.
5.8	9.3	Banco Atlantico, left.
6.6	10.6	Traffic light. Airport to left.
6.7	10.7	More "topes".
6.8	10.9	Mgas, right. Comercial Mexicana Center, left. Topes.
Mgas 7.1	11.4	Housing development, right. Traffic light.
7.3	11.7	Infonavit, "topes".

» **INFONAVIT (Instituto Nacional de Fomento a la Vivienda del Trabajador)** is the government housing program. The federal government build these apartment-like complexes. People qualify to buy them with no down payment and very little per month for long-term payments. To qualify, they must: fall under a certain income level, be married with 2 kids, work. They must be recommended by an employer or union. True, some people have managed to buy some units who do not qualify, then rent them out, but this is being cleaned up. On the whole, it is a very worthwhile endeavor. You'll notice, too, that the people who live here have a real pride in their surroundings, unlike our "projects."

7.8	12.5	End divided highway.
8.8	14.1	Conasupo warehouse, left.
9.3	14.9	Army camp, left.
9.8	15.7	Farmers' market, right.
10.0	16.0	Dyna agency, right.
13.8	22.1	Coca Cola, right.
16.8	26.9	"Alice Does Live Here" ranch. KM 300
32.8	52.5	Slow past school as you enter village of **Leona Vicario**, a record-holding 10 "tope" town.
41.1	65.8	Thru village of **Valladolid Nuevo**, with 3 "topes".
42.4	67.8	Thru village of **Cristobal Colon** and its 2 "topes".

(Over, please)

180-W-1A
PUERTO JUAREZ – VALLADOLID

MI.	KM.	
45.2	72.3	Thru village of **Santo Domingo** and more "topes".
51.0	81.6	Up thru village of **Tintel** with 3 "topes".
51.8	82.9	Thru settlement of **El Pocito** with its "topes".
54.8	87.7	Straight thru village of **Ignacio Zaragoza**, 4 "topes". KM 240
56.8	90.9	Customs check point as you cross state line. You may or may not have to show papers. Leave Quintana Roo (named after Andres Quintana Roo, layer and writer born in Merida, Yucatan, who was president of the Chilpancingo Congress which formulated the Declaration of Independence) and enter Yucatan.
60.8	97.3	Ruins of Coba at left. Thru village of **Nuevo Xcan** and slow for "topes".
66.0	105.6	Mgas at right. Over 7 "topes" thru town of **Xcan**.
80.8	129.3	Nice tourist stop, left.
83.0	132.8	Slow for 5 "topes" as you drive straight thru village of **Catzin**.
88.0	140.8	Enter little town of **Chemax**, home of 4 "topes". Mgas, left. Curve right at fork.

☞ **C**obá and Tulúm — this is a shortcut that local residents have been using for the past few years. We haven't logged it, but it's pretty straight forward until you get to Cobá. There you'll have to ask.

95.8	153.3	Pass side road (right) to village of **Xalau**.
99.8	159.7	Take left fork (curve left) unto bypass around **Ticuch**.
103.0	164.8	Handicraft stand, right.
103.8	166.1	Enter **Valladolid** over short stretch of divided highway, arriving at Av. heroes del 4 de Junio. TURN RIGHT onto Av. Heroes del 4 de Junio, following MERIDA-CUOTA and CHICHEN-ITZA signs.
103.9	166.2	TAKE YOUR FIRST LEFT onto Calle 39. Do not go straight. May be a sign for Casa de los Arcos. You are on a one way street.
104.2	166.7	After 5 blocks, veer right with water plant at your left.
104.6	167.4	Topes.
104.8	167.7	Long stone fence, right. Uniroyal, church at left.
104.9	167.8	**Restaurant Casa de los Arcos**, left.
105.0	168.0	Light, stop sign. Cathedral and plaza, left. Hotels **El Mesón del Marqués** and **María de la Luz**, right.

Merida, Chichen-Itza, follow Log 180-W-1B. For Chichen-Itza Merida toll road, turn right. For free road to Merida, go straight on one way.

End of Log.

(Next Page, Please)

JUNE 1992   180-W-1B TOLL
VALLADOLID – MERIDA

MEXICO TRAVELOG
Puts over 40 years of experience at your side! Copyright © Sanborn's TGP Inc.

VALLADOLID – CHICHEN-ITZA – MERIDA – 100.5 MI OR 160.8KM – MOSTLY DIVIDED, SOME TOLL – DRIVE TIME 2 HOURS

SCENIC RATING — 3

» **NOTE: This log will take you by the famous Mayan archaeological ruins at Chichen-Itza, where there are several good hotels and on to Merida.**

MI.	KM.	
0.0	0.0	As you come into **Valladolid**, begin short stretch of divided and come to Av. Heroes del 4 de Junio. Turn right onto Ave. Heroes del 4 de Junio, following the Merida-Cuota and Chichen-Itza signs.
0.1	0.2	Take your first left. Do not go straight. May be a sign for Casa de los Arcos. You are on a one-way street.
0.4	0.6	After five blocks veer right with water plant at your left.
0.8	1.3	Topes.
1.0	1.6	Long stone fence, on right. Uniroyal and church at left.
1.1	1.8	**Restaurant Casa de los Arcos**, at left.
1.2	1.9	Light, stop sign. Cathedral and plaza at left. Hotels **El Mesón del Marqués** and **María de la Luz** ahead on left. For Chichen-Itza — Merida toll road, TURN RIGHT.

H

Merida free road, go straight on one way. Stub Log 180-N-1S will take you to archaeological ruins.

1.7	2.7	Topes. Go one block to stop sign; then straight ahead.
2.1	3.4	Sharp curve left. (Still on 1-way) Turn sharp right onto divided (Hwy #295).
2.5	4.0	Electrical generating station, at left.
4.8	7.7	Sharp left curve.
4.9	7.8	

Merida — Chichen-Itza, TURN LEFT onto toll road.

Tizimín, straight ahead on Hwy #295.

6.4	10.2	Tourist stop at right with restaurant, shops and rest rooms. KM 153
20.4	32.6	Iguana Xing. Scenic value is enhanced by highly colored painted rocks. Mexican NPA project.
30.4	48.6	Pay toll at KM 115.

Chichen-Itza and Piste exit here and follow Log 180-South-8-Stub.

Merida, straight ahead.

59.4	95.0	Pass exit for **Kantunil**. KM 68
61.4	98.2	Toll road ends and joins free road (left).
69.9	111.8	Take right fork to bypass **Xocchel**.
72.9	116.6	Straight and bypass little town of **Hoctun**. Hospital at right.
75.4	120.6	Curve right around Tahmek (gas in town). KM 40
80.4	128.6	Curve right around **Holactun**.

(Over, please)

180-W-1B TOLL
VALLADOLID – MERIDA

JUNE 1992

MI.	KM.	
86.4	138.2	Keep right. Left fork goes to **San Bernardino**.
87.9	140.6	Veer right. Left fork goes to **Tepic**. KM 20

MI.	KM.	
94.1	150.6	Bend left past bypass around village of **Teya**.
Rv 95.4	152.6	**Oasis RV Campgrounds** with 50 spaces (30 E) and pool. (Folks, this opened Oct. 1992, they offer discount to Sanborn's Mexican Club members.) KM 10
95.6	153.0	Take left fork. Straight is to village of **San Pedro**.
96.0	153.6	Come to junction Hwy #184.

Merida, TURN RIGHT onto divided highway.

Campeche and Chetumal, TURN LEFT

96.7	154.7	Topes.
97.0	155.2	Careful as you approach periférico junction, TURN LEFT.
97.7	156.3	**Pacaptun Subdivision**, right.
98.7	157.9	Topes. Over bumpy railroad crossing (LOOK-&-LISTEN).
99.2	158.7	Slow for "topes" and ahead down two-way street narrowing slightly just ahead.
H 100.0	160.0	Pink **Casa Guerrero** at left and on straight ahead street is now one way.
R 100.3	160.5	Gas at left. Straight ahead on brick street past market at right. Watch for traffic lights ahead. Small plaza at right and another market at left.
100.8	161.3	Come to Calle 60 and end of log. See "Eat and Stray— Merida" for lodging.
100.5	160.8	

Uxmal and it archaeological ruins, straight ahead and follow the Merida — Uxmal Special Log.

Campeche via Becal, also straight ahead and pick up Log 180-N-2.

End of Log.

(Next Page, Please)

JUNE 1992   **180-W-1B LIBRE**
VALLADOLID – CHICHEN-ITZA – MERIDA

MEXICO TRAVELOG
Puts over 40 years of experience at your side! Copyright © Sanborn's TGP Inc.

STUB LOG FROM VALLADOLID TO CHICHEN-ITZA AND ON TO MERIDA ON FREE ROAD

SCENIC RATING — 3

» NOTE: Use this log if on your way to Merida you wish to visit BALANKANCHE CAVES (guides available) and the famous Mayan arcaeological zone of CHICHEN-ITZA, where there are several good hotels.

MI.	KM.	
0.0	0.0	Leave **Valldolid** by way of Merida-libre (free) road.
0.8	1.3	Over narrow-gauge railroad that runs all thru these parts.
1.8	2.9	Side road (left) to **"Cenote Dzitnup"**, (go swimming in a cave) 2.5 miles away (admission charged).
3.3	5.3	Straight thru village of **Ebtun**, mostly at right with its prison at left.
6.3	10.1	Past village of **Cuncunal** mostly at left.
14.0	22.4	Pass microwave station at right. Over "topes" and thru village of **kaua**.
21.3	34.1	Thru village of **Xcalacoop**, slow for "topes", curve right past cemetary on right.
22.0	35.2	Side road (right) over to GRUTAS ("caves") DE BALANKANCHE.

» GRUTAS DE BALANKANCHE are really somethin'. In addition to being quite interesting, there is a pool with blind fish and shrimp at the cave's end. Part of this cave was discovered as late as 1959 by a tourist guide. Guided tours are scheduled at 8-9-10-11 in the morning and 2-3-4 in the afternoon (admission charged; children under 6 not admitted).

H

23.0	26.8	**Hotel Dolores Alba** at right.
23.8	38.1	Pass side road to **Hotels Mayaland, Hacienda Chichen,** and **Villa Arqueológica**.
25.8	41.3	Slow now and come to fork. Left is to the Archaeological zone (For ecological reasons, the road that once went thru the archaeological zone now ends at the ruin's entrance.) and straight is to Merida.
26.3	42.1	RV Park at right. Then **Pirámide Inn** at left (it's called "Pirámide" Inn because of a little ancient pyramid on its grounds just behind motel. **Hotel Misión Chichen-Itza** at right. (For info on these accommodations in area, see "Eat and Stray — Chichen-Itza".)
27.3	43.7	**Restaurant Fiesta** at right. Over "topes" and pass side road (right) to **Dzitas**. Gas at right as you enter **Piste**.
28.3	45.3	"Topes" an into village of **Yokdzonot** (just sneeze it!).
39.3	62.9	Thru village of **Libre Unión** with its "topes".
41.4	66.2	Slow for "topes" and straight thru village of **Holca**.
47.6	76.2	Begin four lanes. Careful for "topes". Thru village of **Kantunil**. At plaza pass side road (right) to **Izamul** (meaning "City of the Hills" according to books of Chilam Balam), 15 miles away, an ancient Itza town of 15,000. Its archaeological zone is of interest, particularly the temple standing on Kinich Kakmo, a huge pyramid with the highest staircase of any Mayan structure. Also on site is a 1549 Franciscan convent.
49.8	79.7	Merida libre is joined by toll road from Valladolid at right. Rejoin Log 180-N-1B at mile 61.4

End of Log.

ROUTE SELECTION

RS-MAYA-4

FOR MERIDA MAP AND EAT & STRAY, TURN BACK TO PAGE 45

MERIDA—CANCUN—PLAYA DEL CARMEN—COZUMEL—CHETUMAL, SEE PAGES 55-61

MERIDA—CAMPECHE—ISLA AGUADA—ESCARCEGA, SEE PAGES 79-85 (Campeche Eat & Stray on Page 33)

JUNE 1992   1 of 2   180-N-2
MERIDA – CAMPECHE

MEXICO TRAVELOG
Puts over 40 years of experience at your side!   Copyright © Sanborn's TGP Inc.

MERIDA (CALLES 60 & 65) – UMAN – BECAL – CAMPECHE – 118 MI OR 188.8 KM – DRIVE TIME 3 HOURS

SCENIC RATING — 3

MI.	KM.	
0.0	0.0	Here in downtown **Merida** at corner of Calles 60 and 65, with Banco del Atlántico at right, Proceed ahead (west on one-way Calle 65). Careful as there's usually a lot of traffic as well as pedestrians. Bancomer at left in next block, then cross Calle 62 at traffic light.
1.0	1.6	Zoological garden at right. Then come to stoplight and turn left onto busy, divided Itzaes Blvd.
M*gas* 1.8	2.9	Gas at right. Ford and VW agencies at left and Coca-Cola too.
2.5	4.0	Sign says MEXICO, UMAN, & AEROPUERTO (airport) straight ahead. **Hacienda Inn** at right.
H 2.8	4.5	Federal highway patrol station at right. Then LP gas at right.
3.0	4.8	Gas at right. Pass **Hotel Posada Maya** at right.
3.5	5.6	Slow for "topes" and pass big cement plant "Maya" at right.
4.0	6.4	Entrance (left) to Merida Airport. Ahead for you.
5.5	8.8	"Periférico" (loop) at left to **Chichen-Itza, Cancun** and **Progreso** etc.
M*gas* 5.8	9.3	Gas at right.
8.5	13.6	Mosaic plant at right.
9.5	15.2	Enter town of **Umán** (and follow CAMPECHE 180 signs). Gas at left. **TURN RIGHT**, slow for "topes", and ahead on one-way street.
10.0	16.0	Careful now! Come to junction Hwy #160 and Hwy #180 to Becal. Turn right here at plaza. Then left at far side. Then right and ahead and past little triangular plaza with market behind.

Uxmal Archaeological zone, straight on will take you there over Hwy #261 (follow the Merida-Uxmal- Special and Uxmal-Campeche-Special Logs). Go ahead and take it if you wish; after Uxmal you'll eventually pick up this log again at Mile 100.5)

13.0	20.8	Co-op pig farm at right.
16.0	25.6	Over "tranvía" (narrow-gauged railroad tracks) and thru village of **Hacienda Poxila,** slow for "topes" and over another "tranvía" the transportation system used for hauling sisal (henequen) from the fields to the factories. Note all the cattle ranches through this area that formerly was henequen fields. Since henequen was formerly one of Yucatan's number one crop, let us tell you a little about it.

HENEQUEN, once big business in the Yucatan, has experienced a severe decline in recent decades due to nylon and other synthetic fibers. In the olden days just about all Yucatan's economy was based on henequen, and hardly a day passed without a freighter sailing from Puerto Progreso, north of Merida, with rope and twine made from the henequen plant. Each wealthy henequen grower had a magnificent hacienda with his factory workers' homes also on the home place, and his acres and acres of henequen surrounding it all. You will still see an occasional henequen field as you travel through this area.

(Over, please)

180-N-2
MERIDA – CAMPECHE

MI.	KM.	
		The motive power behind the **TRANVIA** is the "Mexican jeep" or burro. In the olden days the field workers cut the spike leaves off the henequen plant and loaded them onto a little rail flatcar which was pulled to the sisal factory by burro. Most "tranvías" have been pulled up, now that trucks tote what small amount of henequen is now harvested to the mills, but now and then you'll still see one in operation.
20.5	32.8	Take left fork onto bypass around village of **Chochola**.
22.3	35.7	Merge with road at right coming from town.
29.3	46.9	Curve right onto bypass around village of **Kopoma**.
30.8	49.3	Merge with road (left) coming from town.
36.0	57.6	Power substation at left.
36.3	58.1	Slow for bumpy main line railroad crossing (LOOK & LISTEN).
36.8	58.9	Take right fork or bypass around little town of **Maxcanu** over to left.
38.5	61.6	Merge with road at left coming from town. Gas at left.
46.8	74.9	Curve left onto bypass around **Halacho**.
47.8	76.5	Gas station at left. Note basket-and-car-seat stands.
48.5	77.6	Merge with road (right) coming from town. Skip truck inspection at left.
50.0	80.0	Cross state line: Leave Yucatan enter Campeche.
51.0	81.6	Skip another truck inspection at left. Take right fork onto bypass around town of **Becal** over to left. Then a short mile later, cross main line railroad (LOOK & LISTEN).
52.5	84.0	Merge with road (left) coming from town.
54.5	87.2	Take left fork for bypass around little town of **Tepakan**.
55.8	89.3	Take left fork for bypass around **Dzitbalche** and **Calkini**.
62.3	99.7	Pass side road (left) to **Bacabchen**.
66.8	106.9	Thru village of **Pocboc**. Slow for "topes".
68.8	110.1	Pass abandoned hacienda and church community of **Hacienda Blanca Flor** (White Flower).
69.0	110.4	Straight thru village of **Santa Cruz**.
70.8	113.3	Bear left onto bypass around **Hecelchaken**.
75.0	120.0	Onto bypass around **Pomuch**.
82.0	131.2	Thru little town of **Tenabo**. Pas gas station. Slow for "topes", and then another at plaza at right with church on left.
88.3	141.3	Cemetery at right and thru **Tinun**. Careful for topes.
97.8	156.5	Thru village of **Nilchi**.
100.5	160.8	Come now to junction with old Hwy #180. TURN RIGHT when coast is clear and proceed ahead on Hwy #180. (Note: This is where you'd join this highway if you'd taken Hwy #261 back at mile 10.5 on this log.)
108.3	173.3	Pass side road (left) to **X-Campeu**
111.5	178.4	Thru old stone village of **Castamay**. Slow for "topes".
114.5	183.2	Careful for series of curves ahead. then bend left. Road at right is to **Kala Hampolol**. Start nice bypass around **Campeche**.
120.5	192.8	Pass side road (right) to downtown **Campeche** and to Campeche's airport. Road at left is to **China**.
122.0	195.2	Pass access road (right) to Campeche, 4 Km or 2½ Mi away.
125.5	200.8	Come now to junction with side road into Campeche and to Av. Escencia and end of log.

Champoton, straight ahead and start Log 180-North-3A.

Campeche and to Hotels Baluartes or Ramada Inn, follow stub log below:

MI.	KM.	
0.0	0.0	Having taken right side road at Av. Escenica exit off Hwy #180, proceed ahead.
1.0	1.6	Take left fork at this crossroads and follow PEMEX sign and wind down. Right fork is to Av. Escenica ("Scenic" Avenue).
1.5	2.4	Pemex tanks at left. TURN RIGHT on waterfront boulevard.

(Next Page, Please)

MEXICO TRAVELOG
Puts over 40 years of experience at your side! Copyright © Sanborn's TGP Inc.

MI.	KM.	
2.5	4.0	Come to striking magnificent "glorieta" of a man holding a torch, sort of like our own Statue of Liberty, commemorating Mexico's freedom from the rule of Spain. Now onto divided parkway and enter city of **Campeche**, population 162,000, and capital of state of Campeche. Its name is derived from the mayan words "kim" and "pech" which mean "tick of the serpent".
3.3	5.3	Come now to road fork and take left fork. Ahead to yonder "glorieta".
3.8	6.1	At "glorieta" go on around and aim for shoreline drive.
4.3	6.9	Take left fork here and continue on shoreline. (If you wish to contact the tourist department, their office is in this building in fork - but on right side.)
4.5	7.2	Note lagoon at right and fancy ultra-modern state senate building. Then highrise state capitol and farther along is another ancient fort.
H 4.8	7.7	Come now to **Hotel Baluartes** ("forts"). **Ramada Inn** (Ph: (981) 6-2233; Fax: 1-1618.) is next door. (For info on these and other accommodations in the area, see "Eat & Stray — Campeche".)

When you're ready to return to the highway, just retrace your steps.

End of Log.

MEXICO TRAVELOG
Puts over 40 years of experience at your side! Copyright © Sanborn's TGP Inc.

CAMPECHE (AV. ESCENICA EXIT) TO CHAMPOTON (JUNCTION HIGHWAY #261) - 39.5 MI or 63.2 KM — DRIVE TIME 1 HOUR

SCENIC RATING — 3

» **CARSICK ALERT: You may want to take Dramamine.**

MI.	KM.	
0.0	0.0	On bypass at junction with road (right) to Av. Escenica and to **Campeche**, proceed ahead.
3.5	5.6	End of bypass. Road (right) is to waterfront town of **Lerma**.
6.5	10.4	Pass side road (right) to **Playa Bonita**, a public beach. *When writers refer...*
10.0	16.0	Now alongside gulf for spell.
14.5	23.2	Slow now and take left fork for bypass around little town of **Seybaplaya**.
18.3	29.3	Merge with old road (right) coming from town. Gas at left.
21.0	33.6	Roadside park at right. Then beachfront community of **El Pedregal**.
22.0	35.2	Slow now and come to **Hotel Mision Si-Ho Playa** at right on beach, once an old abandoned hacienda falling to pieces, but somebody came along and did a magnificent job of fixing it up (82 a/c rooms; restaurant specializing in seafood; bar; pool; tennis; fishing and hunting; AE, MC, VI).
23.0	36.8	Settlement of **Costa Blanca** ("White Coast"). *To themselves as we...*
23.5	37.6	More beach homes, and past little settlement of **Acapulquito** ("Little Acapulco") at right.
25.0	40.0	Thru **Villa Madero** and slow for pair of "topes".
27.0	43.2	Village of **Haltunchen** over at left. Side road (left) is to railroad village of **Hool**.
27.5	44.0	Pass side road (left) to **EDZNA** (sometimes spelled "Etzna") **RUINS**.
28.5	45.6	**Ciudad del Sol** ("Sun City") Subdivision at left. Then social security hospital, also at left. Pass side road (left) to **La Joya**.
30.0	48.0	Slow for sharp right curve over little bridge. *And to the reader as you...*
34.0	54.4	Alongside sand dunes and palms with green waters of bay beyond.
37.0	59.2	Over bridge and enter coastal town of **Champoton**, population 12,000. Ahead down waterfront past gas station at left.
38.0	60.8	Past Bus depot and social security (I.M.S.S.) hospital at left.
39.0	62.4	Past Hotel **Venecia** ("Venice") at left. *It's 2 against 1.* —Judith Rascoe
39.3	62.9	Bay at right and "rastro" (slaughterhouse) at left.
39.5	63.2	Come now to junction of inland Hwy #261 (left).

Villahermosa (and Palenque) via inland Highway #261-186, **TURN LEFT** here and proceed down one-way narrow street thru town and start Log 261-South-1.

Isla Aguada and on to Villahermosa via ferry on older Gulf Highway #180, continue **STRAIGHT** here. Start Isla Aguada Special-North. There's only one ferry now and it's a pleasant drive, great for birders and nature lovers. Some times the road is rough, so RV's take note. There's a very nice RV park, hotel, cabin layout at Isla Aguada (open in winter, but sporadic in summer).

End of Log.

(Next page, please)

MEXICO TRAVELOG
Puts over 40 years of experience at your side! Copyright © Sanborn's TGP Inc.

CHAMPOTON (JUNCTION HWY #180) TO ESCARCEGA (JUNCTION HWY #186) 51.0 MI OR 81.6 KM – DRIVE TIME 1 – 1½ HOURS

SCENIC RATING — 1

» NOTE: You'll see some village names that have an X in front of them. In Maya this is pronounced "sh". For example, a village named X-Moo would be pronounced "Shmoo"; one named X-Nuk would be pronounced "Schnook".

MI.	KM.	
0.0	0.0	Starting here at junction Hwy #180-261 with the Gulf to your right, TURN LEFT and proceed down narrow one-way street thru town. Follow ESCARCEGA sign.
1.0	1.6	Rice processing plant at left.
1.5	2.4	Pass Lienzo de Charro (rodeo arena) at right.
3.5	5.6	Pass side road to **Ulumal** and **Pustunch**.
8.4	13.4	Thru village of **Vicente Guerrero** named after a revolutionary hero, general, and president (1829-1831). Slow for "topes".
13.8	22.2	Curve right and then thru big **Ejido Pixtun**.
18.0	28.8	Thru stretched-out village of **José María Morelos y Pavón**, named for one of Mexico's greatest revolutionary heroes (1765-1815), the man with the terrible headaches.
26.0	41.6	Pass side road (left) to railroad village of **Aquiles Serdan**, a revolutionary hero (1876-1910) and forerunner of the Mexican Revolution.
27.2	43.5	Bend right and thru village of **X-Bacab**. Then pass side road (left) to **Pixoyal**.
29.7	47.5	Past lumber mill over to right. Then thru **Ejido Revolución**.
32.2	51.5	Pass side trail to microwave tower.
36.7	58.7	Thru community of **Cantemo**.
41.7	66.7	Thru **Villa Carranza** at left. Then thru community of **La Esperanza**.
44.0	70.4	Now up and down thru several miles of rock cuts.
50.5	80.8	Past school at right.
51.0	81.6	Come to junction Hwy #186 and end of log. There is Mgas around corner at right. Left for Escarcega.

Chetumal, TURN LEFT and follow Log 186-East-3.

Villahermosa, TURN RIGHT and follow Log 186-West-2.

End of Log.

(Next page, please)

ROUTE SELECTION   RS-MAYA-5

PALENQUE—ESCARCEGA, GO TO PAGE 107 START LOG 186-W-2

CANCUN — PLAYA DEL CARMEN, NEXT PAGE (87), START LOG 307-S-1

JUNE 1992 • PTO JUAREZ – F. CARRILLO PUERTO

MEXICO TRAVELOG
Puts over 40 years of experience at your side! Copyright © Sanborn's TGP Inc.

PUERTO JUAREZ (JCT HWY #180) — FELIPE CARRILLO PUERTO (JCT HWY 184) — 140 MI OR 224 KM — DRIVE TIME 2½-3 HOURS

SCENIC RATING — 3

» NOTE: This Log takes you past Puerto Morelos and Playa del Carmen, the "jumping off" places, to Cozumel Island. Also it takes you past fabulous Cancún (deluxe hotels, marina, international airport, etc.) and past Tulúm archaeological "zona" (interesting Mayan ruins), and past Caleta Xel-Ha natural aquarium).

MI.	KM.	
0.0	0.0	Starting here at Av. J. Lopez Portillo and Av. Tulúm with plaza at right and Goodyear at left, TURN RIGHT (south) onto divided Av. Tulúm. "ZONA HOTELERA" and "CANCUN, CHETUMAL" signs at right. Blanco Store at right. Enter resort town of **Cancún**.
0.2	0.3	Stoplight. Go halfway around "glorieta" (circle) and proceed straight ahead (follow CHETUMAL sign). **Suites Paraiso Hotel** at right. **McDonald's** at left. **Comercial Mexicana** at left. Bus station at right.
0.7	1.1	Cross Av. Uxmal at "glorieta" (go halfway around) and proceed ahead. **Restaurant Bananas** (on access street) and **Novotel** at right. **Pizza Hut** at right. Bancomer at left
1.2	1.9	Come to "glorieta". Careful for stop light and straight ahead (follow TULUM and AEROPUERTO signs). Left is to Zona Hotelera and Av. Cobá. English AA is ½ block on right at Plaza América Shopping Center, 2nd floor, room 33 (meets daily at 6:15 PM). At right is **Super Deli**. At left, next to VW agency is good **Hotel América** (The best in town, also American Express office). The **American Hospital** (Viento #15 SM4, Ph: 84-6133 or 84-6068) is over on your left, opposite Hotel América.
3.0	4.8	Regular gas station at right. Shortcut to Merida at right (Hwy #180).
5.8	9.3	Beer warehouse (Superior brand) and distributing office at right.
6.3	10.1	**Ejido Alfredo V. Bonfil** at right.
9.3	14.9	Central de Abastos (Farmer's market) at right.
10.0	16.0	Pass side road (right) to Cancun's International Airport. Continue straight ahead following CHETUMAL sign. Under overpass there's a right turn for Zona Hotelera (Cancun).
13.6	21.8	End divided highway.
22.5	36.0	Gas station, right. Pass side road (left) to seashore town of **Puerto Morelos** where you can catch the commercial ferry to **Cozumel**. Ferry departs daily for Cozumel at 6 AM, but be here by 4:30 AM. It departs from Cozumel for mainland at 2 PM (Monday at 5 PM). The crossing takes 2-3 hours, depending on winds and tides. RV's awaiting departure of ferry can overnight in ferry parking lot.
		Hotel La Ceiba & Ojo de Agua blew away, but on the plaza is the ** **Hotel Villas Latinas**, a modern 2 story hotel on the water. If you kept going straight and didn't turn off to the square, you'd pass the *** **Hotel Posada Amor**, PH: (987) 100-33), one of my favorites. They are simple, natural cabañas in a garden-type setting. Reasonable price. The owner is very friendly and proud of his electronic organ. The adjacent restaurant is simple, hearty and healthy. Highly recommended.
		There is a neat couple who rent nice cabañas close by, ** **Rancho Libertad**. Jack there does personal growth workshops. The cabañas are roomy, with ceiling fans and economical. Someday they plan to have a hot tub — not a jacuzzi.

(Over, please)

307-S-1
PTO JUAREZ – F. CARRILLO PUERTO
JUNE, 1992

MI.	KM.	
H		Farther down the road are the **** **Villas Marina** — PH: (90) 987-411-47 (cellular can be called from Cancun or Pto. Morelos) anywhere else call (91-987) 4-1147. US: 1-800-3-CAN-CUN. They're run by Tom and Vicki Sharp. They also have the **Caribbean Reef Room** restaurant. Both are first-class, luxury-type places. Closer to town is the **Villas Shanti**, a Yoga retreat, run by Jean and Jack Loew. They operate by reservations only and cater to Yoga groups, but you can contact John Mastromarino at the **Villas Clarita**, one block closer to town than Villas Shanti. He has nice apartments for rent too. You can also reach him at the **Palapa Pizza Restaurant** on the plaza. Phone: (987) 1-0042 Fax: (987) 1-0041. Less expensive is **Los Aricefes** — across from the back of Villas Shanti (on the main road that runs from the plaza, on the beach side) — 8 rooms, 1 Br. and kitchenettes. No credit cards. See "Eat & Stray Playa del Carmen" for more info on lodging.
23.4	37.4	Jardín Botánica Dr. Alfredo Parrera Morín (Botanical Garden), left.
30.4	48.6	**Playa Paraíso Condos** at left.
37.6	60.2	At left, **Cabañas Capitán LaFitte** Apdo. Postal 1463, Merida Ph: (99) 23-0485, 24-1548, Fax 23-7142 USA 800-538-6804 (23 cabañas; ceiling fans; restaurant; bar; fishing boats, scuba diving).
38.5	61.6	Pass side trail (left) to **Punta Bete**. Right now ** **Kailuum** is still down the road a piece, but they'll be moving sooner or later. It's a rustic, fancy tent hotel. They have these huge tents with beds and good mosquito netting right on the beach. There is communal dining and the whole place is operated by a real conservationist. There's no electricity and they don't want any. They're closed Sept-Oct.
39.5	63.2	Pass side trail (left) to **Xcalacoco Campground**. Phone: (99) 23-0485 or 24-1545.
41.6	66.6	At left, **Shangri La Caribe** (70 rooms, 2-bed semi-cabañas, Ph: (987) 2-2888 & Fax; open Nov 15 - Apr 30) and **Las Palapas** (just as nice) Ph: (987) 2-2972 Fax 4-1678.
		Superior Beer at left.
42.5	68.0	Come now to side road (left) to seaside town of **Playa del Carmen**, the "jumping off" place to **Cozumel**. Turnoff is beyond the sign. Turn at **Restaurant El Faisán y el Venado**.
H		**PLAYA DEL CARMEN**, with a Mexican-Caribbean flavor all its own, boast an airport, 9 nice residential subdivisions, many small but good restaurants and several arts and crafts shops. This place has developed tremendously in the past few years, but is still "funky" and a different world than Cancun, so if you don't like Cancun, you'll probably like this place. I do. From Playa del Carmen, 3 passenger ferries depart daily at 5:30, 7:30, 9:30, 10:15, 10:30, 11:00 AM, 12:15, 2:30, 5:30, 6:30, 7:30, 9:00 PM from pier across from **Hotel Las Molcas** where tickets may be purchased. Departures from Cozumel back to mainland are at 4:00, 6:30, 8:00, 9:00, 11:00 AM, 2:00, 4:00, 4:30, 5:30, 6:00, 6:30, and 8:00 PM (times subject to change). The trip takes about 45 to 50 minutes each way. See "Eat & Stray" for hotels. KM 290
46.5	74.4	**Xcaret** is well developed and pricey, but a pretty nice placed to spend the day — especially if you have kids.
Rv 53.0	84.8	Pass side road (left) to little town of **Pamul** and to **Cabañas Pamul Trailer Park** with 63 spaces; electricity; water; dump station; showers; toilets; restaurant; bar; fishing trips. Reservations: Av. Colon # 501-c Dept.-d-211, Merida, Yuc. 97000. Phone and Fax (98) 25-9422.
55.5	88.8	**Puerto Aventuras** on the left. Modern, highrise resort complex.
58.0	92.8	Pass side road (left) to **Xpu-há**, sand camping.
60.2	96.3	Pass **Kantenáh**, for the adventures.
62.5	100.0	Artisans and restaurants at right.

» One lizard you'll see around here is the Basilisk which reaches the length of a yard; its color is green and brown while its crest is reddish. According to Mayan legend, he obtained the crest that runs down his back when he won a race with a deer. The Lord of the woods had placed a bench at the finish line for the winner. The deer arrived first, of course, but when he started to sit down, the Basilisk shouted, "Look out, you big galoot! I was here first." Sure enough, the wily lizard was already on the bench. How did he out run the deer? He didn't. He hitched a ride on the tail if the deer and jumped off just before he sat down. That just goes to show — sometimes you win by chasing tail.

| H 64.0 | 102.4 | Pass side road (left) to **Villas Akumal Caribe**. |

(Next Page, Please)

JUNE 1992 **EAT & STRAY PLAYA DEL CARMEN**

PLAYA DEL CARMEN

AREA CODE — 987   Copyright © Sanborn's TGP Inc.

SLEEPING AROUND PUERTO MORELOS

** **HOTEL VILLAS LATINAS** —MOD— On the plaza a modern 2 story hotel on the water.

*** **HOTEL POSADA AMOR** —ECON— PH: (987) 1-0033), one of my favorites. They are 20 simple, natural cabanas is d'garden-type setting. Reasonable price. The owner is very friendly and proud of his electronic organ. The adjacent restaurant is simple, hearty and healthy. Water sports: Diving. Highly recommended.

** **RANCHO LIBERTAD** —ECON— There is a neat couple who rent nice cabanas close by, Jack there does personal growth workshops. The cabanas are roomy, ceiling fans and economical. Someday they plan to have a hot tub — not a jacuzzi.

**** **VILLAS MARINA** —UPPER— PH: (90) 987-411-47 (cellular can be called from Cancun or Pto. Morelos) anywhere else call (91-987) 4-1147. US: 1-800-3-CANCUN. They're run by Tom and Vicki Sharp. They also have the **Caribbean Reef Room Restaurant**. Both are first-class, luxury-type places.

*** **VILLAS SHANTI** —UPPER— A Yoga retreat, run by Jean and Jack Loew. Take last left before plaza. They are on Av. Niños Heroes 7 blocks on right (0.6 Mi. from road into town). They operate by reservations only and cater to Yoga groups, but you can contact John Mastromarino at the Villas Clarita. Reservations: Apdo. Postal # 789 Cancun, Q.R. 77500 Phone: (987) 1-0040 or P.O.Box # 464, Glen, N.H. 03838 Phone: (603) 383-6501

*** **VILLAS CLARITA** —UPPER— One block closer to town than Villas Shanti. John has nice apartments for rent too. (No kids under 12) You can also reach him at the Palapa Pizza Restaurant on the square. Phone: (987) 1-0042 Fax: (987) 1-0041

** **LOS ARICEFES** —MOD— Less expensive, 8 rooms, 1BR and kitchenettes. No credit cards.

SLEEPING AROUND PLAYA DEL CARMEN

** **QUINTA MIJA** (Mi= Micah, Ja= Jacab) —MOD— Apdo #54 — Perhaps my favorite little hotel in Mexico — take a left as you enter town (1 block before beach), go 4 blocks past Chicago Restaurant, and it's on your left. It's a tucked-away paradise, but only for special people like me. It ain't fancy and it ain't air-conditioned and it ain't for disco Joes. What it is nice-sized two story kitchenette-condos which are homey, functional and reasonably priced. Ceiling fans. Atmosphere is warm and cozy. Nice little pool. Parking. Caribbean-style bar. English spoken. Owned by a nice couple, Greg & Sally who hail from Colorado. PH: 3-0111. In US, call 1-800-538-6802, or (303) 674-9615.

** **COSTA DEL MAR** —MOD— 5th Av & 6th St., across street from Chicago. 3 story, moderate A/C hotel. Not on the beach, but reasonably priced. Plumbing is U.S. style so you can flush paper — unusual in inexpensive hotels here. English spoken. PH & FAX: 2-0231. In Houston (713) 783-4322.

** **BLUE PARROT HOTEL** —MOD— On the beach and several styles of rooms, from simple to private bungalows, also restaurant. Popular. English spoken. MEX PH: 3-0083, FAX: 3-0049. P.O. Box 64. US PH: 1-800-634-9547, (904)775-6660.

HOTEL DELFIN —ECON— Apdo. Postal # 38, Playa del Carmen, Q. Roo 77710 PH: 3-0176 — simple, reasonable, a block from beach.

(More Goodies on other side)

**EAT & STRAY
PLAYA DEL CARMEN**   JUNE, 1992

**   **KAI LUUM** —MOD— KM298 (Punta Bete) A rustic fancy tent hotel. No electricity. Communal dining. English spoken. Reservations: Write to Camtel Ventures, Box 2664, Evergreen, CO 80439 USA.

****   **LAS MOLCAS** —UPPER— This is a first-class highrise with A/C. Restaurant. Bar. CATV. Pool. It's to the right of the ferry dock, but an easier entrance before you get to town. Follow signs. AE, MC, VI. Ph: (Merida) (99) 21-6661.

EATING PLAYA DEL CARMEN

***   **CHICAGO** —UPPER— Good U.S. style restaurant owned by Bill & "Chicago" Jeanette Harris. Seafood, steaks, ribs and sports bar. Everything there is first-class quality. 5th ?Ave. & 6th St. PH: 3-0208.

**   **DA GABI RESTAURANT** —MOD— Shucks, folks, I can't say enough good things about this place. One block towards town form Quinta Mija and 1/2 block towards beach, on left. It has really good pasta and other Italian food, seafood, croissants, healthy food and atmosphere. Open 7-10:30 AM for breakfast & 6-11 PM for dinner. Reasonable prices and outdoor dining.

SLEEPING AROUND AKUMAL

***   **CLUB AKUMAL CARIBE, and VILLAS MAYA** —UPPER— 21 rooms, 40 bungalows A/C kitchenettes; restaurants; palapa bar; dive shop, (rentals and instruction available); gift shop; pool; quiet lagoon with tropical fish; lots of coconut palms; plus 4 miles of beautiful beach. Phone:(987) 2-2532. VI, MC, AE.

***   **LAS CASITAS AKUMAL** —UPPER— Nice palapas, pool. Pricey. PH: (987) 2-2554, USA 1-800-AKUMAL. V, MC.

***   **AKUMAL CANCUN** —UPPER— 82 A/C rooms, tennis courts, less expensive. AE, MC, VI. PH: (987) 2-2453 & FAX: (987) 2567.

**   **AVENTURAS DE AKUMAL** —UPPER— A posh hotel; restaurant, bar; pool.

*   **CAPHE-HA** —MOD— Guest house on beach at Tulum turnoff in the Sian Ka'an ecological preserve. Reservations: Guy Frankel in Sidona, Arizona, Phone: (602) 282-4435 or in New York, Jeff Frankel, Phone: (212) 219-2198.

CAMPING, PARKING AND PLUGGING IN!

*   **XCALACOCO CAMPGROUNDS** —ECON— (Punta Bete) Good for tents and hammocks; showers and toilets. Phone: (99) 23-0485 or 24-1545.

*   **RV CAMPAMENTO LA RUINA** —ECON— (Puerto del Carmen) Off Calle 2, towards beach. Nicely run place with a little ruin. Hookups. Friendly.

  "CABAÑAS PAMUL" TRAILER PARK —ECON— KM274 63 Spaces; electricity; water; dump station; showers; toilets; restaurant; bar; fishing trips. Reservations: Av. Colón # 501-C, Dept. D-211, Merida, Yuc. 97000 Phone and Fax: (99) 25-9422.

12 STEP PROGRAMS

AA (English) — At Puerto Morelos, 1 Km. beyond Villas Shanti on left just before dead end (it's a sand road). It's a 2-story house and may have "AA" sign. There's a large dog in yard.

END OF EAT & STRAY

(Please turn page!)

COZUMEL ISLAND

This very pleasant, restful get-away place is approx a dozen miles off the east coast of the Yucatan Peninsula and it's 30-odd miles long and about 9 miles across. A flat and jungle-like brush covers the island. A Spanish explorer name of Juan de Grijalva discovered the island in 1518 and a year or so later Cortez came along and paid a visit. Later such famous pirates as Henry Morgan and Jean Lafitte used the island for a hide-out. Incidentally, Cozumel means "tern" or "sea swallow" in Mayan and the official name of the town is "San Miguel de Cozumel".

As you'll note on the map there are a number of ancient pre-Columbian Mayan (or possibly Toltec?) archaeological ruins scattered around the island. Most of the ruins aren't very well maintained and neither are they particularly spectacular, especially after you've visited Chichen Itza or Uxmal. An expedition from Harvard and Arizona University uncovered ruins of some interest called "San Gervasio" containing about 200 separate buildings including two temples dating from the 13th to 15th centuries.

Chankanaab, about 4.5 miles south of town, is a marine life preservation lagoon, an underwater natural park, and botanical garden. Meaning "small sea", Chankanaab is a natural fish sanctuary inhabited by jillions of multi-colored tropical coral, turtles, crabs, lobsters, etc. The beautiful clear blue water changes to shades of green and aqua at various times of day. A subterranean channel connects Chankanaab with the sea causing the surface to rise and fall with the tide. Scuba and snorkel gear is for rent and cold drinks are available.

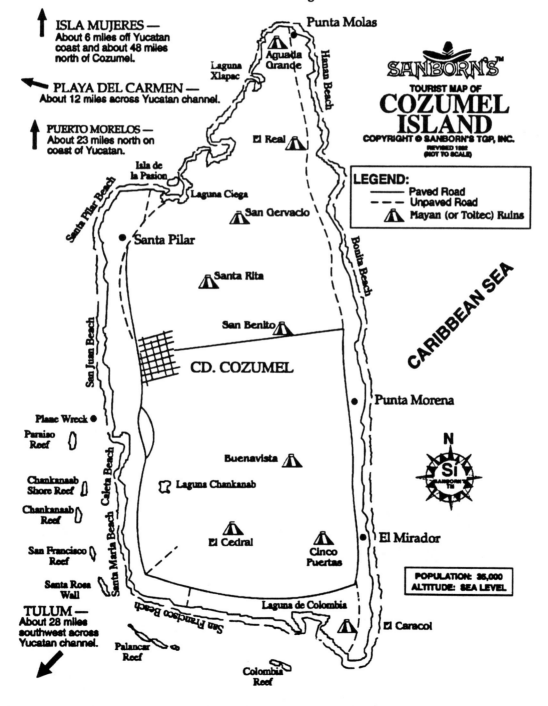

WHAT TO DO IN COZUMEL

ROBINSON CRUSOE TOUR — Boat trip (*Acali* or *Matanzeros*) to San Francisco or Palancar Beach. Enroute divers will dive for conch. Lunch and refreshments are included. Take your snorkel gear along. Tour departs daily from Cozumel Caribe Hotel at 9 AM and from El Presidente Hotel at 9:30, returning at 3 PM and 3:30 respectively.

GLASS-BOTTOM BOAT — Cruises depart around 10 AM from the pier or you can request that you be picked up at your hotel. Arrangements can be made at *Aqua Safari, Viajes y Deportes del Caribe*, or through your hotel.

TULUM BOAT TRIP — Ferry over to mainland (weather permitting) for a visit to the Tulum archaeological site. Depart by ferry around 9:30 AM and return about 7 PM. Take your scuba and snorkel gear. Trips to Tulum and other archaeological sites can also be arranged by private plane - contact *Turismo Aviomar* at Rafael Melgar 29 (phone 2-03-62) or your hotel.

FISHING — Arrangements can be made by the *Boat Association* at the pier (phone 2-00-80) or through your hotel.

SCUBA DIVING — A dive trip with *Aqua Safari* or *Discover Cozumel* includes boat trip to reef, guide, all dive gear, 2 dives, 2 tanks of air, and lunch (with all drinks). Trip departs at 9:30 AM (6-10 divers) and returns at 4 PM. Divers are required to show a C card. Also available is a 2-hour diving trip at night from 7-9 PM. Reservations for either trip should be made a day in advance. **WATER SKIING** — Available at most beachfront hotels.

PUERTO MORELOS CAR/PASSENGER FERRY SERVICE — Depart from Puerto Morelos at 7 AM and from Cozumel at 11 AM from pier near El Presidente. Trip takes approximately 4 hours. Call 2-0827 for departure times.

PLAYA DEL CARMEN PASSENGER FERRY — Three 75-minute round trips daily between Playa del Carmen and Cozumel. Tickets can be purchased at ferry office in front of Hotel Molcas just across from pier an hour prior to departure. The schedule is as follows:

LEAVE COZUMEL	LEAVE PLAYA DEL CARMEN
4:00 AM	5:30 AM
6:30 AM	7:30 AM
9:00 AM	10:15 AM
11:00 AM	12:15 PM
1:30 PM	2:30 PM
4:00 PM	5:30 PM
6:30 PM	7:30 PM

PLAYA DEL CARMEN — CANCUN BOAT SERVICE
Several departures daily from Cozumel from marina near Aviomar Turismo via Catamaran water jet. Contact Turismo Aviomar, Av. Rafael Melgar 13; phone 2-0588 or 2-0477. Also have jet boat.

PLAYA DEL CARMEN — COZUMEL FLIGHT SERVICE
Flights daily via Air Tri-Lander Aircraft. 4 flights each way, 11 minutes long. Flights leave Playa del Carmen at 9:26 AM, 11:26 AM, 3:20 PM and 5:20 PM. Flights leave Cozumel at 9:00 AM, 11:00 AM, 3:00 PM and 5:00 PM.

VEHICLE RENTAL — Cars, motorcycles, and bicycles can be rented at *Ruben's* on the south side of the plaza, *Aquila, Pancho Rentals, Rentador Caribe, Avis, Hertz*, or at your hotel.

SIGHTSEEING, TOURS, ETC. — There are several good travel agencies in the area including "Fiesta Cozumel Holidays" located on the waterfront (phone 2-0522 or 2-0433; "Viajes y Deportes del Caribe", Hotel El Presidente (phone 2-0322 or 2-0923) or "Aviomar" next to Joaquin's on waterfront (phone 2-0477). They can arrange for transfers, cruises, safaris, excursions, fishing, and scuba expeditions, rental cars, etc. A good tour operator is Barbara Navarreze, Calle 20 NTE Door Cov. Sindicato de Guias Y Similores de Q. Roo. Ph: 2-3041.

SIESTA — 1 PM TO 5 PM. Stores are closed. The place is dead. Take a nap.

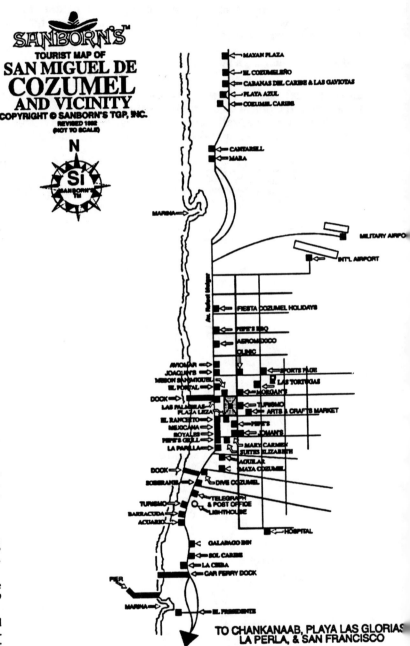

JULY 1991

**EAT & STRAY
COZUMEL, QR**

COZUMEL

AREA CODE — 987   Copyright © Sanborn's TGP Inc.

| SLEEPING AROUND |

* **AGUILAR** —MOD— 20-room air-con motel at south edge of town at AV. 5 Sur & Calle 3 Sur. No restaurant. Pool. Parking. Ph: 2-0307.

* **BARRACUDA** —MOD— 4-story, 30-room beachfront air-con hotel at south edge of town. No restaurant. Diving equipment rental, instruction, and trips. Parking. AE, MC, VI. Ph: 2-0002.

** **CABAÑAS DEL CARIBE** —MOD— Tropical 57-room air-con hotel at north end on Carretera Santa Pilar. Restaurant. Bar. Pool (plus natural salt-water pool). Travel agency. Gift shop. Parking. AE, MC, VI. Ph: 2-0017 or 2-0072.

** **CANTARELL** —MOD— 3-story, 109-room air-con north beach hotel. Restaurant. Bar. 2 pools. Gift shop. Parking. AE, MC, VI. Ph: 2-0144. FAX: 2-0016.

CASA DEL MAR —MOD— 98-room, 8-cabana air-con hotel. Restaurant. Pool. Bar. Ph: 2-1665. In US Toll free: 800-621-5277.

** **COZUMEL CARIBE** —MOD— 12-story, 245-unit air-con beachfront tropical hotel at north end. Restaurant. Bar. Pool. Tennis. Shuffleboard. Gift shops. Parking. AE, MC, VI. Ph: 2-0100 or 2-0021.

*** **EL COZUMELENO** —MOD— VALUE. 5-story, 100-room beachfront hotel at far north end. Wonderful atmosphere. A delightful place. Info on friends of Bill W. ask in resturant. Restaurant. Bar. Pool. Tennis. Shops. Parking. AE, MC, VI. Ph: 2-0344, 2-0149, or 2-0050. FAX: 2-0381.

EL PIRATA —ECON— 2-story, 21-room downtown hotel a half-block south of plaza at 5a Av. Sur 3a. Some air-con. No restaurant. Parking. Ph: 2-0051.

**** **EL PRESIDENTE** —UPPER— 5-story, 192-room luxury air-con beachfront hotel about 3 1/2 miles south of town. Restaurant. Bar. Disco. Large pool. Tennis. Games. Shops. Car rental. Parking. AE, MC, VI. Ph: 2-0322.

*** **FIESTA AMERICANA SOL CARIBE** —UPPER— 220-room, 10-story luxury air-con hotel on beach across from La Ceiba. Restaurant. Coffee shop. Bar. Beach club. Mariachi club. Disco. Pool. Tennis. Boutique. Travel agency. Tobacco shop. Parking. AE, MC, VI. Ph: 2-1711 or 2-0700 Fax: 21301 US: 800-FIESTA-1.@E&S STARS = *

GALAPAGO INN —MOD— 24-room air-con hotel about 1.5 miles south of town on beach. Restaurant. 3-7 day diving packages. Parking. Ph: 2-0663. Caters to divers.

** **LA CEIBA** —UPPER— 11-story, 112-room air-con hotel about 3 miles south of town just before El Presidente. Restaurants. Bars. Pool. Whirlpool. Tennis. Car rental. Scuba shop. Complete water sports center including certified scuba instructors. Parking. AE, MC, VI. Ph: 2-0379.

** **LA PERLA** —MOD— 30-room air-con beachfront hotel on road to Chankanaab (Kilometer 2). Restaurant. Bar. Pool. Dock. Robinson Crusoe Cruise. Parking. AE, MC, VI. Ph: 2-0188.

*** **MARA** —MOD-UPPER— 4-story, 48-room air-con hotel on north beach just before marina. Restaurant. Bar. Pool. Parking. AE, MC, VI. Ph: 2-0300 or 2-0194.

MARY CARMEN—MOD—2-story, 27-room air-con hotel a half-block south of Pepe's Restaurant at 5a AV. Sur 11. No restaurant. Parking. Ph: 2-0581.

(More Goodies on other side)

EAT & STRAY
COZUMEL, QR

JULY 1991

* **MAYA COZUMEL** —MOD— Small, 2-story, 39-room air-con hotel on south side. No restaurant. Pool. Parking. AE, MC, VI. Ph: 2-0011.

*** **MAYAN PLAZA** —MOD-UPPER— 12-story, 94-room elegant Mayan-style hotel on far north end on San Juan Beach. Restaurant. Bar. Pool. Tennis. Shops. Parking. AE, MC, VI. Ph: 2-0411 or 2-0072.

* **MESON SAN MIGUEL** —MOD— 4-story, 97-room air-con hotel on downtown plaza a half-block from main dock. Restaurant. Pool. Parking. AE, MC, VI. Ph: 2-0233.

* **PLAYA AZUL** —MOD— 3-story, 64-room air-con hotel on north beach. Restaurant. Bar. Pool. Tennis. Parking. AE, MC, VI. Ph: 2-0043 or 2-0199.

PLAYA LAS GLORIAS —MOD— 163-room hotel on Av. Rafael Melgar KM 1.5. Restaurant. 2 Bars. Pool. Parking. AE, MC, VI. Ph: 2-2000 or 2-1937.

SUITES ELIZABETH —MOD— 5 air-con apartments, each with kitchenette and sitting room, downtown a block south of plaza and a half-block from waterfront at Calle Salas 44. No restaurant. Parking. Ph: 2-0330.

EATING COZUMEL

** **ACUARIO** —MOD— Nice restaurant located on south side where aquarium once stood. Enjoy excellent steaks, soups, lobster, fish, conch, shrimp, turtle (seasonal), and oysters. Open noon till midnight. AE, MC, VI.

** **EL PORTAL** —MOD— Good restaurant downtown across from plaza. Features seafood, lobster, venison, and Lebanese dishes. Open 7 AM-11 PM.

*** **EL RANCHITO** —MOD— Mexican cafe in nicely remodeled colonial home converted to restaurant at Av. Melgar #141. Tex-Mex, seafood, and steaks. Indoor and outdoor dining. Open 7:30 AM till 11 PM. Closed Sunday. AE, MC, VI. Ph: 2-1154.

** **LAS GAVIOTAS** —MOD— Good international and Mexican-style restaurant at Cabanas del Caribe. Mariachi show Mondays and Wednesdays, 6:30-7:30 PM, 8:30-9:30 PM; Mexican folkloric show Fridays at 7:30-9:30 PM. AE, MC, VI. Ph: 2-0017.

** **LAS PALMERAS** —MOD— Open-air restaurant overlooking ocean across from pier at Av. Juarez & Rafeal Melgar. American and Mexican food plus seafood. Delicious tropical drinks. Great spot for "people watching". Open for breakfast, lunch, and dinner. AE, MC, VI. Ph: 2-0532

** **LAS TORTUGAS** —MOD— Mexican restaurant at Av. Diez North #82. Extensive Mexican food menu plus seafood steaks. Open 11 AM-12 AM. MC, VI.

*** **MORGAN'S** —MOD— Fine restaurant, a downtown landmark, at Av. 5 and Juarez, named after Henry Morgan, the 17th-century pirate. Offers seafood and international cuisine. Open 12 PM till 4 PM for lunch; 6:30 PM till 11 PM for dinner. Disco 9 PM till 3 AM. AE, MC, VI. Ph: 2-0584.

** **PEPE'S BBQ** —MOD— Western-style restaurant on waterfront. Specialties include steaks, seafood, ribs, and Mexican food. Live country music from 8 PM till closing. Open 5 PM till 1 AM. AE, MC, VI.

** **PEPE'S GRILL** —MOD— Gourmet restaurant on Av. Rafael Melgar facing ocean. Seafood specialties. Live music nightly. Beautiful decor and gracious atmosphere. Open 5 PM till 12 AM. AE, MC, VI.

** **PEPE'S** —MOD— Popular old-time open-air restaurant around corner southeast of plaza. Specializes in steaks, seafood, and Mexican food. Open 7 AM till 12 AM daily. AE, MC, VI.

* **PLAZA LEZA** —MOD— Informal cafe on main plaza. Indoor and outdoor dining. Short orders including sandwiches and tacos plus seafood and steaks. Open 10 AM till 12 AM daily. AE, MC, VI.

(Please turn page!)

*** **ROYALES** —MOD-UPPER— Nice, cool, pleasant restaurant a half block south of plaza on waterfront at Rafael E. Melgar Av. #15.. Steaks, seafood, and Spanish dishes. Open 3 PM-2 AM. Live music 9:30 till 10:30 PM. AE, MC, VI. Ph: 2-1439.

* **SAN FRANCISCO** —MOD— Very rustic thatched-roof open-air restaurant far south of town on Playa San Francisco (as a matter of fact, floors are sand). Features fresh seafood. Open 9 AM till 4 PM daily.

** **SOBERANIS** —MOD— Excellent seafood restaurant on waterfront south of plaza at Av. Melgar #471. Serves seafood plus Mexican food and steaks; good breakfast, too. Open 8 AM till 12 AM. Live music 1 till 6 PM. Ph: 2-0246.

*** **SPORTS PAGE** —MOD— Real sports aficionado's hangout at Av. Cinco Norte #13 & Calle 2 Norte. Fine food and service. Sports paraphernalia throughout. Very clean. Satellite TV. Indoor and outdoor dining. Nice bar. Fish, lobster, steaks, Mexican food, and sandwiches. Open 10 AM till 12 AM daily. MC, VI. Ph: 2-1199.

12 STEP PROGRAMS

TABLA DE SALVACION — 632 S. 20th Av. between 7th & 9th streets. Su M W F 6 PM.

End of Eat & Stray.

(More Goodies on other side)

TravMed - A "Must" For Any American Traveling Abroad!

TravMed takes over where your regular hospitalization and medical plan rarely go... into a foreign country.

Don't take for granted that your U.S. hospitalization plan provides its usual coverage outside the U.S.A. Most plans provide some limited coverage available in the U.S.

If you get sick or have an accident in a foreign country... TravMed can help you locate medical care. With TravMed you can travel knowing you have prepared for the unexpected. You get the help you need to save your business trip or vacation... perhaps even your life.

First, you get MEDEX Worldwide Travelers Assistance around the world!

We give you professional assistance very quickly, often in minutes, after you call us *collect*.

To be sick or hurt in a foreign country can be a traumatic experience.

How do you find a competent doctor who speaks English?

The TravMed solution: pick up *any* phone and call us collect. We'll give you the numbers to call our MEDEX Assistance Coordination Centers, wherever you are in the world.

You'll be answered in English by a multilingual specialist who immediately goes to work to:

- Assist you in locating the right kind of medical care nearest you
- Help you overcome language barriers by directing you to English speaking doctors or translators
- Monitor your progress during the course of your treatment and recovery
- Maintain contact with your family and personal physician back home in the U.S.
- Arrange for emergency evacuation if medically necessary. The service is quick, professional and most helpful!

If you should find it necessary, you may arrange for your own medical care. Your $100,000.00 coverage is then confirmed by a quick *collect* telephone call to one of your MEDEX Assistance Coordination Centers.

***Third, you get a bargain!
TravMed costs only $3.00* a day—
the deductible is only $25.***

* You get $100,000 protection for each trip plus the medical assistance service for group membership rates of only:

$3.00 a day (through age 70) or $5.00 a day (age 71-80)

You pay only a $25 deductible per accident or sickness for required medical care.
All further covered expenses are paid by TravMed.

Second, you get $100,000.00 coverage for medical and hospital expenses, and many other benefits

TravMed provides you with up to $100,000.00 coverage for sickness or accident. This includes:

- Physicians' fees and hospital expenses
- Emergency dental expenses
- Emergency medical evacuation to home or hospital
- Repatriation of remains expenses
- Special trip expenses for accompanying travelers 19 years of age and under to home residence
- Special trip expenses for bringing a family member to your side

And we do more...

TravMed also makes direct payments to the physicians, hospital, and the organization handling evacuation. This gives you added convenience and preserves your cash.

So you are protected from financial hardship and worry.

TravMed®

Enjoy the MEDEX Worldwide Travelers Assistance security that Europeans have known for years

When you buy TravMed you will receive your TravMed/MEDEX Identification card and certificate of coverage directly

MEXICO TRAVELOG
Puts over 40 years of experience at your side! Copyright © Sanborn's TGP Inc.

	MI.	KM.	
H	65.0	104.0	Entrance to **Hotel Club Akumal Caribe** and **Villas Maya**. Although run separately, this complex consists of 21 rooms with A/C, some with kitchenettes and 40 bungalows; restaurants; palapa bar; dive shop (rentals and instruction available); gift shop; pool; quiet lagoon with tropical fish; lots of coconut palms; plus 4 miles of beautiful beach. Phone: (987) 2-2532 Also **Las Casitas Akumal** A/C 14 luxurious villas overlooking the bay. Phone: (987) 2-2554 USA 800-5-AKUMAL. Then pass side road (left) to **Hotel Akumal Cancun** (100 A/C rooms; restaurant; bar; pool; tennis courts; AE, VI, MC. Phone: (988) 4-2272 or (987) 2-2453 Fax 2-2567.
Rv	67.0	107.2	**Hotel Aventuras de Akumal** at left.
	68.0	109.0	Pass side road (left) to beachfront **Playa de Chemuyil** (admission charged) where there is a restaurant, good swimming, and space for self-contained RV's.
	69.4	111.0	Pass side road (left) to **Playa Xcacel**, another beachfront park with space for RV parking.
	70.7	113.1	Pass side road (left) to **Xel-Ha Caleta** ("cove"), a short ½ mile away, which is a fabulous natural aquarium formed by a little salt-water cove where you can swim or snorkel with the beautiful multi-colored fish (equipment available for rent). There are several shops here, as well as a palapa snack bar and an underwater Mayan religious site. (Park closes at 5 PM; admission is charged)
	79.4	127.0	Come to side road.

Tulúm Mayan Ruins, TURN LEFT. Road goes on to Boca Paila fishing resort (25 rooms divided among 9 palm-thatched villas; restaurant; excellent fishing; miles of beach; MAP only

 » TULUM, Mayan for "walled fortress", was first sighted by man in 1518 when Spanish explorer Juan de Grijalva sailed past this area and wrote that the city looked as large as Seville, Spain. The "zona" consists of several buildings, the castle (pyramid-type building) being the most interesting. Also on the site is the carved figure of the Descending God and the temple of the Frescoes. Records indicate that Tulúm flourished in the 11th century and many of the preserved buildings show a Toltec influence as at Chichen-Itza. The "zona" is open daily from 7 AM till 6 PM (admission charged).

Restaurant El Crucero ("The Crossroads") at left. Then Mgas at left. **Restaurant El Faisán y el Venado**, left at entrance to archaeological zone. There's also inexpensive **Motel Acuario** (Customer Sjoerd Bakker of Woodstock, Ont tells us the rooms are clean and reasonable. Fans.). Folks, we drove the road, toward **Boca Paila**. It's is a little rough and goes through the national park area Sian Ka'an. There are several cabaña hotels near the ruins and on down. We do want to warn you about **Osho Oasis**, though. We ate there, and while the vegetarian fare was very good, other folks have advised me that the place is run by "Moonies" and some strange goings on go on there(not recommended). The road to **Punta Allen** is chock-full of frigate birds and I hear the beach has lobsters.

H	80.7	129.1	Pass side road (right) is to the ruins of COBA, 47 KM (28 MI), where there's a good hotel, **Villa Arqueológica**, run by Club Med (40 rooms; restaurant; bar; library; pool; tennis; MC, VI). Archaeologists theorize that when the site is completely cleared, it will be the most expansive of all the Mayan ruins. (Incidently, the tallest pyramid of the region is located here.)
	95.5	152.8	**Chunyaxche** ruins off to left. Then thru community of same name.
	108.5	173.6	Pass side road to **Chumpón**. "Men aren't pigs — pigs are smarter." Carla on *Cheers*.
	111.0	177.6	At left, road to **Vigia Chico**.

(Over, please)

307-S-1
PTO JUAREZ – F. CARRILLO PUERTO

JUNE 1992

	MI.	KM.	
(EAT)	140.0	224.0	At left, **Restaurant Mayan Tianguis.**
	140.5	224.8	Soccer field at left and enter town of **Felipe Carrillo Puerto** (population 20,000), once known as "Chan Santa Cruz", a stronghold of the Mayans up till the 20th century.
	141.0	225.6	Come now to Benito Juárez "glorieta" and junction hwys #184-295. Market building at right.

Chetumal or Belize, go halfway around circle and proceed ahead. Start Log 307-South-2. There is gas at right, next block.

Muna and Merida, TURN RIGHT and start Log 184-North.

H

M*gas*

Incidentally, there's a fair little emergency hotel here called **Hotel Chan Santa Cruz** with 10 clean air-con rooms. To get there, go to corner beyond gas station and turn right at next corner; it is in the second block on right.

End of Log.

(Next Page, Please)

MEXICO TRAVELOG
Puts over 40 years of experience at your side! Copyright © Sanborn's TGP Inc.

FELIPE CARRILLO PUERTO (JCT HWY #184) — BELIZE BORDER — CHETUMAL — 93.5 MI OR 149.6 KM — DRIVE TIME 1½- 2 HOURS

SCENIC RATING — 3

» NOTE: If you are going to Escarcega, we recommend a very early start. Hwy #186 is a lonely road with few services. Please be off it well before dusk.

MI.	KM.	
0.0	0.0	In **Felipe Carrillo Puerto** at Benito Juárez Monument circle, pass **El Faisán y el Venado** ("The Pheasant and the Deer") **Restaurant** at left. Hotel associated with restaurant has good clean rooms, shower, WC, fans (Acknowledgement to Sjoerd Bakker, Woodstock, Ontario). Then pass gas station (clean rest rooms) at right in next block. Better gas up here if going to Escarcega. Straight ahead thru town with Conasupo grocery at right. (but if you wish to go to **Hotel Chan Santa Cruz**, turn right at next corner — it's on right before bank on corner of main plaza) Continuing thru town, slow for "topes" at school, left. Then Social Security Clinic, right.
6.3	10.1	Crossroads (right) to **Laguna Ocom** and (left) to **Chanca Ver.**
11.5	18.4	Thru settlement of **Uh-May**. School, right. Watch two "topes", one before and one after school.
29.5	47.2	Settlement of **A. Quintana Roo** at left. Two "topes".
31.6	50.6	Pass side road (right) to Noh-Bec, 7 Kilometers.
38.9	62.2	Pass side road (right) to big **Chaccbooben** government agricultural project, 7 km. Then thru stretched-out village of **Limones** — See any lime trees?? Note little Mayan pyramid at left in middle of town. Plaza at left and careful for "topes" (three).
42.3	67.7	Pass road (left) to **Majahual**. There's a nice trailer park and cabañas, **Las Palapas, 47.7 miles after turn at Majahual, or 81 miles** from here. Its owned by Deborah and Craig. Allow 2½ hours to drive it. Do not stop at the primitive one about 20 miles after the turn — it's a little funky even for me. (Thanks to Eric Contreras and Jeannie for this information.)
46.3	74.1	Thru community of **Pedro A. Santos**, "topes" (three). Incidentally you can pick up Radio Belize 820 (in English) on your AM dial.
48.8	78.1	Pass junction Hwy #293 (right) to **Valle Hermoso** which leads to Jct. Hwy #184 and all the way back to Merida.
52.5	84.0	Side trail (left) to **Buena Vista** on lake Bacalar. (Lake Bacalar, incidentally, is one of the loveliest lakes in the hemisphere; we'll tell you how to get there in 17 miles.)
62.5	100.0	This is Las Caobas forest preserve thru here. ("Caoba" is Spanish for Mahogany)
67.0	107.2	There's beautiful **Lake Bacalar** over at left.
69.0	110.4	Pass side road (right) to **Reforma**.
70.0	112.0	Veer right with one way road from town on your left.

Bacalar via beautiful shoreline drive, TURN LEFT (not recommended for large RV vehicles). You'll find Hotel Laguna, Phone (Merida) (99) 27-1304 (Chetumal) (983) 2-3517. (There's an easier entrance two miles ahead. Turn left at hotel sign.)

Chetumal or Bacalar bypass, veer right, pick up this log at mile 74.5 below.

(Over, please)

307-S-2
F. CARRILLO PUERTO - CHETUMAL

JUNE 1992

MI.	KM.	
70.3	112.5	Curve right at "T". Watch "topes", pass white church at right. A block beyond old white church, TURN LEFT at "El Universo" bicycle repair shop at right. Proceed down this narrow street for a couple of blocks and pass plaza at left, go one more block till "T", merge with Lake Bacalar shoreline parkway. Note ancient fort over at left built by the Spaniards in the 17th century. If to lakeside restaurants for shrimp, cold drinks, etc., turn left — they're a short ¼ mile ahead.

Chetumal and/or Hotel Laguna, turn right

Follow this terrific drive along side pretty Lake Bacalar which is also called "Lago de los Siete Colores" (Lake of Seven Colors) because at sunrise (or was it sunset?) and certain other times of day, the color of the water is said to change in to different shades of blue.

	MI.	KM.	
	71.9	115.0	On lake shore drive, pass government worker's cottages at right and school complex at left.
H	73.0	116.8	Fancy Pagoda at left.
	73.2	117.1	Pass **Hotel Laguna** at left. Then pass **Los Loquitos RV Park** at left (no-hookups) — it's open sporadically and closed during summer.
Rv			
(EAT)	74.5	119.2	Pass **Restaurant Cenote Azul** at right. Across road is **Cenote Azul Trailer Park** (40 spaces with electricity and water; showers; toilets; dump station; natural swimming "hole"). Come to Hwy #307 again and turn left. KM 15
			Back on Hwy #307 again, did you enjoy your side-sortie alongside lovely Lake Bacalar?
	80.6	129.0	Nice agricultural experimental farm at right.
	81.9	131.0	Thru Community of **Xul-Ha** and slow for "topes".
	84.0	134.4	Come now to junction Hwy #186 and slow for merging traffic. This is end of Hwy #307. Proceed ahead on Hwy #186 east toward Chetumal and/or Belize border.

Escarcega, go right and start Log 186-West-1. Better gas up in Chetumal if you're low. We've heard there's unleaded in Xpujil, but didn't verify it.

	86.1	137.8	Past road worker's community of **Huay Pix** over at right. Then bridge over **Estero Chac**.
	90.7	145.1	Come now to junction (right) with side road down to **Belize Border**.

Belize, turn right and start Log "Belize Special" after crossing free bridge.

It's a couple of miles down to border village of **Subteniente Lopez**, which is Spanish for "Second Lieutenant Lopez". Incidentally, Subteniente Lopez was in charge of this border post during the Huerta-Carranza "revolution" and was killed by opposing soldiers in Chetumal, so the village was named in his honor.

Chetumal, continue ahead on Hwy #186 and follow this log.

	MI.	KM.	
Rv	91.5	146.4	Pass road junction (left) with Av. Insurgentes that'll take you to **Calderitas** and on to **Sunrise on the Caribbean RV Park** and to Chetumal Zoo. Note monument to Andres Quintana Roo (1787-1851), patriot & poet, for whom this state was named. Mgas, left, begin 4-lane highway.
Mgas	93.1	149.0	Penitentiary, right and courthouse next door. Sports stadium and Hwy police station, right.
	94.0	150.4	Enter city of **Chetumal** (population 80,000). Airport at left and past Dyna, Ford and VW agencies at right. **Motel Paradise** at right; city hall at left and park just beyond.
	94.8	151.7	Go ½-way 'round glorieta with spire. Proceed ahead on Av. Obregon. Pass Nissan dealer, left.
	95.3	152.5	Go halfway 'round "La Patria" monument. **MGAS**, left. Then **topes**.
	95.6	153.0	Pass **Hotel Casablanca**, right. Then City Hall and plaza, left. There seems to be a cop on every corner in this town, so drive carefully. I got a ticket here.
	95.9	153.4	Cross Av **Juarez**, with **Bancomer** and **Banamex** on corners. Ahead for one block.

(Next Page, Please)

F. CARILLO PUERTO - CHETUMAL

MEXICO TRAVELOG
Puts over 40 years of experience at your side! Copyright © Sanborn's TGP Inc.

MI.	KM.	
96.0	153.6	Come now to junction with Av. de los Heroes and end of log.

If to bayfront boulevard, ahead another block and turn right. If to town's better hotels, turn left onto Av. de los Heroes and on up the street for 4 blocks and you'll see **Los Cocos** at left; **Continental Caribe** is just ahead on right. And if you'll glance at your map of Mexico, you'll agree that this is **the** jumping-off spot!

H

End of Log.

(Over, please)

THE WALL STREET JOURNAL.

© 1992 Dow Jones & Company, Inc. All Rights Reserved

VOL. XC NO. 3 ★★ SOUTHWEST EDITION — FRIDAY, JULY 3, 1992 — DALLAS, TEXAS — 75 CENTS

What's News—

Business and Finance

THE FED CUT interest rates on the heels of a report showing that the unemployment rate rose to 7.8% in June, its highest point since 1984, while payrolls sank. Analysts said the data signal the weakness, but not the end, of the recovery. The Fed lowered the discount and Fed funds rates each by half a point, to 3% and 3.25% respectively, their lowest levels since 1963.
 Banks slashed their prime rates to 6% from 6.5% in response to the Fed's move, and interest rates paid by consumers are expected to fall as well. But the lower consumer rates aren't likely to create the demand needed for an economic revival, analysts said.
 (Articles in Column 6 and on Page A2)

★

 Bond prices soared on the unemployment rate's jump and the Fed's rate cut. But stocks slid and the dollar declined. The Dow Jones industrials fell 23.81 points to 3330.29. Long-term Treasury bond prices leaped about 1% points, pushing their yields down to 7.63% from 7.74%. Short-term interest rates plunged to 20-year lows.
 Gold prices jumped on speculation that the Fed's action will spark inflation. Platinum prices also advanced.
 (Articles on Pages C1 and C16)

★

 Olympia & York reached an accord in principle with its Canadian creditors on a plan for paying its operating expenses. The pact could break a logjam that has held up the real estate giant's Canadian debt restructuring.
 (Article on Page A3)

★

 Stock mutual funds posted losses averaging 2.59% for the second quarter, trailing the S&P 500's 1.9% gain and marking the funds' worst performance since 1990's third period. Money market funds climbed 0.86%. Taxable bond funds were up 3.5%.
 (Article on Page C7)

★

 U.S. securities firms' earnings rose 15% in the second quarter from a year earlier, but were down 27% from the first period, analysts said. The slowdown reflects declines in underwriting revenue and trading profits, and a pause in mutual fund sales.
 (Article on Page C1)

★

 AT&T and its two big unions unveiled details of a contract accord that both sides said would help the phone giant become more competitive while giving workers more job security.
 (Article on Page A3)

★

 The House approved overwhelmingly a package of business tax breaks, including incentives to invest in depressed areas. The measure would also create a write-off for some assets acquired in takeovers.
 (Article on Page C19)

World-Wide

 CONGRESS VOTED for a third extension of emergency jobless aid.
 Passage of the $5.6 billion measure, which would be financed with tax-raising provisions, came two days before the current program of emergency federal benefits was to begin expiring. Sponsors said the legislation eventually would help 1.5 million people. The House voted 396-23 for the extension until next March, and the Senate followed with a 93-3 vote. Republican support for the measure was influenced by yesterday's report of a rise in the jobless rate.
 (Article on Page C13)
 Bush's signing of the bill will be the final action this year on an issue that has divided the parties since last summer, when the president twice killed earlier bills and hurt his political standing.

★

 THE U.S. SAID it would begin humanitarian relief flights to Sarajevo today.
 Two Air Force cargo planes are to depart from Germany today to join an international airlift into the besieged Bosnian capital. Meanwhile, the Pentagon said its warships had been pulled out of the Adriatic off Yugoslavia. In Washington, Bush repeated his reluctance to deploy U.S. ground troops in the region. Milan Panic, a Serb emigrant who is now a U.S. businessman, agreed to become premier of the new, smaller Yugoslavia. *(Article on Page A3)*
 As a U.N. convoy totaling more than 1,000 men took up temporary positions near Sarajevo's airport, artillery bombardments reportedly continued.

★

 The House approved a $252.65 billion defense spending bill intended to minimize industry layoffs and to provide funding for pet projects of the military services. The measure also calls for the financing of some costly projects opposed by the White House.
 (Article on Page A8)

★

 Bush vetoed a bill that would have allowed people to register to vote when they apply for a driver's license, saying it would be "an open invitation to fraud and corruption." It was the 31st veto of his presidency. The measure also would have made registration forms available at unemployment and public assistance offices.

★

 The Army and Navy have completed a world-wide withdrawal of their tactical nuclear weapons, Bush announced, fulfilling a pledge he made last year. The withdrawal involves 1,700 ground-based nuclear arms in Europe and 700 nuclear bombs and cruise missiles on submarines and surface ships.
 A Senate panel approved the Start nuclear arms-reduction pact signed a year ago by the U.S. and the former Soviet Union. The Senate Foreign Relations Committee voted to send the treaty to the full Senate.

★

 Miyazawa said in Washington that Japan views resolution of a dispute with Russia over four islands as a test of Russia's readiness to cast off its Stalinist past. In Moscow, Yeltsin accused Tokyo of not contributing its share to his reform efforts.

★

 Indianapolis researchers believe they found the reason women after menopause often develop weak bones. The scientists said lab studies show that lack of the hormone estrogen leads to an overproduction of bone scavenger cells that carve pits and craters in the skeleton. Their report is in today's issue of the journal Science.

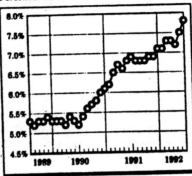

Unemployment Rate
Percent of labor force, seasonally adjusted.

UNEMPLOYMENT in June rose to a seasonally adjusted 7.8% of the civilian labor force from 7.5% the preceding month, the Labor Department reports. (Article on page A2.)

If a Chicken Crosses A Road in Mexico, It Will Be Noted

Mike Nelson's Travelogues Are Rich in Detail and Written To Lure Americans South

By MATT MOFFETT
Staff Reporter of THE WALL STREET JOURNAL

 SIERRA MADRE MOUNTAINS — A mile high on a precarious Mexican road, Mike Nelson edges his Volkswagen van toward a steep downslope. "Hold on to your britches," he shouts, as the van starts barreling down the mountain. Reaching bottom, Mr. Nelson spies four wooden crosses beside the road. Nearby is the twisted remains of a car bumper. It's not for nothing that this road is called *El Espinazo del Diablo*, the Devil's Backbone.
 But then, Mr. Nelson didn't get the name "Mexico Mike" by just sticking to the beaten track. Mr. Nelson, 41 years old, with a graying beard, drives 40,000 miles a year mapping Mexico's modern highways and unpaved back roads. He visits places as diverse as Mexico City, the largest metropolis in the world, and villages seldom seen by foreign travelers. His observations fill the minutely detailed Mexico travelogues published by Sanborn's, a McAllen, Texas, vendor of auto insurance.
 Among other things, the travelogues pinpoint danger zones like the deadly slope on the Devil's Backbone. There aren't any flashing lights or warning signs at the top of the descent, just the well-kept shrine to crash victims at the bottom.

Please Turn to Page A8, Column 4

Looking Inward

With Cold War Ov[er,]
Many Western Lea[ders]
Face Domestic Ma[laise]

The New World Order [Yields]
Fewer Economic Be[nefits]
Than Many Hoped

Modest Goals for G-7 M[eeting]

By GERALD F. SEIB
Staff Reporter of THE WALL STREET [JOURNAL]

 WASHINGTON — Vaclav Hav[el, presi]dent of Czechoslovakia and unoff[icial phi]losopher of the New World Orde[r, had a] sobering message for the leade[rs of the] industrialized world as they gath[er to]day for their annual economic su[mmit.]
 The collapse of the Commu[nism] "has put Western policy making [in a state] of shock," Mr. Havel declares. [" ...] is the West somewhat confused [by the] tremors in the East — it is beg[inning to] shake a little itself, and the struc[ture of] former certainties is beginning [to come] loose."
 Odd as it seems, President [Bush and] the other leaders of the worl[d's seven] leading industrialized nations a[re a politi]cally jittery lot as they prepare [to meet] in Munich Monday for their firs[t summit] since the demise of the Soviet U[nion. They] might have expected the end o[f the Cold] War to win them praise and se[cure their] hold on power. Instead, the sam[e kind] of post-Cold War discontent [that] produced Ross Perot in the U.S.[, a wave] of deep economic malaise, disen[chantment] with established political leade[rs and bu]reaucracies, a sense it's now s[afer to look] for alternatives — are flowing [through the] industrialized world.

Out of Favor

 "It's incredible," says Ja[mes Schle]singer, former defense secret[ary and di]rector of central intelligence. "[Bush's low] approval ratings of Helmut K[ohl rival] many at 25%, 30%. Mitterran[d is dis]proved of by the [French] [people.] Everywhere you go you find [disenchant]ment." In fact, the leader [coming in] with the broadest personal p[opularity at] home probably won't be from [any of the] so-called Group of Seven i[ndustrial] nations, the U.S., Canad[a, Britain,] France, Germany, Italy and J[apan. It will] be Russian President Boris Ye[ltsin, who's] stopping by for a chat, says [Robert Hor]mats, vice chairman of Gol[dman Sachs] International.
 The result is that the G[-7 leaders] are so focused on internal p[roblems that] they are ill-prepared to take t[he bold and] risky steps necessary to gen[erate coordi]nated economic growth, finis[h]ing global trade treaty or s[hore up democ]racy in Russia.
 "People have lost their be[arings," says] Francois Heisbourg, a fo[rmer senior] French government aide wh[o is now direc]tor of the International Insti[tute for Strate]gic Studies in London. "The[y are focus]ing on its domestic prioriti[es. They] are looking at their internal [problems.]"

 Tokyo stock prices r[ose yester]day, sending the Nikkei [index up] 432.56 points, or 2.7%, to [conclude] a three-day increase of 6.[...]
 (Article on Page [...])

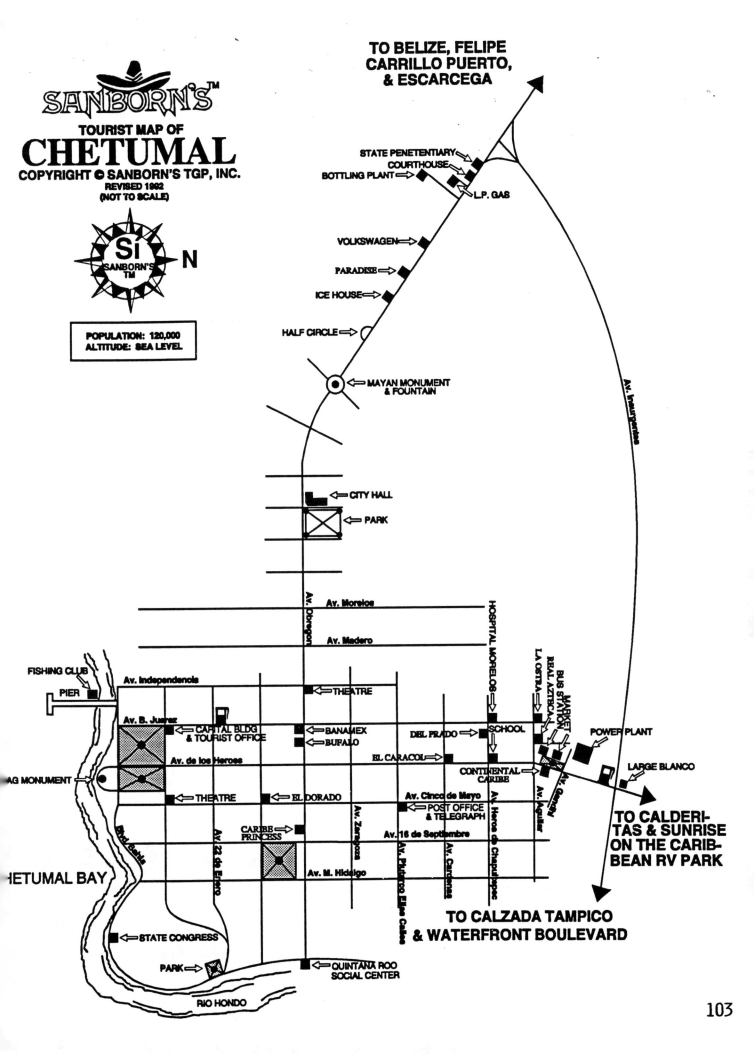

General Info
CHETUMAL, Q. ROO

CHETUMAL is what you call an "emerging" city. Up until 1961 there were no roads into town, no trains, no buses, no airlines — only small ships because the harbor was not deep enough for big ones. It was a pretty grubby hurricane-prone little place. No water, no sewers, no paved streets. No nothing. Many of its inhabitants were shady characters by the law in various Mexican states and foreign countries.

This town has progressed a long, long way since 1961. It's a "free port" which accounts for its dozens of mercantile stores that sell just about everything from all over the world. It has potable water, storm-and-sanitary sewers, well-lighted paved streets and divided boulevards, attractive public buildings, pretty residences, and friendly people. The bayfront layout is quite impressive — the capitol building, the pier, the flag glorieta out over the water, the park, the whole works. It's really "coming" — and how it has improved over what it was many years ago.

JUNE 1992

EAT & STRAY
CHETUMAL

CHETUMAL

AREA CODE — 983   Copyright © Sanborn's TGP Inc.

CHETUMAL, (population 110,000) founded in 1898 by Admiral Othon Pompeyo Blanco, is the capitol of the beautiful and romantic state of Quintana Roo and is located in the southeastern part of the Yucatan Peninsula, near Río Hondo, the natural border between Mexico and Belize. It has a pleasant climate (average temperature is 26 C.) The coolest month is January. You can find wonderful landscapes among vestiges of the ancient Mayan civilization. It is also a duty-free port, offering to shoppers many articles imported from all over the world.
NOTE: Here are some inportant emergency phone numbers: Federal Police, 2-0193; City Police, 2-1500; Traffic Police, 2-1984; Fire Dept., 2-1578; Red Cross, 2-0571; Harbour Captain, 2-0244; Immigration Dept., 2-0221; Tourist Information, 2-3663 or 2-0266

SLEEPING AROUND CHETUMAL

* **CASA BLANCA** — ECON — 27 clean units. Parking. MC, VI. Av. Alvaro Obregón #312 Ph: 2-1248

* **CARIBE PRINCESS** — MOD — Good 38-room, 3-story A/C hotel on Av. Alvaro Obregón just a few blocks from bay. Restaurant. Bar. Parking. Ph:2-0520

*** **CONTINENTAL CARIBE** — MOD — Good 71-room, 3-story A/C hotel Av. Heroes #171. Restaurant. Piano Bar. Disco. Pool. Servibars in rooms. Parking nearby. MC, VI. Ph:2-1100 or 2-1702

*** **DEL PRADO** — UPPER — The best A/C hotel, 2 blocks south of market at corner of Av. Heroes & Chapultepec. Restaurant. Bar. Pool. Servibars in room. Disco. Parking. Hertz Rent-A-Car in lobby. Ph:2-0544.

*** **LOS COCOS** — UPPER — Very good 80-rooms. Very friendly. 2 story A/C hotel at Av. Heroes and Chapultepec. Travel agency (helpful). Good restaurant. Bar. Disco. Pool. Small playground. Enclosed parking. AE, MC, VI. Ph: 2-0544 Fax: 2-0920.

EL DORADO — ECON — Good enough 22-room, 2-story A/C hotel at Av. Cinco de Mayo #42. Most rooms A/C. Bar. On street parking. Ph:2-0315 or 2-0316.

PARADISE — ECON — Emergency 48-room, 2-story motel on highway at edge of town Zona Industrial #1. Some rooms A/C. Restaurant. Pool. Parking. Ph: 2-0072.

PRINCIPE — MOD — Nice, clean, 48-room 3- and 5-story A/C hotel on Av. Heroes #326. Restaurant. Bar. Parking. AE, MC, VI. Ph: 2-4799 or 2-5167.

* **REAL AZTECA** — ECON — Clean, comfy 30-room A/C hotel at Calle Belice #186 behind central bus station. Restaurant. Piano bar. Private parking. P: 2-0720 Or 2-0666.

EATING CHETUMAL

*** **CASA BLANCA** — UPPER — Very nice, fancy restaurant at Av. Francisco I. Madero #293 serving steak, seafood, chicken, and veal. Open 1 PM til midnight. Ph: 2-2791.

** **LA OSTRA** — MOD — Good restaurant in north part of town just west of bus station across from hospital an Av. Efrain Aguilar. Good steaks, seafood, and service. MC, VI. Ph: 2-0452

(More Goodies on other side)

**EAT & STRAY
CHETUMAL**

CAMPING, PARKING & PLUGGING IN!

SUNRISE ON THE CARIBBEAN — ("Zaztal Yoo Canaab" in Mayan) — 26-space facility on beach in nearby town of Calderitas, 4.5 miles west of junction bypass and road into Chetumal. 15 spaces with electrical and water hookups. Ask for location of drinking faucet. Cold showers. Toilets. Grassy pads. Boat ramp. Grocery accross street. 1 fresh water faucet.

End of Eat and Stray.

(Please turn page!)

ROUTE SELECTION RS-MAYA-6

CHETUMAL—CANCUN—USE PAGES 107-113

ESCARCEGA—PALENQUE, USE PAGE 107 TO ESCARCEGA TURNOFF, THEN TURN TO PAGE 113 AND START LOG 186-W-1

JUNE 1992

MEXICO TRAVELOG
Puts over 40 years of experience at your side! Copyright © Sanborn's TGP Inc.

CHETUMAL – BELIZE BORDER – FELIPE CARRILLO PUERTO – 96 MI OR 153.6 KM DRIVE TIME 1½-2 HOURS GOOD HIGHWAY, MOSTLY 2-LANE

SCENIC RATING — 3

» NOTE: If you are going to Escarcega, we recommend a very early start. Hwy #186 is a lonely road with few services. Please be off it well before dusk.

MI.	KM.	
0.0	0.0	Starting here on Av. Obregon at corner of Av. de los Heroes, proceed ahead with Banamex on left at next corner and the theater next block on right. (Incidentally, you can pick up Radio Belize in English, 820 on your AM dial)
1.0	1.6	Pass park and city hall, right. There seems to be a cop on every corner in this town, so drive carefully. I got a ticket here. Pass **Hotel Casablanca**, left.
1.3	2.1	Mgas, right. Go ½-way around "La Patria" monument. Pass Nissan dealer, right.
1.8	2.9	Pass **Motel Paradise** and VW Ford and Dyna agencies, left. Airport, right.
2.7	4.3	Past highway police station and Sports Stadium, left. Courthouse and penitentiary also at left.

Mgas

Rv

4.3	6.9	4-lane highway ends. **Mgas**, right. Better gas up here if going to **Escarcegas**. If they are out, there's a station in Tulúm. Pass road junction (right) with Av. Insurgentes that goes to **Calderitas** and on to **Sunrise on the Caribbean RV Park** and to Chetumal Zoo. Note monument to Andres Quintana Roo (1787-1851), patriot and poet, after whom the state was named.
5.1	8.2	Come now to Junction (left) with side road down to **Belize** border.

Belize, turn left and start Log "Belize Special" after crossing free bridge.

It's a couple of miles down to the border town of **Subteniente Lopez** which is Spanish for "Second Lieutenant Lopez". Incidentally, Subteniente Lopez was in charge of this border post during the Huerta-Carranza "revolution" and was killed by opposing soldiers in Chetumal, so the village was named in his honor.

9.7	15.5	Cross bridge over **Estero Chac** and past road worker's community of **Huay Pix** over at left.
11.8	18.9	Come now to junction of Hwys #186 and #307 (begins here).

Escarcega, go left and start Log 186-West-1.

Rv

13.9	22.2	Thru community of **Xul-ha** and slow for "topes".
15.2	24.3	Nice Agricultural Experimental farm, left.
21.3	34.1	Pass side road (right) to **Restaurant Cenote Azul** and **Cenote Azul Trailer Park** (40 spaces with electricity and water; showers; toilets; dump station; natural swimming "hole") and to **Hotel Laguna** (Ph: (Merida) (99) 27-1304, (Chetumal) (983) 2-3517. It is also a scenic route thru town (not recommended for large RV vehicles) by Lake Bacalar, one of the lovliest lakes in the hemisphere.
25.6	41.0	Pass side road (right) to **Lake Bacalar**.
26.8	42.9	Pass side road (left) to **Reforma**.
28.0	44.8	Beautiful Lake Bacalar continues at right.
32.5	52.0	This is Las Caobas forest preserve thru here. (Caoba is Spanish for Mahogany)
43.3	69.3	Side trail (right) to **Buena Vista** on Lake Bacalar.

(Over, please)

307-N-1
CHETUMAL – FELIPE CARRILLO PUERTO

JUNE 1992

MI.	KM.	
47.0	75.2	Pass junction Hwy #293 (left) which leads to **Valle Hermoso** and to Jct. Hwy #184 and all the way back to **Merida**.
49.5	79.2	Thru community of **Pedro A. Santos**, slow for "topes" (three).
53.5	85.6	Pass road (right) to **Majahaul**. There's a nice trailer park and cabañas, **Las Palapas**, 47.7 after turn at Majahual, or 81 miles from here. It is owned by Deborah and Craig. Allow 2½ hours to drive it. Do not stop at the primitive one about 20 miles after the turn — it's a little funky even for me. (Thanks to Eric Contreras & Jeanie, of McAllen, TX for this informantion.)
56.9	91.0	Thru stretched out village of **Limones** — See any lime trees?? Plaza at right and careful for "topes" (three). Note little Mayan pyramid at right in middle of town. Then pass side road to big **Chaccboben** government agricultural project. 7km.
64.2	102.7	Pass side road to village of **Noh-Bec**, 7km.
66.3	106.1	Settlement of **A. Quintana Roo** at right. Two "topes".
84.3	134.9	Pass school at left. watch for two "topes" one before and one after school and thru settlement of **Uh-May**.
89.5	143.2	Crossroads (right) to **Chanca Ver** and (left) to **Laguna Ocom**.
95.8	153.3	Enter town of **Felipe Carrillo Puerto** (population 20,000) once known as "Chan Santa Cruz", (a stronghold of the Mayans up till the 20th century), with Social Security clinic at left. Slow for "topes" at school at right. (If you wish to go to **Hotel Chan Santa Cruz** turn left two blocks before "glorieta" (circle) — it's on right near bank on corner of main plaza.) Pass **El Faisán y el Venado Restaurant** at right. (Hotel associated with restaurant has good clean rooms, showers, WC, fans (Acknowledgement to Sjoerd Bakker, Woodstock, Ontario). Gas station on left. Then come to Benito Juárez Monument circle and end of log.

Cancun and Puerto Juárez, go halfway around circle and proceed ahead. Start Log 307-North-2.

Valladolid, go 2/3-way around circle and take Hwy #295 North.

Muna and Merida, go 3/4-way around circle and to the left and start log 184-North.

End of Log.

(Next Page, Please)

JUNE 1992   1 of 2
FELIPE CARRILLO PUERTO – PUERTO JUAREZ

MEXICO TRAVELOG
Puts over 40 years of experience at your side! Copyright © Sanborn's TGP Inc.

FELIPE PUERTO CARRILLO (JCT HWY #184) – CANCUN – PUERTO JUAREZ (JCT HWY #180) – 140 MI OR 224 KM DRIVE TIME 2-3 HOURS

SCENIC RATING — 3

MI.	KM.	
0.0	0.0	Starting here in **Felipe Carrillo Puerto** (population 20,000), once known as "Chan Santa Cruz", a stronghold of the Mayans up till the 20th century, at Benito Juárez Monument "glorieta" (circle) with market building at left, proceed ahead, north.
0.5	0.8	Pass soccer field at right and out of town.
1.0	1.6	At right, **Restaurant Mayan Tianguis.**
30.0	48.0	Pass side road (right) to **Vigia Chico.**
32.5	52.0	Pass side road to **Chumpón.** "Men aren't pigs — pigs are smarter" — Carla on *Cheers*.
45.5	72.8	Thru community of **Chunyaxche.** Chunyaxche ruins off to right.
60.3	96.6	Pass side road (left) is to the ruins of **COBA**, 47 Km (28 Mi), where there's a good hotel, **Villa Arqueológica**, run by Club Med (40 rooms; restaurant; bar; library; pool; tennis; MC, VI). Archaeologists theorize that when the site is completely cleared, it will be the most expansive of all the Mayan ruins. (Incidentally, the tallest pyramid of the region is located here.)

H

Valladolid, Merida. This is a shortcut to the aforementioned places. It's sticky getting through Cobá, but if you ask enough people, you'll get out of town.

61.6	98.6	Mgas at right. Come to side road.

M*gas*

Tulúm Mayan ruins TURN RIGHT and on to Boca Paila fishing resort (25 rooms divided among 9 palm-thatched villas; restaurant; excellent fishing; miles of beach; MAP only.

 » TULUM, Mayan for "walled fortress", was first sighted by man in 1518 when the Spanish explorer Juan de Grijalva sailed past this area and wrote that the city looked as large as Seville, Spain. The "zona" consists of several buildings, the castle (pyramid-type building) being the most interesting. Also on the site is the carved figure of the Descending God and the temple of the Frescoes. Records indicate that Tulúm flourished on the 11th century and many of the preserved buildings show a Toltec influence as at Chichen-Itza. The "zona" is open daily from 7 AM till 6 PM (admission charged).

Restaurant El Crucero ("The Crossroads") at left. Restaurant Faisán y Venado, left at entrance to archeological zone. There's also inexpensive **Motel Acuario** (Customer Sjoerd Bakker of Woodstock, Ont tells us the rooms are clean and reasonable, fans). Folks, we drove the road, toward **Boca Paila**. It's is a little rough and goes through the national park area Sian Ka'an. There are several cabaña hotels near the ruins and on down. We do want to warn you about **Osho Oasis**, though. We ate there, and while the vegetarian fare was very good, other folks have advised me that the place is run by "Moonies" and some strange goings on go on there (not recommended). The road to **Punta Allen** is chock-full of frigate birds and I hear the beach has lobsters

(Over, please)

FELIPE CARRILLO PUERTO – PUERTO JUAREZ

MI.	KM.	
70.3	112.5	Pass side road (right) to **Xel-Ha Caleta** ("cove"), a short ½ mile away, which is a fabulous natural aquarium formed by a little salt-water cove where you can swim or snorkel with the beautiful multi-colored fish (equipment available for rent). There are several shops here, as well as a palapa snack bar and an underwater Mayan religious site (Park closes at 5 PM; steep admission is charged).
Rv 71.6	114.6	Pass side road (right) to **Playa Xcacel**, a beachfront park with space for RV parking.
EAT 73.0	116.8	Pass side road (right) to another beachfront park, **Playa de Chemuyil** (admission charged) where there's a restaurant, good swimming, and space for self-contained RV's.
74.0	118.4	**Hotel Aventuras de Akumal** at right.
H 76.0	121.6	Pass side road (right) to **Hotel Akumal Cancun** (100 A/C rooms; restaurant; bar; pool; tennis courts; AE, MC, VI. Ph: (988) 4-2272 or (987) 2-2453 Fax 2-2567. Then pass side road (right) to **Hotel Club Akumal Caribe** and **Villas Maya**. Although run separately, this complex consists of 21 rooms with A/C, some with kitchenettes and 40 bungalows; restaurants; palapa bar; dive shop (rentals and instruction available); gift shop; pool; quiet lagoon with tropical fish; lots of coconut palms; plus 4 miles of beautiful beach. Ph: (987) 2-2532. Also **Las Casitas Akumal** A/C 14 luxurious villas overlooking the bay. Ph: (987) 2-2554, USA 800-5-AKUMAL.

» **One lizard you'll see around here is the Basilisk, which reaches the length of a yard; its colors are green and brown while its crest is reddish. According to Mayan legend, he obtained the crest that runs down his back when he won a race with a deer. The Lord of the woods had placed a bench at the finish line for the winner. The deer arrived first, of course, but when he started to sit down, the Basilisk shouted, "Look out, you big galoot! I was here first." Sure enough, the wily lizard was already on the bench. How did he out run the deer? He didn't. He hitched a ride on the tail if the deer and jumped off just before he sat down. That just goes to show — sometimes you win by chasing tail.**

77.5	124.0	Artisans and restaurants at left.
79.8	127.7	Pass **Kantenáh**, for the adventures.
82.0	131.2	Pass side road (left) to **Xpu-Há**, sand camping.
84.5	135.2	**Puerto Aventuras** on right. Modern, high rise resort complex.
Rv 87.0	139.2	Pass side road (right) to little town of **Pamul** and to **Cabañas Pamul Trailer Park** with 63 spaces; electricity; water, dump station; showers; toilets; restaurant; bar; fishing trips. Reservations: Av. Colón # 501-C Dept. D-211, Merida, Yuc. 97000. Phone and Fax: (99) 25-9422.
EAT 93.5	149.6	Pass side road (right) to **Xcaret**, well developed and pricey, but a pretty nice place to spend the day — especially if you have kids.
97.5	156.0	Come now to main road to seaside town of **Playa del Carmen**, the "jumping off" place to Cozumel. Turn at **Restaurant El Faisán y el Venado**. PLAYA DEL CARMEN, with a Mexican-Caribbean flavor all its own, boast an airport, 9 nice residential subdivisions, many small but good restaurants, several arts and crafts shops. This place has developed tremendously in the past few years, but is still "funky" and a different world than Cancun, so if you don't like Cancun, you'll probably like this place. I do. From Playa del Carmen, 3 passenger ferries depart daily to Cozumel at 5:30, 7:30, 9:30, 10:15, 10:30, 11:00 AM, 12:15, 2:30, 5:30, 6:30, 7:30, 9:00 PM from pier across from Hotel Las Molcas where tickets may be purchased. Departures from Cozumel back to mainland are at 4:00, 6:30, 8:00, 9:00, 11:00 AM, 2:00, 4:00, 4:30, 5:30, 6:00, 6:30, and 8:00 PM. The trip takes about 45 to 50 minutes each way. See "Eat & Stray" for hotels. KM 290
98.4	157.4	Superior Beer at right. Also, **Shangri La Carribe** (70 rooms, 2-bed semi-cabañas, Ph: (987) 2-2888 & Fax; open Nov 15 - Apr 30) and **Las Palapas** (just as nice) Ph: (987) 2-2972 Fax 4-1678.
100.5	160.8	Pass side trail (right) to **Xcalacoco Campground**. PH: (99) 23-0485 or 24-1545.
101.5	162.4	Pass side trail (right) to **Bunta Bete**. Right now ** **Kailuum** is still there, but they'll be moving sooner or later. It's a rustic fancy tent hotel. They have these huge tents with beds and good mosquito netting right on beach. There's communal dining and the whole place is operated by a real conservationist. There's no electricity and they don't want any. They're closed Sept-Oct.

(Next Page, Please)

JUNE 1992   2 of 2   **FELIPE CARRILLO PUERTO – PUERTO JUAREZ**

MEXICO TRAVELOG
Puts over 40 years of experience at your side! Copyright © Sanborn's TGP Inc.

MI.	KM.	
102.4	163.8	At right, **Cabañas Capitán LaFitte**. Apdo. Postal # 1463 Merida, Yuc. 97000 Phone: (99) 23-0485, 24-1548, Fax 23-7142; USA 800-538-6804 (23 cabañas; ceiling fans; restaurant; bar; fishing boats; scuba diving).
109.6	175.4	**Playa Paraiso Condos**, right.
116.6	186.6	Jardín Botánica Dr. Alfredo Parrera Morín (Botanical Garden), right..
118.5	189.0	Pass gas station, left. Then pass side road (right) to seashore town of **Puerto Morelos** where you can catch the commercial ferry to **Cozumel**. Ferry departs daily for Cozumel at 6 AM, but be here by 4:30 AM. It departs from Cozumel for mainland at 2 PM (Monday at 5 PM). The crossing takes 2-3 hours, depending in winds and tides. RV's awaiting departure of ferry can overnight in ferry parking lot. Hotel La Ceiba & Ojo de Agua blew away, but on the square is the ** **Hotel Villas Latinas**, a modern 2 story hotel on the water. If you kept going straight and didn't turn off to the square, you'd pass the *** **Hotel Posada Amor**, PH: (987) 100-33), one of my favorites. They are simple, natural cabañas is a garden-type setting. Reasonable price. The owner is very friendly and proud of his electronic organ. The adjacent restaurant is simple, hearty and healthy. Highly recommended. There is a neat couple who rent nice cabañas close by, ** **Rancho Libertad**. Jack there does personal growth workshops. The cabañas are roomy, ceiling fans and economical. Someday they plan to have a hot tub — not a jacuzzi. Farther down the road are the **** — **Villas Marina** — PH: (90) 987-411-47 (cellular can be called from Cancun or Pto. Morelos) anywhere else call (91-987) 4-1147. US: 1-800-3-CAN-CUN. They're run by Tom and Vicki Sharp. They also have the **Caribbean Reef Room** restaurant. Both are first-class, luxury-type places. Closer to town is the **Villas Shanti**, a Yoga retreat, run by Jean and Jack Loew. They operate by reservations only and cater to Yoga groups, but you can contact John Mastromarino at the **Villas Clarita**, one block closer to town than Villas Shanti. He has nice apartments for rent, a too. You can also reach him at the **Palapa Pizza Restaurant** on the plaza. Phone: (987) 1-0042 Fax: (987) 1-0041. Less expensive is **Los Aricefes** — across from the back of Villas Shanti (on the main road that runs from the plaza, on the beach side) — 8 rooms, 1 Br. and kitchenettes. No credit cards. See "Eat & Stray Playa del Carmen" for more info on lodging.
127.4	203.8	Begin divided highway.
131.0	209.6	Pass road to Cancun's International Airport. Cancun's Zona Hotelera, EXIT RIGHT and follow your nose
131.7	210.7	Central de Abastos (Farmer's market) at left.
134.7	215.5	**Ejido Alfredo V. Bonfil** at left.
135.2	216.3	Beer warehouse (Superior brand) and distributing office at left.
138.0	220.8	Shortcut to Merida, left (Hwy #180). Regular gas at left.
139.8	223.7	Enter resort town of **Cancun**. At right next to VW agency is good **Hotel América** (the best in town. also **American Express** office. The American Hospital (Viento #15 SM4 Ph: 84-6133 or 84-6068) is over to your right, opposite Hotel América. At left is **Super Deli**. English AA is ½ block on left at Plaza América Shopping Center, 2nd floor, room 33 (meets daily at 6:15 PM). Come to "glorieta". Careful for stoplight. Right is to Zona Hotelera and Av. Cobá.
140.3	224.5	Bancomer at right. **Pizza Hut** at left. **Novatel** and **Restaurant Bananas** (on access street) at left. Cross Av. Uxmal at "glorieta" (go halfway around).
140.8	225.3	Bus station at left. **Commercial Mexicana** and **McDonald's** at right. **Suites Paraiso Hotel** at left. Stoplight. Go halfway around "glorieta" and ahead.

(Over, please)

307-N-2
FELIPE CARRILLO PUERTO – PUERTO JUAREZ

JUNE 1992

MI. KM.
141.0 225.6 Come to junction Av. J. Lopez Portillo with Blanco store at left.

Puerto Juarez, TURN RIGHT and follow Log 180-S-8B at mile 98 till end of log.

Valladolid and Merida, TURN LEFT (Hwy #180) and follow Log 180-W-1A starting at mile 4.8.

End of Log.

(Next Page, Please)

JULY 1992

MEXICO TRAVELOG
Puts over 40 years of experience at your side! Copyright © Sanborn's TGP Inc.

JUNCTION HWY #307 — ESCARCEGA (JUNCTION HWY #261) — 158 MI OR 252.8 KM — DRIVE TIME 3 — 3½ HOURS. GET AN EARLY START.

SCENIC RATING — 1

This is still the shortest way to Escarcega, but sometimes this road is so rough you'll be barking when you've finished it. Nov. — Apr. is usually the worst. In summer it usually gets patched. Go slow or you'll be looking for a "taller muelles" (spring shop) — especially RV's. If it's bad, the worst is between the Quintana Roo state line and Escarcega. Going up to Merida and down will take you 2 days of hard driving, or 3 normal days, if you want to avoid this route. Ask a Green Angel what it's like lately. Scenery is low scrub jungle and flat nothing. It's little travelled, so if you break down, you'll have a long wait. The Green Angels do patrol it, twice a day.

All along this route you'll be driving through villages whose names are preceded by an "x", which in Mayan, is pronounced "sh". For example, a village named "X-Moo" would be pronounced "schmoo" or one named "X-Nuk" would be pronounced "schnook". Thanks to Sanborn's regulars, George & Dot Young. They spend every winter on the Yucatan and suggest everybody learn a few words of Maya. They say local folks really appreciate it.

» **NOTE: We recommend a very early start. Hwy #186 is a lonely road with few services. Please be off it well before dusk. There's gas at the junction to A. Obregon, 4 MI west of here on this log (or in Chetumal, 10 MI east of here on Hwy #186), but then not again till X-Pujil, 60½ MI from this junction. The next worthwhile accommodations are at Escarcega, 158 MI (But they're somewhat less than desirable; at Palenque, 290 MI; and at Villahermosa, 358 MI.**

MI.	KM.	
0.0	0.0	Starting here at junction Hwy #307 (10 MI east of Chetumal), proceed west on Hwy #186.
1.8	2.9	Pass side road to **Juan Sarabia**, 3 Km away. School at right. Watch for "topes". *Men think...*
3.5	5.6	Over bridge and thru village of **Ucum**. School at left and slow for "topes".
4.2	6.7	Pass side road (left) to **A. Obregon**, 15½ MI. Gas (regular) at left.
4.8	7.8	Pass little village of **Carlos A. Madrazo**, left. *Women can't be...*
13.8	22.1	Curve left and thru village of **Gonzales Ortega**. Careful for "topes". Pig crossing.
19.3	30.9	Thru little village of **Nachi Cocom**. 3 "topes". *Trusted too far...*
25.2	40.3	Pass side road (left) to neat ruins of **Kohunlich**, 5 MI.

» **KOHUNLICH was first discovered in 1968 by looters of pre-Hispanic treasures and was rediscovered in 1970 by archaeologist Victor Segovia Pinto. This site is a huge Mayan city, possibly the largest find yet made in the Americas, with over 200 buildings uncovered thus far. Among them is a ball court, oldest among all known Mayan cities, and the "Piramide de los Mascarones" ("Pyramid of the Masks"). The eight Mayan stucco masks flanking the pyramid's central stairway are the only ones of their kind, some still having their original colors. Also uncovered was the ingenious hydraulic system for collecting and conserving rain water. Sr. Segovia has done a superb job of restoration and landscaping.**

	25.4	88.6	Pass immigration check point and "topes". *Women think men...*
	26.0	41.6	Thru **Francisco Villa**, named after a lad better known as "Pancho" Villa.
	31.3	50.1	Thru little town of **Nicolás Bravo**. Skip livestock inspection at far end. There are 5 "topes".

(Over, please)

186-W-1
JCT HWY #307 — ESCARCEGA

JULY 1992

MI.	KM.	
38.5	61.6	Down and over bridge. Altitude is 600 ft.
42.3	67.7	Pass side road to **Caobas**. Then ahead pull over to right for customs check.
45.5	72.8	Come to state line — leave Quintana Roo and Enter Campeche.
48.8	78.1	Thru village of **La Mosa** and curve right and out. Skip Agr. Inspection at left, then "topes".
62.5	100.0	Down into **X-Pujil**. Gas at right. Side road (right) to settlement of Zoh Laguna. Trail (left) to ruins of **Río Bec**.

» **RIO BEC, so named because they were once a large ceremonial center mostly around the Río Bec, is unique in that it is surrounded by a moat and contains over 20 temples, several of which are still standing including a large palatial structure. Jungle-like trails lead to all the major structures of this lost city.**

66.5	106.4	Archaeological ruins of **Becan** over to right.

» **BECAN, a good-size Mayan city, was discovered in 1934 by a Carnegie Institute expedition under the guidance of Karl Ruppert. The city was constructed around 800 A.D. and its most prominent structure is "Temple B" measuring 55 feet in height and 58 feet in length. It has excellent carved stonework and six rooms. Archaeologists rank it in importance with Uxmal's "Governor's Palace" and Palenque's "Temple of the Sun".**

68.0	108.8	Pass side trail (left) to ruins of **Chicanna**, about ½ mile down dirt road.

» **CHICANNA has several structures of the late Classic Río Bec style which are pretty well preserved. One exhibits a complex facade that has been restored by the Middle American Research Institute of Tulane University. This facade was built in the "Chene" style similar to the one at Hochob (and reproduced in the national museum in Mexico City).**

Can't be trusted...

107.8	172.5	Microwave relay tower at left and wind down.
115.0	184.0	Thru settlement of **Constitución** and slow for 2 "topes". Km 70.
117.0	187.2	Slow for "tope" and thru village of **X-Bonil**.
118.0	188.8	Ejido Santa Lucía at left. "The secret of staying young is to live honestly, eat slowly and lie about your age." — Lucille Ball.
124.0	198.4	Pass side road (left) down to **Silvituc**.
124.5	199.2	Lake Nah over to left. Then thru lumbermill village of **Centenario**. 2 "topes".
126.0	201.6	Curve wide right past village of **López Mateos**, mostly at left.
132.7	212.3	Thru community of **Justicia Social**.

Too near. — MM.

135.8	217.1	Pass settlement of **El Lechugal**, mostly at right.
142.8	228.5	Slow for 2 "topes" and past **Ejido La Libertad**.
151.3	242.1	Thru village of **Matamoros**. Watch out for 3 "topes".
152.7	244.3	Slow for poorly banked left curve. The Eiffel Tower, dead ahead.
157.0	251.2	Into little town of **Escarcega** (population 17,000) and slow for "topes". Incidentally, Escarcega is a chicle town — for many years it was headquarters for chicle hunters. (The place ought to be called "Wrigleys" instead of Escarcega.)
157.5	252.0	Bus station at right. Then LOOK-AND-LISTEN as you cross railroad — trains do run on this Merida main line. Social security hospital (I.M.S.S.) at left.
157.9	252.6	Pass **María Isabel Hotel & Restaurant**, not exactly like the María Isabel (Sheraton) in Mexico City, But there's nothing finer in Escarcega and the rates aren't quite as high as those of its Mexico City counterpart and it's A/C, clean and comfy. VI only. There's also the **Hotel Escarcega** at right.
158.6	253.8	Bend right a little and come to junction Hwy #261 and end of log.

Villahermosa, TURN LEFT and Start Log 186-W-2. Mgas is just ahead at right.

Champoton, Campeche and Merida, TURN RIGHT and follow Log 261-N-1.

End of Log.

(Next Page, Please)

MEXICO TRAVELOG
Puts over 40 years of experience at your side! Copyright © Sanborn's TGP Inc.

ESCARCEGA (JUNCTION HWS #186 & #261) — PALENQUE JUNCTION — 115 MI OR 184 KM — DRIVE TIME 2½ HOURS

SCENIC RATING — 1

	MI.	KM.	
Mgas H	0.0	0.0	Here at junction Hwys #186 & #261, west edge of a little railroad town of **Escarcega**, proceed ahead past gas station at right. They have Mgas, but watch 'em like a hauk, they got me! MM. Then **Motel Ah-Kim-Pech** at left (strictly emergency). Watch for 2 "topes".
	0.8	1.3	Pass Military camp at left.
	1.5	2.4	LP gas at left and tall microwave relay tower **El Tormento**, right.
	4.2	6.7	Past forestry experiment station at right (visitors welcome)
	6.7	10.7	**Ejido Kilometer 36**, at right.
	15.7	25.1	Pass side road (right) to **Sabancuy**.
	16.9	27.0	Slow for "topes" and curve left thru village of **18 de Marzo**, then another "tope".
	19.5	31.2	Big mahogany mill at left. Then pass **Ejido Pital**, right.
	26.0	41.6	Over "tope" and thru village of **Manantel**, then 2 more "topes".
	28.0	44.8	Pass side road (left) to **Nueva Chontalpa**.
			Anecdote: The truck driver stopped suddenly on the highway, and the car behind crashed into him. The truck driver was sued. "Why didn't you hold out your hand?" the judge asked the truck driver. "Well," said the truck driver, "if he couldn't see the truck, how in the world could he see my hand?"
	38.0	60.8	Nice gas (regular) station at left. Then pass side road to **Candelaria**.
	42.1	67.4	Pass little **Ejido Ojo de Agua**, right.
	49.4	79.8	Pass settlement of **Buenavista**, right. Then cross bridge over Río Candelaria.
	62.0	99.2	Gas station and so-so restaurant at right.
			Definition: A Pedestrian is a man who thought there were a couple of gallons left in the tank.
	64.2	102.2	Thru settlement of **Aguacatal**, 2 "topes". Then over Río Chumpán. **Km 195**.
	79.0	126.4	Wide place of **Vista Alegre**.
	82.0	131.2	Landscape (fields) looks like Holland.
	88.6	141.8	Side road (right) to **Palizada**. Skip truck inspection station at right.
	89.5	143.2	Come to state line — leave Campeche and enter Tabasco. Then pass side road (right) to **Balancán** (where Cuauhtemoc, the last Aztec emperor, is believed to have been hanged by Cortez, his Spanish captor) and on down to railroad and lumber town of **Tenosique**, birthplace of martyred statesman Pino Suárez (1869-1913), who was Madero's vice-president.
	95.0	152.0	Pass side road (left) to little river town of **Chable**. Cemetery at right and come to toll house (clean restrooms) and pay toll. Then proceed ahead, up and over bridge across famous Río Usumacinta, a very important river.

» Originating in Guatemala, **RÍO USUMACINTA** runs into the jungles and is the boundary between Guatemala and Mexico. The brown waters of the Usumacinta (meaning "place of the sacred monkeys"), along with those of the Grijalva, empty into the Gulf and together they compose one-third of the water in all rivers in Mexico. It is navigable (more than half its length is more than 20 feet in depth) and is the only means of transportation and communication for all the ranchers and lumber mills up in the wilds. Incidentally, Río Usumacinta is also the state line — leave Tabasco and enter Chiapas.

Mgas

| | 95.5 | 152.8 | Over bridge and several more ahead. |

(Over, please)

186-W-2
ESCARCEGA — PALENQUE JCT

MI. KM.
101.9 163.0 Pass Mgas station at left. Then pass side road (left) to **Emiliano Zapata**, a very interesting tropical town.
115.0 184.0 Slow now! Come to junction (left) with road down to **Palenque** and archaeological ruins, 22 MI, and side road (right) to **Catazaja** and end of log. Gas just ahead beyond junction on left.

Villahermosa, STRAIGHT AHEAD and start Log 186-West-3.

Palenque, TURN LEFT and start Palenque Special log.

End of Log.

(Next Page, Please)

JULY 1992   **PALENQUE SPECIAL**
PALENQUE, CHI

MEXICO TRAVELOG
Puts over 40 years of experience at your side!   Copyright © Sanborn's TGP Inc.

PALENQUE JCT (HWY #186) — PALENQUE STATION, PALENQUE TOWN, AND ON TO MAYAN RUINS - 22 MI OR 35.2 KM — DRIVE TIME 30 MIN — 1 HOUR

SCENIC RATING — 4

This side road will take you down to Palenque and the famous Palenque archaeological ruins. Prior to the construction of Hwy #186, the only way to get there to visit these magnificent Mayan ruins was either by private plane or by train - and it was indeed a chore! Don't hesitate to take this very worthwhile side-sortie.

MI	KM	
0.0	0.0	Having turned off Hwy #186 at gas station, proceed ahead south — **watch for livestock and "topes".**
2.4	3.8	Pass Conalep de Palenque Vocational School. *If all the cars...*
4.2	6.7	Slow now for left curve.
7.5	12.0	Pass Palenque county line (63,000 population).
9.0	14.4	Curve left and pick up railroad at right. *In Mexico were in a line...*
11.5	18.4	Pass Hotel Hacienda at right, a motel del paso.
12.7	20.3	Slow now for sharp dangerous curve left.
13.5	21.6	Over "tope" and then pass side road (left) to **La Libertad**. Then slow, slow for very bumpy **RR XING**. Then curve right and slow for **tope** in front of railroad depot over at right. Pass **Hotel Santa Ursula** and **Hospedaje El Kichan** at right also. Then curve left thru community of **Paka-Na** or **Estación Palenque** and over another **tope**.
15.1	24.2	Pass Palenque's airport at left.
15.6	25.0	Pass VW agency, right and curve right.
16.0	25.6	Past LP gas at right. *Some idiot would try to pass. — MM.*
16.4	26.2	Past **Hotel Plaza Palenque** at left.
16.5	26.4	Slow for poorly banked left curve with **Hotel Maya Tucán** at right and **Mayorca** at left. Then pass **Tulija Hotel** at left. Good garage next door. Both built by enterprising fellow named "Choyote" in his 60's.
17.0	27.2	Careful now. Come to fork at white "Cabeza Maya" (Maya head). (To get to Doctor's office take left fork to Quaker State on right and Hotel Tulija. Turn left, pass market, he's on left.)

Ruins, take right fork.

Palenque, take left fork.

      Los Tulipanes motel at left; **La Canada** also at left.

17.5	28.0	Having taken right fork, pass side road left to hotel **Nututun** and **Agua Azul State Park**. Go straight ahead over "topes". This road eventually ends at junction with old Pan American Highway #190 below San Cristobal de las Casas. It is a fine blacktop road, but a little twisty. You'll also find *deslaves* during the rainy seasons — May-July and late Nov.-Jan. (Log 199 South takes you here.) If you are over 30 feet long (or your rig is), then go to La Ventosa and cross Hwy #185. Don't even think about Hwy #187 from Villahermosa.
18.2	29.1	"Topes". Slow down.
18.7	29.9	Pass **Hotel Los Leones** at right, then **Kin-Ha Hotel & Trailer Park** at right.
19.5	31.2	Slow for sharp downgrade right curve. Motel **Chan-Kah** (Little Village) at left.

(Over, please)

PALENQUE SPECIAL
PALENQUE, CHI

MI	KM	
20.0	32.0	"Tope". Pass entrance to Palenque National Park. Then curve right.
Rv 20.8	33.3	Mayabell RV Park at left. Past Cascades Monument.
21.7	34.7	Now sharp left and wind up. Then sharp right and up some more.
22.0	35.2	Curve left and come to archaeological "zona" and stop at little toll house at right. Pay admission and parking charge and turn into parking lot at left and lock car. Then walk on up past gate into clearing which is where the action begins — better wear a hat.

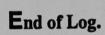
You should get yourself a guide if you really want to enjoy this unusual attraction. Also, bear in mind that the "zona" is open 8 AM till 5 PM. And there's a little refreshment stand at right behind toll house. A sound and light show is planned. Let us know when it starts.

End of Log.

(Next Page, Please)

ROUTE SELECTION RS-PAL-1

SAN CRISTOBAL OR GUATEMALA (& back) START LOG 199-S (PAGES 119 THRU 132)

OTHERWISE SKIP TO CONTINUATION OF DIRECT ROUTE (colored sheet), AND START LOG 183-W-3 (PAGE 138)

JULY 1992   1 of 2   199—SOUTH
                                 PALENQUE, CHI — JCT. HWY #190

MEXICO TRAVELOG
Puts over 40 years of experience at your side! Copyright © Sanborn's TGP Inc.

PALENQUE — OCOSINGO — JCT HWY #190 — 126.5 MILES OR 202.4 KM — DRIVE TIME — 5 — 6½ HOURS — CURVY — NO MAGNA

SCENIC RATING — 4

» PLEASE INQUIRE LOCALLY (i.e. truck drivers, highway patrols, or Green Angels) ABOUT CONDITIONS! During rainy seasons (May — July & late Nov — Jan), "deslaves" (washouts) inevitable. Road will be passable, but one-lane in spots. Some sharp curves. If you're rig's over 30 feet, we don't recommend this route. Go to Acayucan & cross on Hwy #185. Don't try Hwy #187 from Villahermosa — it's worse!

The good news is it's a great shortcut from the Yucatan and Palenque to the nice colonial city of San Cristobal de las Casas. The bad news is has more curves than Raquel Welch and Dolly Parton combined. That's more curvaceous than even I like. Buses and trucks use it, so it's not a deserted highway. Not recommended for large RV's. Thanks to a nice fellow who's name I didn't catch and Richard Snapp of Shreveport, LA, who helped me with info on this road.

	MI.	KM.	
	0.0	0.0	Having turned south (left) here at junction with road to Palenque ruins, continue ahead toward mountains. Watch out for the people on road side carrying firewood, bananas, corn husks for tamales etc. Pass AGUA AZUL 62 KM. sign (38 miles) and also OCOSINGO 118 KM. sign.
(EAT)	0.9	1.4	Pass lake and pretty restaurant.
	1.1	1.8	Over bridge. The first 15 minutes of a rain storm are the most dangerous for drivers. Park and wait it out.
	1.9	3.0	Hotel Nututun on left, natural river pools.
H	3.0	4.8	Uphill winding, grade 2°. On 2 lane mountain roads, you'll sometimes see a sign with arrows crossing the lanes. This means you are supposed to switch lanes (drive in the left lane) — temporarily. The theory is that you can see oncoming traffic on blind curves better. You can! On curves in general, slow before going into them. Accelerate slightly at the apex.
	3.6	5.8	Down winding.
	5.5	8.8	Jog right for bypass around Chancol off to left.
⛰	6.5	10.4	Careful for slippery curves thru here. We all know to use our transmission as a brake (even automatics), don't we?
	7.0	11.2	Hairpin curve.
	10.0	16.0	Altitude 1,500 feet. Then down winding.
	11.0	17.6	Sometimes a washout here. Careful. (ALWAYS slow before going around a curve — you never know when a chunk of highway has departed or a hurry-worry driver has decided to pass.)
	11.5	18.4	Pass side road to Mijol-Ha. 0.8 miles away.
	12.5	20.0	Uphill and downhill winding, beautiful scenery.
	15.5	24.8	Village of San Miguel down to left. Note the corrugated aluminum roofs.
	18.5	29.6	Pass turnoff to Salto de Agua.
	19.1	30.6	Over bridge. Then thru Ejido Santa Maria. Pass queen bee farm.
⛽	20.3	32.5	Emergency gas and diesel on left, the old fashioned way from barrel.
	23.3	37.3	Careful for narrow section of road. This is B. Traven country. He set many of his "Jungle" novels around here. If you want to understand Mexico, he has a unique insight.
	24.0	38.4	Straight stretch for passing.
	25.3	40.5	Thru community of Ursulo Galvan.

(Over, please)

199—SOUTH
PALENQUE, CHI — JCT. HWY #190

MI.	KM.	
25.9	41.4	Straight stretch.
27.6	44.2	Over **Rio Tulija**. Then straight stretch.
30.0	48.0	Caution for rough road thru here.
31.2	49.9	Mayan community of **Yobchib**. Then sharp curve over bridge and up hill.
31.8	50.9	**Chilón** county line. Pass road side shops. Brightly colored embroidered goods, cheaper.
33.0	52.8	Great valley view on right.
34.3	54.9	Slow for **Escuela** (school) **Zapata**.
35.3	56.8	Thru **Tzinteel** village.
36.0	57.6	Pass side road (right) to CASCADAS DE AGUA AZUL (Agua Azul Waterfalls).

» Over OK paved, windy downhill 2.7 mile, 6° grade road. The falls are a series of over a thousand falls, not all of which can be reached by foot. The area is a nice spot for a picnic, to take pictures, and to just hike the trail around the falls and enjoy nature's handiwork. Agua Azul has a primitive camping area and there is a grassy spot where trailer camping is permitted. Kids wash cars — negotiate price, usually about ½ or less of what they ask. Trail above falls to picnic area. Kids selling bean empanadas and sweet buñuelos (fried flour tortillas sprinkled with sugar). Many birds. Small day use fee. No security. Boondocking only. Use your own judgement. The cross at the head of falls is for a frenchman who dared the falls and lost!

40.3	64.5	Thru coffee village of **Xhanil**.

» This is coffee country, and the little shrub-like plants alongside the highway are coffee plants. Coffee grows best at from 800-5,000 feet, with higher-altitude coffee considered best. When ripe, the coffee bean resembles a red bead on the shrub and must be hand-picked as coffee beans do not ripen simultaneously. After picking, the red husk is removed and the golden-colored bean is placed in the sun to dry. After drying, the dry bean is washed several times to remove its membrane and is then shipped to outlets where it is roasted, ground, and packaged. Harvest season in this area is November thru January. Other sections of Mexico which grow coffee are Tapachula, Jalapa, Veracruz, parts of Oaxaca, parts of Michoacan, and around Patzcuaro and Morelia.

48.0	76.8	Community of **El Chich** down side road (left). Then **Escuela Pedro Moreno** at left.
51.0	81.6	**Paso del Macho** and thru school zone.

» If thru here during corn harvest time, you'll see the Mayan practice of doubling over the stalk enabling the ears to hang down. This helps shed any late-season rains and also keeps the kernels dry and helps protect the ears from the birds till harvested. Corn plays an important role in Mayan culture.

56.3	90.1	**Laratzac** down to right. Then thru **Tunapaz**.
61.0	97.6	**Tulu** down side road (left), but ahead for you to Ocosingo, 13 miles.
62.5	100.0	**Xotxotja** (pronounced "shoat-shoat-ha"), mostly down to right.
72.3	115.7	Lumber mill and registered Swiss cattle farm to right.
73.5	117.6	Enter town of **Ocosingo**, largest in these parts. Gas station at right.
74.3	118.9	Pass side road (left) to ruins of TINANA. It's 5-10 miles of unimproved road, but okay except during rainy season. Worthwhile visit. Stone casket museum (talk about "perpetual care!"). Sorry, large RV's better forgo this one. (If you've made it this far, the curves continue, but surface usually better, by the way).
76.0	121.6	Take leave of Ocosingo.
83.5	133.6	Community of **Nueva Esperanza**.
86.0	137.6	Thru **Cuschuja**.
86.5	138.4	Government sawmill at left.
87.3	139.7	Thru **La Florida**. Then another small settlement of La Florida.
89.5	143.2	Community of **Abasolo**.
93.0	148.8	Settlement of **Corralito**. Then **Tobilja** down side road (right).
102.0	163.2	Note **Oxchuc**, a good-size town for these parts, over to right.
107.0	171.2	Thru **Chempil**.
112.0	179.2	Stretched-out town of **Huixtan**.

(Next Page, Please)

MEXICO TRAVELOG
Puts over 40 years of experience at your side! Copyright © Sanborn's TGP Inc.

MI.	KM.	
117.0	187.2	**Careful for landslide zone** (there are frequently boulders on highway and detours around them).
120.0	192.0	**Puerto Humoso.**
123.1	197.0	**Las Huertas** sawmill at right and then community of **Chivero** (sheep).
126.5	202.4	Come to junction with Hwy #190. Congratulations! You made it!

San Cristobal de las Casas, turn right. Magna in San Cristobal, west end, near Parador Real.

Comitan and Guatemala, turn left. Magna in Comitan.

End of log!

(Over, please)

StateWide

Down Mexico Way

"Mexico Mike" Nelson writes the book on seeing Mexico by automobile.

"MEXICO MIKE" NELson's day began, appropriately enough, deep in the heart of Mexico at the Villas Arqueologicas hotel, a low-key resort run by Club Med in the shadows of the Aztec pyramids of Teotihuacán. He had already revised the fee to the archaeological site, evaluated the parking lots, and ducked into a few restaurants. Now Nelson, as the chief travel logger for *Sanborn's Mexico Travelog*, was headed on a circuitous route through the states of Hidalgo, Mexico, and Puebla.

But less than an hour after Nelson hit the road, he was hopelessly tangled in rush-hour traffic in Ecatepec de Morelos, an industrial suburb on the northeastern edge of Mexico City. No matter which direction he turned—when he could turn—he couldn't locate the toll road to Pachuca, the capital city of Hidalgo. In one half-hour span, he dropped coins in the same toll booth three times. Muttering his whereabouts into a cassette recorder, he started to lose his cool, honking his horn and shouting epithets at cars and buses trying to cut him off as only the locals of Mexico City can. When he finally found the sign for the Pachuca toll road, he made one last comment into the recorder: "Okay. Forget all that."

A traveler should never lose his cool in traffic, according to Sanborn's *Travelog*, the guide given to motorists who buy Sanborn's Mexico auto insurance. Since Mexico Mike writes the travelog, he should have remembered Rule of the Road number 10: "DO go with the flow—especially in city traffic." But his reaction to the bumper-to-bumper crawl was understandable, considering how hassle-free this road-logging trip had been until now. Two days earlier, Nelson was measuring the tunnel leading into the ghost town of Real de Catorce and determined that it is too tight for RVs. The day before, he had gotten a lead on Mexico's largest orchid garden and sampled the waters of a renowned spa in San Miguel de Allende. "It's kind of like being a truck driver," he said. "Everybody thinks I'm on vacation when I'm doing these trips. But that jam was no picnic."

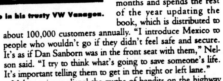

Mike Nelson tours all of Mexico in his trusty VW Vanagon.

Touring Mexico by highway can be a picnic as long as cultural differences, road conditions, and the fear of the unknown don't get in the way. That's why Dan Sanborn started writing the *Travelog* back in 1948 as a service for his insurance customers. The mile-by-mile description reassures drivers unfamiliar with Mexico that they're on the right track and educates them about taboos such as driving at night. "Mexico is open range. I can personally attest that you can't see a black cow at night," Nelson says. Other advisories warn motorists to stay out of Mexico City on the day that vehicles with license plates ending in certain numbers are banned from the road—if you get caught, you'll pay a fine. Otherwise, Nelson writes, be friendly, and the highway is a fine way to see Mexico.

Mike Nelson got hooked on the *Travelog* in 1957, when his family drove from the Valley to San Luis Potosí. Seven-year-old Mike was the navigator, and his bible was the loose-bound book with the yellow cover. "I knew then I wanted to be a writer, so I thought writing a book like this was a great way to make a living," he said. "Dan Sanborn became my hero. I wanted to be like him."

For the last four years, Nelson has *been* Dan, or, more specifically, the executive vice president in charge of publishing for Sanborn's Mexico Insurance Services (Dan Sanborn is retired and lives in McAllen). That means Nelson drives nearly 25,000 miles of Mexico's highways for a total of four months and spends the rest of the year updating the book, which is distributed to about 100,000 customers annually. "I introduce Mexico to people who wouldn't go if they didn't feel safe and secure. It's as if Dan Sanborn was in the front seat with them," Nelson said. "I try to think what's going to save someone's life. It's important telling them to get in the right or left lane."

Nelson tries to dispel the myths of bandits on the highway and crooked police. "I haven't seen a bandit yet," he observed. "And the only experiences I've had with cops have been when they've helped me. Not everyone's one hundred percent honest, but the vast majority are."

The payoff on this day was the view that unfolded outside the windshield. Amber waves of grain framed by rows of giant maguey cactus contrasted with an endless parade of rumbling trucks and noisy buses as well as proverbial peasants leading proverbial burros. The route went from spacious four-lane toll roads to bumpy, congested stretches of two-lane blacktop. Nelson kept a sharp eye out for *topes*, the speed bumps that slow traffic on major and secondary roads, noting every detail by scribbling into one of two pads, speaking into his tape recorder, or cuing his assistant logger.

Mexico Mike couldn't be in a rush if he wanted to. His road vehicle, a 1980 VW Vanagon, negotiates steep inclines like an ancient Mack truck with emphysema and requires oil and transmission checks frequently enough for Nelson to become familiar with repair shops along the way. But those attributes simply force Nelson to adhere to Rule of the Road number 8: "DON'T get in a hurry." Still, he comes prepared. A mechanic's creeper and spare parts are stowed in the back. A pen on a string dangles around his neck, his back is comforted by two orthopedic cushions, and his shoulder belt has extra padding. The van's control panel is augmented by a compass, an altimeter, a stopwatch, cassette tapes, and a Swedish odometer from Dan Sanborn himself.

Three hours after the morning traffic jam, Mexico Mike approached a highway junction marked by three restaurants. Nelson stopped at one, La Posta—done up like a rustic hunting lodge—long enough to enjoy a pleasant meal of rabbit *mojo de ajo*, quail eggs, and coffee. Afterwards, a chat with the owner led to a description of the owner's hometown of Pahuatlán, thirty miles distant in Hidalgo. The land there was *muy divina*, he said, marked with waterfalls and lush forests.

The observant Mexico Mike jots down details on his notepad.

It sounded intriguing enough for Nelson to make an unscheduled detour. After Nelson backtracked and tooled through ten miles of verdant pastures and a settlement named Honey, the road twisted to reveal a stunning vista of a deep valley below steep, craggy peaks high enough to catch the clouds. In the hour it took to drive the next fifteen miles, the scenery changed dramatically from mountainsides of tall, cool pines to tropical slopes choked with banana plants.

Finally, at Pahuatlán, the asphalt gave way to cobblestones surrounded by whitewashed buildings with red-tiled roofs. Nelson inspected the town's two hotels; dropped into an artisan's shop, where he bought some paper made by Nahua Indians; and inquired about the number of foreigners who visit. He concluded that the place was romantic enough to spend more time in with the right companion. But because the shadows were growing longer, he wanted to push on. He had heard of sulfur springs near Huauchinango, thirty miles east. True to his calling, he had to check it out. —J.N.

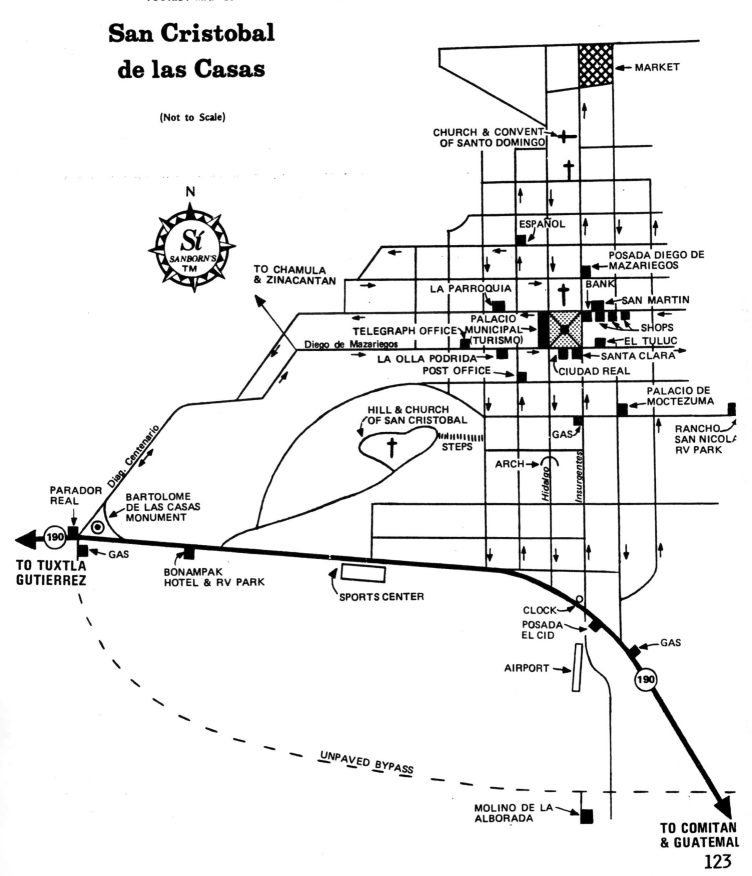

<u>SAN CRISTOBAL DE LAS CASAS</u>, population 93,500, is one of Mexico's most charming towns. It received its name from Friar Bartolome de las Casas, a great defender of Indian rights long before this practice became popular. Founded March 31, 1528 by Captain Diego de Mazariegos, one of Hernan Cortez' officers, the town is the fourth oldest on the American continent.

Due to its remote location the town is off the beaten path of the masses of tourists, although it is popular with French and other European tourists. Part of San Cristobal de las Casas' charm is that it lies in the beautiful valley of Jovel at an altitude of near 7,000 feet, and is surrounded by mountains and pine forests dotted with quaint little Indian villages. It has retained a unique blend of Spanish colonial and Indian heritage. Just as common as Spanish in the market and in the surrounding villages are the Tzotzil and Tzeltal languages.

With its cobblestone streets and many old buildings, parts of San Cristobal de las Casas still feel 16th century, and many of its buildings are works of art in themselves. The Temple of Santo Domingo was built in baroque style between 1547-60. Its altar and pulpit are fashioned of finely fitted pieces of carved wood. Also of interest are the large Indian market (closed Sunday because several surrounding villages have Sunday markets) where inhabitants of aforementioned villages come to buy and sell produce, merchandise, and artifacts and a smaller tourist market near the downtown plaza. There're also the Na-Bolum Museum of Archaeology at the estate of the late explorer-anthropologist Franz Blum at Calle Vicente Guerrero #34, the craft shops on Guadalupe Street, and the National Indian Institute where the natives are instructed in agriculture, literacy, nutrition, and hygiene. Nearby places of interest include the Grutas ("caves") of San Cristobal, magnificent Sumiero Canyon in the Tierra Colorada Mountains, and the colorful Indian towns of Zinacantan, San Juan Chamula, and Tenejapa. The town's biggest fiesta is held July 17-24 in honor of their patron saint, St. Cristobal.

If you need assistance of any kind, check with the tourist office ("turismo") located on the ground floor of the municipal palace across from the plaza. And take note that the town virtually closes down from about 2 PM-4:30 PM for a <u>long</u> lunch break ("siesta" time). Remember to plan your day accordingly.

SANBORN'S
WHERE TO EAT & STAY
San Cristobal de las Casas

HOTELS & MOTELS

*** <u>BONAMPAK</u> — Nice 50-room air-con motor hotel a couple blocks off Hwy #190 on Calzada Mexico. Restaurant. Bar. Parking. No pets. AE, DI, MC, VI. Phone 8-1621.

* <u>CIUDAD REAL</u> — 33-room converted hacienda on main plaza at 31 de Marzo #10. Good restaurant. Bar. On-street parking. No pets. AE, CB, DI, MC, VI. Phone 8-0187.

* <u>ESPANOL</u> — Old colonial 36-room hotel 2 blocks north of plaza at Calle Primero de Marzo #15. Restaurant. Bar. Parking. No pets. AE, DI, MC, VI. Phone 8-0045, 8-0203, or 8-0412.

** <u>MOLINA DE LA ALBORADA</u> — Pleasant, relaxful 10-room ranch-hacienda hotel high on knoll overlooking valley and town. Dining room. Horses. Space for few RV's. Parking. Pets OK. VI. Phone 8-0935.

*** <u>PARADOR CIUDAD REAL</u> — 48-room motel at Diagonal Centenario #32 at north entrance to town. Restaurant. Laundromat. Emergency RV parking. Parking. Pets OK. No credit cards. 8-0187.

*** <u>POSADA DIEGO DE MAZARIEGOS</u> — Attractive 52-room air-con hotel a block north of plaza on Calle Ma. Adelina Flores #2. Good restaurant. Bar. Curio shop. Travel agency. Car rental. Parking. No pets. AE, DI, MC, VI. Phone 8-0621.

<u>POSADA EL CID</u> — 60-unit motel on highway just beyond road to airport. Restaurant. Parking. No pets. MC, VI. Phone 8-0984 or 8-1181.

** <u>SANTA CLARA</u> — 40-room hotel at Av. Insurgentes #1 on main plaza, once the home of San Cristobal's founder, Diego de Mazariegos. Good restaurant. Bar. Parking. No pets. MC, VI. Phone 8-1140.

RESTAURANTS

* <u>EL TULUC</u> — Little cafe-style restaurant at Francisco Madero #9, a block from main plaza. Excellent Chiapan coffee and "comida corrida" (blue-plate special) for lunch. Open 9-11 AM for breakfast; 11 AM-1 PM for coffee; 1-5 PM for lunch; 5-7 PM for coffee; and 7-10:30 PM for a la carte dinner. Closed Tuesdays. No credit cards.

** <u>LA OLLA PODRIDA</u> — Simple but nice restaurant a couple blocks off main plaza at corner of Diego Mazariegos and Allende. Excellent Mexican and Italian dishes and steaks. Good service. Bakery. Open 6 AM-11:30 PM daily. MC, VI.

RV FACILITIES

<u>BONAMPAK</u> — 26-space RV facility in conjunction with hotel (13 spaces with all hookups; 13 without). Showers. Toilets. Restaurant. Bar. Pets OK. Phone 8-1621.

<u>LA AMISTAD</u> — 22-space park (12 spaces with all hookups; 10 with electricity and water) set among pines 18½ miles south of town on Hwy #190 in little village of Teopisca. Showers. Toilets. Picnic tables. Pets OK.

<u>MOLINA DE LA ALBORADA</u> — See above.

<u>PARADOR CIUDAD REAL</u> — See above.

<u>RANCHO SAN NICOLAS</u> — 25-space RV park at end of Calle Francisco Leon. Electrical and water hookups. Showers. Toilets. Pets OK.

Copyright © Sanborn's TGP, Inc.

Since you'll sometimes visit friends or go places not covered in the *Travelog*, we offer the following tips on what to do when you're lost. Of course you'll never get lost with the *Travelog* — or almost never.

HOW TO ASK DIRECTIONS

1. Keep the questions short. Even if your Spanish is okay, the most direct questions get the best answers. If you don't speak much, a simple "**A**" (pronounced "*ah*" like at the doctor's) *Mexico* ?" (or the name of the closest big city in the general direction you're heading). Coupled with a smile, that'll get you just about anywhere.

2. NEVER ask how long it will take! The answer will depend on how long it took the person you asked, the last time he went. If he rode a bicycle, he'll tell you it takes quite awhile. Ditto for distances. Usually, you'll get a "lejos" (far), or "cerca" (near). These, like travelling times, are subjective.

3. Maps often cause more confusion and take more time than pointing. Use them sparingly.

4. Folks will always tell you how to get somewhere, even if they don't know. It's considered impolite to just say no. Don't you be nasty and get impatient, even if you've been the way he recommends. Nod politely, say "Gracias", and find somebody else. If two people say the same thing, you've got a pretty good shot at getting where you're going.

5. Kids are the worst to ask. They have a hard time understanding gringo Spanish and often have vivid imaginations. Look for an adult.

6. Women will sometimes ignore you, because they were taught not to talk to strangers.

7. Gas station attendants usually know, but they may not have time to talk. Ask a driver getting gas.

8. A little roadside tienda is a good choice, as there are usually a few folks sitting around who would love to help you out. If two of them agree on a route, take it! It won't hurt to buy a refresco while you're there. If they have returnable bottles, you'll have to pay a deposit if you take it out. The deposit's often more than the soda. Taverns are best avoided.

9. Cops can be helpful.

10. If the directions are convoluted, the person giving them has never been where you want to go. Thank him and find someone else. Any directions that start off "... dos (or tres) cuadras ..." (2 or 3 blocks) are suspicious. What that really means is that you should go two or three blocks away and maybe you'll find somebody who can help you.

190-South-6B
San Cristobal-Guatemala

SAN CRISTOBAL DE LAS CASAS THRU COMITAN TO CD. CUAUHTEMOC (GUATEMALAN BORDER) — 107 MILE

With most of the winding behind, the highway straightens out somewhat from here to the Guatemalan border. You'll encounter lots of Indian communities thru here, so careful for folks alongside the road — it should be fairly easy to spot 'em because of their colorful attire.

* *

0	Here at monument to Fray San Bartolome de las Casas, proceed ahead on Hwy #190. . Then sports center at right.
1	Supermarket at left and Pepsi at right.
1½	Blue-and-white church at left. . Pass road (right) to airport and to Molino de la Alborada, a ranch-type hotel. . Then Posada El Cid at right and LP gas, also at right. . Gas ⛽ at left.
3	"Periferico Norte" (north bypass) at left and road to Tenejapa. . Then merge with "Periferico Sur" (south bypass) at right. . Then pass ecology institue at right and social security clinic, also at right.
7-	Side road (right) to GRUTAS ("caves") DE SAN CRISTOBAL. . If speleology interests you, the caves are open from 8-5 daily (admission charged). . Note pines lining both sides of highway.
8	Side road (left) to Ocosingo and on to Palenque. . If to either of these towns, turn left and start Log 199-North; presently the road is paved except for two stretches totaling 25 miles, and although these surfaces are "improved", the highway is <u>not</u> recommended for large RV's.

Back on Hwy #190 heading east. . .

8½	Instituto Nacional de Investigaciones Forestales ("National Institute of Forest Investigations") at left.
10+	Curve right and up thru Mitziton. . Careful along highway thru here for four-wheeled wooden carts used for hauling wood (or people). . Then curve left and easy winding thru thick, lush forest.
13½+	Village of Betania.
15½	Settlement of Belem ("Bethlehem") at left and past little chapel at right.
18½	Road workers' campo of Siberia at left. .Then La Amistad RV Park at right (22 spaces among pines with water and electrical hookups, 12 with sewer; toilets, showers; picnic tables; popular during winter months).
20½	Curve right and straight into Teopisca (population 35,000) and ahead thru town. . Plaza and church at left.
22-	Gas ⛽ at left, and take leave of Teopisca.
24-	Junction (right) with Hwy #24 to Villa Las Rosas.
24½+	Pass Amatenango to right where an unusual type of floral design pottery is produced.
26½	Establos ("stables") San Nicolas, a ranch-farm to right.
29¼	Side road (left) to Napite and thru settlement of Tulanca.
33½	Past side road (left) to Cruz Quemada somewhere among the rocks. ("Cruz Quemada" means burned cross — Ku Klux Klan way down here?). . Pass side road (right) to Laguna Chamula
41	Thru scattered community of Laguna Larga.
42-	Thru village of El Durazno at right.
44½	Village of San Francisco at right.
51	Side road (right) to Colonia Hidalgo (population 84,733).

(over, please)

SAN CRISTOBAL DE LAS CASAS-COMITAN-CD. CUAUHTEMOC (190-South-6B)

55	Slow as you enter town of <u>Comitan de Dominguez</u>, better known as "Comitan" and start sloping divided boulevard. . then at left is Hotel Los Lagos de Montebello (52 rooms; restaurant-bar; pool; parking; no pets; MC, VI). . If it's growing late don't hesitate to put up here since there are no accommodations in Ciudad Cuauhtemoc, and if you're heading for Guatemala, there is no lodging till Huehuetenango, 102 miles. . Gas ⛽ at left and then again at right ⛽. . Then pass social security clinic at right. . Divided ends.
	By the way, there's a Guatemalan Consulate here in Comitan and if you're heading that way, this is a good place to get your tourist card (if you don't already have it). . Tourist cards for Guatemala must be obtained in advance.
59-	Pass gas ⛽ at right. . Then customs and immigration check.
62	<u>Colonia Francisco Sarabia</u> at right. . Then side road (left) to <u>Pamala</u>.
64	Side road (left) to Comitan's airport.
66-	Slow now for a "SANBORN'S EXTRA".
	If you have an hour or two to spare, turn left here and drive 26 miles to MONTEBELLO NATIONAL PARK where there's a chain of 16 beautiful mountain lakes surrounded by scenic forest. Some of the blue-green lakes are in Mexico and some in Guatemala. And at the end of the paved road is a "mirador" encircled by three lakes with parking and picnic tables where you can soak up the postcard view. Located on a good dirt road 7 miles southeast of the national park's entrance is pleasant Lago Tziscao RV Park (electrical hookups; toilets; cold showers; small restaurant). Incidentally, admission is charged to enter the national park.
67	Thru settlement of <u>Trinitaria</u>. . You're now 1712 meters (5617 feet) above sea level.
74½	Wide left horseshoe curve and on down.
93¼	Curve right and over bridge over Rio Grijalva and thru community of <u>San Gregorio</u>. . Immigration check point at left — be prepared to stop, although you might be waved on.
104½	Gas ⛽ at left. . Then curve right and thru <u>El Jocote</u>.
106	Side road (right) to <u>Comalapa</u> and on to <u>Huixtla</u>, 26 miles north of Tapachula on Hwy #200, but don't tackle it as it's not yet paved completely.
107	Into border community of <u>Ciudad Cuauhtemoc</u>. . Pull over to left and stop for customs — turn all your papers in. . Come to end of log (2 miles from Guatemalan border).

190-North-1A
Guatemala-San Cristobal

CD. CUAUHTEMOC (GUATEMALAN BORDER) THRU COMITAN TO SAN CRISTOBAL DE LAS CASAS — 109 MILES

NOTE:— Highway #190, also known as the Pan American Highway, is good but winding in spots. It's a very scenic drive thru lots of Indian communities so be careful for folks on the road — it should be fairly easy because of the colorful outfits they wear. And if you're wondering why everything is so green and lush, it's because the state of Chiapas gets close to 25% of the entire country's water resources.

* *

0	After obtaining your tourist cards at MIGRACION and car permit at ADUANA ("Customs"), having your luggage inspected, and having tourist stickers placed on your vehicle windshield, you're officially welcome to Mexico. . Proceed ahead and wind thru Grijalva River Valley.
2½	Into border community of Ciudad Cuauhtemoc and pull over to right for immigration and customs check — have papers ready.
3½	Side road (left) to Comalapa and on to Huixtla, 26 miles north of Tapachula on Hwy #200. But don't tackle it as the road is paved only to Motozintla, 42 miles from here and the remaining 25 are practically impassable.
5-	Thru community of El Jocote. . Gas at right (next gas at Comitan, 46 miles).
16	Enter community of San Gregorio. . Stop at right for last immigration and customs check. Then over bridge over Rio Grijalva and out.
22½	Pass side road (right) to Las Delicias, 12 miles.
28½	Side road (left) to Limon.
42¼	Thru settlement of Trinitaria (altitude 5,617 feet).
43½+	Slow for a SANBORN'S EXTRA. . .

If you have an hour or two to spare, turn right here and drive the 26 miles to MONTEBELLO NATIONAL PARK where there is a chain of beautiful mountain lakes surrounded by scenic forests. Part of the 16 blue-green lakes are in Mexico and the rest in Guatemala. At the end of the paved road is a "mirador", a place where you can park and soak up the post card view, encircled by three lakes with picnic tables available. Lake Tziscao is located on a good all-weather road seven miles southeast of the park's entrance (electrical hookups; toilets; cold showers; small restaurant). . Incidentally, admission is charged to enter the national park.

45½	Side road (right) to Comitan's airport.
47¼	Pass side road (right) to Pamala. . Then Colonia Francisco Sarabia at left.
49	Slow for customs check.
51	Lumber mill ("Cia. Forestal de Chiapas") at left. . Slow as you enter town of Comitan de Dominguez, better known as "Comitan". . Start divided and pass social security clinic and gas, also at left (next gas at Teopisca, 36 miles). . Then Hotel Los Lagos de Montebello at right (60 rooms; heated pool; parking; no pets; MC, VI; phone 2-0647).
58½	Side road (left) to Colonia Hidalgo.
65-	Village of San Francisco at left.
68	Thru scattered community of Laguna Larga.
75	Pass side road (left) to Laguna Chamula. . Then pass side road (right) to Cruz Quemada somewhere among the rocks. (Incidentally, "Cruz Quemada" means burned cross — Ku Klux Klan 'way down here?)
79½	Thru settlement of Tulanca. . Then side road (right) to Napite.

(over, please)

CD. CUAUHTEMOC-COMITAN-SAN CRISTOBAL DE LAS CASAS (190-North-1A)

82½ Establos ("stables") San Nicolas, a ranch-farm over to left. . Along highway thru here careful for four-wheeled wooden carts used for hauling wood or people.
84 Past Amatenanco to left where an unusual type of floral design pottery is produced.
84¾ Junction (left) Highway #24 to Villa Las Rosas.
86¾ Slow now as you enter Teopisca. . Gas at left (next gas at San Cristobal de las Casas, 20 miles). . Jog left-right past plaza on left and church on right. . Note tepee-style Conasupo grain storage bins off to left.
90 Entrance (left) to La Amistad RV Park (22 spaces among pines; electrical and water hook-ups; 12 with sewer; showers; toilets; picnic tables). . Pass roadworkers' campo of Siberia at right.
93 Little community of Belem at right. . Little chapel at left.
98½ Thru Mitziton.
100½ Side road (right) to Ocosingo and one day to Palenque — but don't tackle it now!
102 Side road (left) to GRUTAS ("caves") DE SAN CRISTOBAL. . (If speleology interests you, the caves are open from 8-5 daily; admission charged.)
105 Merge left with Periferico Sur (south bypass). . A half-mile further on merge with Periferico Norte (north bypass) and road to Tenejapa.
107- Gas at right (next regular gas, 2 miles). . LP gas at left and enter outskirts of nice little town of San Cristobal de las Casas (population 40,000), the "gem of Chiapas" and the state's oldest Spanish settlement. . Try to spend some time here in this historic town — there's lots to see and accommodations are good.

Back on highway, pass Posada El Cid at left. . If to downtown, turn right here at clock on right onto one-way street (see map). . Street at left goes to airport and to Molino de la Alborada Hotel.

107¾ Supermarket at right and Pepsi at left. . Then sports center at left.
109 Come now to monument to Fray San Bartolome de las Casas at right, first bishop of Chiapas and champion of the Indians. . Road at right is to San Cristobal de las Casas proper. Gas just ahead (regular only) at left. . End of log. . See "Where to Eat & Stay in San Cristobal de las Casas" for information on accommodations.

If to Tuxtla Gutierrez or Villahermosa, start Log 190-North-1B.

ROUTE SELECTION

CONTINUATION OF DIRECT ROUTE

JULY, 1992   **199-NORTH**
                                                                  JCT. HWY #190 — PALENQUE, CHI

MEXICO TRAVELOG
Puts over 40 years of experience at your side! Copyright © Sanborn's TGP Inc.

JCT. HWY #190 — OCOSINGO — PALENQUE — 126.5 MI OR 202.4 KM — DRIVE TIME — 5 — 6½ HOURS. — CURVY — NO MAGNA.

SCENIC RATING — 4

» **PLEASE INQUIRE LOCALLY (i.e. truck drivers or Green Angels) ABOUT CONDITIONS!** During rainy seasons (May — July & late Nov — Jan), "deslaves" (washouts) inevitable. Road will be passable, but one-lane in spots. Some sharp curves. If you're rig's over 30 feet, we don't recommend this route. Go to La Ventosa & cross on Hwy #185. Don't try #187 to Villahermosa — it's worse.

The good news is it's a great shortcut from San Cristobal de las Casas or Guatemala to the Yucatan and Palenque. The bad news is has more curves than Raquel Welch and Dolly Parton combined. That's more curvaceous than even I like. Buses and trucks use it, so it's not a deserted highway. Not recommended for large RV's. Thanks to a nice fellow who's name I didn't catch and Richard Snapp of Shreveport, LA, who helped me with info on this road.

MI.	KM.	
0.0	0.0	Having turned north (right) here at junction of #190 onto Hwy #199, proceed ahead.
3.4	5.4	**Las Huertas** sawmill at left and then community of **Chivero** (sheep).
6.5	10.4	**Puerto Humoso.** Careful. (ALWAYS slow before going around a curve — you never know when a chunk of highway has departed or a hurry-worry driver has decided to pass.)
9.5	15.2	**Careful for landslide zone** (there are frequently boulders on highway and detours around them).
14.5	23.2	Stretched-out town of **Huixtan.** Careful for slippery curves thru here. We all know to use our transmission as a brake (even automatics), don't we?
19.5	31.2	Thru **Chempil.** This is B. Traven country. He set many of his "Jungle" novels around here. If you want to understand Mexico, he has a unique insight.
24.5	39.2	Note **Oxchuc,** a good-size town for these parts, over to left.
33.5	53.6	Settlement of **Corralito.** Then **Tobilja** down side road (left).
37.0	59.2	Community of **Abasolo.**
39.2	62.7	Thru **La Florida.** Then another small settlement of La Florida.
40.0	64.0	Government sawmill at right.
40.5	64.8	Thru **Cuschuja.**
43.0	68.8	Community of **Nueva Esperanza.**
50.5	80.8	Enter outskirts of **Ocosingo.**
52.2	83.5	Side road (right) to ruins of **TINANA.** It's 5-10 miles of unimproved road, but okay except during rainy season. Worthwhile visit. Stone casket museum (talk about "perpetual care!"). Sorry, large RV's better forgo this one. (By the way, if you've made it this far, the curves become more intense and surface gets more uneven — usually.)
53.0	84.8	Enter town of **Ocosingo,** largest in these parts. Gas station at left.
54.2	86.7	Lumber mill and registered Swiss cattle farm to left.
64.0	102.4	**Xotxotja** (pronounced "shoat-shoat-ha"), mostly down to left.
65.5	104.8	**Tulu** down side road (right), but ahead for you to Ocosingo, 13 miles.
70.2	112.3	**Laratzac** down to left. Then thru **Tunapaz.**

(Over, please)

199-NORTH
JCT. HWY #190 — PALENQUE, CHI

JULY 1992

» If thru here during corn harvest time, you'll see the Mayan practice of doubling over the stalk enabling the ears to hang down. This helps shed any late-season rains and also keeps the kernels dry and helps protect the ears from the birds till harvested. Corn plays an important role in Mayan culture.

MI.	KM.	
75.5	120.8	Paso del Macho and thru school zone.
78.5	125.6	Community of El Chich down side road (right). Then Escuela Pedro Moreno at right.

» This is coffee country, and the little shrub-like plants alongside the highway are coffee plants. Coffee grows best at from 800-5,000 feet, with higher-altitude coffee considered best. When ripe, the coffee bean resembles a red bead on the shrub and must be hand-picked as coffee beans do not ripen simultaneously. After picking, the red husk is removed and the golden-colored bean is placed in the sun to dry. After drying, the dry bean is washed several times to remove its membrane and is then shipped to outlets where it is roasted, ground, and packaged. Harvest season in this area is November thru January. Other sections of Mexico which grow coffee are Tapachula, Jalapa, Veracruz, parts of Oaxaca, parts of Michoacan, and around Patzcuaro and Morelia.

86.2	137.9	Thru coffee village of Xhanil.
89.5	143.2	Side road (left) to CASCADAS DE AGUA AZUL (Agua Azul Waterfalls). There are few pull outs on this road.

» Over OK paved, windy downhill, 2.5 mile, 6° grade road, The falls are a series of over a thousand falls, not all of which can be reached by foot. The area is a nice spot for a picnic, to take pictures, and to just hike the trail around the falls and enjoy nature's handiwork. Agua Azul has a primitive camping area and there is a grassy spot where trailer camping is permitted. Kids wash cars — negotiate price, usually about ½ or less of what they ask. Trail above falls to picnic area. Kids selling bean empanadas and sweet buñuelos (fried flour tortillas sprinkled with sugar. Many birds. Small day use fee. No security. Boondocking only. Use your own judgement. The cross at the head of the falls is to a frenchman who tumbled to his death.

90.2	144.3	Thru community of Tzinteel.
92.2	147.5	Slow for Escuela (school) Zapata.
93.2	149.1	On left Coffee is sold. The state of Chiapas is noted for its good coffee.
93.6	149.8	Salto de Agua county line.
94.0	150.4	Thru Mayan community of Yobchib. Then sharp curve over narrow bridge.
95.5	152.8	Pass road (right) to Agua Clara.
96.0	153.6	Caution for rough road thru here. Wide spot for passing.
96.7	154.7	Short straight stretch of about 1 mile.
97.6	156.2	Over Rio Tulija.
98.4	157.4	Finca Tulija entrance marked by orange painted disking disks.
98.9	158.2	Straight stretch — ½ mile long.
99.9	159.8	Emergency gas stop, (reg. only) from barrels.
101.0	161.6	Straight stretch for 1 mile.
101.2	161.9	Thru community of Usulo Galvan.
103.2	165.1	Careful for narrow section of road.
104.8	167.7	Over bridge. then thru Ejido Santa María. Emergency gas — regular from barrels. Rural Conasupo store.
106.3	170.0	Santa María queen bee farm.
106.6	170.6	Salto de Agua, careful, trucks.
108.3	173.3	Straight stretch of ½ mile.
110.0	176.0	Village of San Miguel down to right.
112.0	179.2	Downhill — 6° grade winding.
113.0	180.8	Thru village, many people on road. Then uphill.
113.8	182.1	Pass turnoff to Misol-Ha, 0.8 miles away.
115.5	184.8	Sometimes a washout here.
116.4	186.2	Passing zone.

(Next Page, Please)

JULY 1992   199-NORTH
JCT. HWY #190 — PALENQUE, CHI

MEXICO TRAVELOG
Puts over 40 years of experience at your side! Copyright © Sanborn's TGP Inc.

MI.	KM.	
☞ 118.2	189.1	Careful for slippery curves thru here. We all know to use our transmission as a brake (even automatics), don't we? Then pass turnoff to **San Manuel**. Downhill and windy.
118.8	190.1	Entering county (Municipio) of Palenque.
119.8	191.7	Jog left for bypass around **Chancol** off to right. Palenque **10 KM**.
121.4	194.2	Downhill and windy.
122.2	195.5	Pass water purification plant. Then over bridge and wind on down
H 123.4	197.4	Over bridge and past **Nututun Hotel**. Then straight stretch for 1 mile.
125.3	200.5	Come now to junction with road to **Palenque ruins**.

Palenque ruins, turn left and begin pink "Palenque Special" at mile 17.5

Downtown Palenque, take right fork.

Hwy #186, Villahermosa or Yucatan, continue ahead 17.5 miles to junction with Hwy

M*gas*   #186. Magna at Emiliano Zapata, 13.3 miles east of junction.

End of log!

(Over, please)

MEDEX

WORLDWIDE TRAVEL ASSISTANCE

Assistance Services for Worry-Free Travel:

- Locating the right kind of medical care nearest you.

- Overcoming language barriers by directing you to English speaking doctors or translators.

- Monitoring your progress during the course of your medical treatment and recovery.

- Maintaining contact with your family and personal physician back home.

- Coordination of your insurance coverages.

- Arrangement of emergency medical transportation if necessary... and more!

MEDEX Travelers Assistance Identification

MEDEX

Group Number: 567

Valid Dates: Sanborn's liability policy period

WHEN TO CONTACT MEDEX FOR ASSISTANCE

Call the nearest MEDEX Coordination Center if:

- You are hospitalized or are about to be hospitalized.
- You are involved in an accident requiring medical care.
- You have difficulty locating medical care.
- You have a medical problem and require translation services.
- You have any serious travel difficulties.

In an emergency—go immediately to the nearest physician or hospital without delay, then contact the nearest MEDEX Assistance Coordination Center.

HOW TO CONTACT MEDEX FOR ASSISTANCE

1. Call MEDEX at one of the numbers listed below. You can call 24 hours a day, 7 days a week. (When a toll-free number is not available, call the nearest Assistance Center collect.)
2. Give the MEDEX Coordinator your name and group number.
3. Explain the nature of your illness, injury or medical problem and the type of help you need.

IN MEXICO TOLL FREE
95-800-010-0061

IN THE USA & CANADA
1-800-527-0218

IN THE UNITED KINGDOM
0800-252-074

COLLECT FROM ANYWHERE IN THE WORLD
1-410-321-4426   Baltimore, MD
44-273-202141   Brighton, England

JULY 1992   186-W-3
PALENQUE JCT — VILLAHERMOSA

MEXICO TRAVELOG
Puts over 40 years of experience at your side! Copyright © Sanborn's TGP Inc.

PALENQUE JUNCTION — VILLAHERMOSA (JUNCTION HWY #195) — 73 MI OR 116.8 KM — DRIVE TIME 1½ — 2 HOURS

SCENIC RATING — 3

» This is a fine inland route thru nice green ranching country, and a good alternate to the older Gulf Coast route (Hwy #180). It's fairly straight good paved road and since it's a truck route, it's well traveled.

0.0	0.0	Starting at junction (left) with side road to **Palenque**, proceed ahead on Hwy #186, gas (regular only) at left. KM 118.
2.0	3.2	Pass "Programa Hule" — Rubber tree program station.
5.6	9.0	Thru village of **Cuauhtemoc**.

» **Cuauhtemoc (1502-1525)** was the 11th & last Aztec Emperor. The son of Emperor Ahuizotl & princess Tilalcaptl, he was educated in the Calmecac school for nobles. Cortes made him a prisoner on Aug. 13, 1521 & had him killed by hanging him by his feet like a common criminal, on Feb. 28, 1525. He was 23. He was betrayed by Malinche, who acted as interpreter. To this day, a "Malinche" is a woman who cannot be trusted — that's the polite version.

6.0	9.6	Cross Cataza county line. I'm a confirmed bachelor. I sent my picture to a lonely hearts club. They sent it back.
8.0	12.8	Pass side road (right) to **Jonuta**.
10.0	16.0	Thru stretched-out village of **Nueva Esperanza** (New Hope). KM 95.
11.7	18.7	Restaurant ranch at right. The first 15 minutes of a rain storm are the most dangerous for drivers. Park and wait it out.
16.0	25.6	Pass side road (right) to **Monte Grande**.
16.5	26.4	Thru little village of **Bajadas Grandes**.
18.8	30.1	Cross Puente de Calzada and its "topes" (before and after). KM 84.
20.0	32.0	Skip inspection station. Watch for trucks. KM 82.
22.5	32.5	Cross state line - leave state of Tabasco and enter state of Chiapas. Note Heliconia flowers at roadside - orange bracts (blooms) like multi-birds of paradise. Then past abandoned customs station at right. KM 78.
23.0	36.8	Truck inspection on right. Do not stop.
27.0	43.2	Up and over bridge across Río Tulija. Then pass side road (left) to **Estación Zopo**.
28.5	45.6	Side road (left) to **Salto de Agua**, not worth visit (we didn't).
29.0	46.4	Cemento Apaseo (cement factory), left
31.0	49.6	Pass side road (left) to **Agua Blanca**.

+ SANBORN'S EXTRA — To AGUA BLANCA, turn off at Km 65. It's 3 Mi to railroad and 1.4 Mi farther to Agua Blanca. Take this gravel road (good - but not for RV's, it has rock "topes"). Heliconia flowers in bloom - orange blossoms. Pass plaza of Las Palomas on left (green benches), Public Library, church on right. Continue straight thru, past second plaza, over pipe bridge, past Telesecundaria, over narrow bridge and past Heliconia Restaurant. Electric light in restaurant. Cross railroad. Then come to Agua Blanca. Nice with water falls, pools, grutas (caves). dry camping, night watchman. It's an unspoiled area: clean, simple restaurant with rest rooms and changing rooms. picnic table, BBQ pit. Natural spring water. Bring insect repellant. Orchids in trees. Small fee charged. (Thanks to A. Corelis, Pto. Vallarta, Jal.)

(Over, please)

186-W-3
PALENQUE JCT — VILLAHERMOSA

MI.	KM.	
34.0	54.4	Thru community of **Manatinero**. Watch for school crossing. **KM 60**.
37.0	59.2	At our passing, observed road crew making potholes. **KM 55**
38.5	61.6	Pass side road (left) to **Estación Zopo** on railroad, 4.3 miles away.
42.5	63.2	Past community of **Puxcatán**. Then cross bridge over Río Puxcatán. Then pass side road (right) to little town of **Macuspana** (a dangerous crossroad). Note nice stadium, also at right, and Monument to Lazaro Cardenas. Although only 200 feet above sea level, Macuspana is a town in the "mountain region" situated on the banks of the river of the same name. Mgas at right. OK bathrooms. Try some crispy fried bananas (like potato chips).
42.8	68.5	Watch for trucks pulling onto highway.
47.0	75.2	New microwave station, left.
47.1	75.4	Come now to dangerous crossroads (right) to **Belén** ("Bethlehem") and (left) to **Jalapa**.
49.0	78.4	7th-Day Adventist Church, right.
50.0	80.0	Thru settlement of **San Juan el Alto** with fancy church at left.
51.8	82.9	Pass another dangerous crossroads (right) to **Ciudad Pemex**, an oil area community, and (left) to Cacao.
52.0	83.2	**Chop Suey Restaurant!!** How'd dat get dere?
55.5	88.8	Pass side road (right) to **Tequila**, then side road (left) to **Zapotillo**.
56.6	90.6	Pass side road (left) to **Ismate**.
60.5	96.8	Come to toll house. Pay toll. "Topes" on both sides.
62.0	99.2	LP gas, right.
63.0	100.8	Pass abandoned motel construction site at right (must have run out of funds??). Divided boulevard begins. **KM 13**.
64.0	102.4	Pass under overpass and side road (right) to airport. Then past settlement of **Dos Montes** at left. **KM 11**.
65.5	104.8	Cross bridge over Río Zapote I. Careful of trucks entering on right.
66.5	106.4	Now over Zapote II bridge. You'll go straight thru town unless overnighting in **Villahermosa**.
69.5	111.2	Come now to fancy glorieta (circle) with monument to Tabscoob "Nuestro Tata ("founding father" or "our forefather").
70.0	112.0	Come to toll house and pay toll. Then over nice bridge over Río Grijalva and under pedestrian overpass. Then pass side street (left) to downtown and **Hotels Manzur, María Dolores** and **Holmeca** — (but you exit at right and go under divided). Continue down on Hwy #186 (Blvd. Grijalva), (Take first exit after bridge for Mgas.) Pass gas station at right on service access road.
70.9	113.4	Central bus depot at right. (Exit here for hotels but not for RV park.) Pass **Hotel Maya Tabasco**, left on access road.
71.0	113.6	Pass exit to Av. Universidad.

Frontera and Isla Aguada on the gulf on Hwy #180, exit right and TURN RIGHT onto Av. Universidad and go toward Comalcalco and Cd. Industrial. Start Isla Aguada Special-South. There's 1 ferry and the last one leaves at 6:30 PM and it's a 3½ hour drive from here, so leave early. Go this way also for Tierra Colorado and Hotel Graham.

71.8	114.9	Cross bridge over Laguna de las Ilusiones. Bend left, then past "Centro de Convivencia Infantil (Kiddy park) at left. Next to park is Villahermosa's pride, the **La Venta Museum**, where 27 Olmec archaeological cultures, including the huge altar with the face of a monkey, are exhibited. Park is open daily from 8:30 AM till 5 PM (admission charged).
72.0	115.2	This street is called Paseo Tabasco. This exit goes to **Holiday Inn. RV Park La Choca** is about ¼ mile west of Holiday Inn. No hookups, but OK. Continue under underpass and pass Tabasco 2000, once the airport and now a housing development. Nice Hotel **Viva Villahermosa** at left (exit ahead).
72.8	116.5	Come now to junction (left) Hwy #195 and imposing monument to Sanches Magallanes. Make U-turn left (go around) at glorieta and stay on lateral road if to **Viva Villahermosa** and **Hyatt Hotels**.

(Next Page, Please)

MEXICO TRAVELOG
Puts over 40 years of experience at your side! Copyright © Sanborn's TGP Inc.

P

M*gas*

Coatzacoalcos, proceed ahead past circle and down Hwy #180 and start Log 180-North-4. Gas just ahead on right.

Tuxtla Gutierrez, San Cristobal de las Casas, etc. on Hwy #195 turn left here at circle and start Log 195-South-1. — NOTE: We don't recommend this road. You really should go back to Palenque and take Hwy #190 instead using Log 199-South. If you have a rig over 30 feet long, go on to Acayucan and cross on Hwy #185. During rainy season (May—July & late Nov.—Jan.) even Hwy #199 may be difficult. Inquire at a highway patrol or ask a Green Angel, or call the Green Angel # in the front of travelog.

End of Log.

(Over, please)

$8.95
$11.90 (Mail Order)

SANBORN'S™ book

To order (or request review copy)
Call 1-800-222-0158
(Order blanks on reverse)

Mexico from the Driver's Seat

Tales of the Road from Baja to the Yucatán

By
"Mexico" Mike Nelson

Essential reading for automobile adventurers

"You know those little gravel roads leading from the highways, headed nowhere in particular? That's where Mike Nelson turns off to bring home Mexcio from the inside looking out. Nobody can lay bare the soul of a country as complex and misunderstood as Mexico, but *Mexico from the Driver's Seat* comes far closer than many books dedicated to Holiday Inn wannabes, cheap straw hats and hamburgers like back home. Take one of those books along. But read *Mexico from the Driver's Seat* before you go. It is sometimes funny, sometimes bittersweet and always a valuable perspective."

Joseph B. Frazier
Associated Press News Editor for Mexico & Central America

"Mr. 'Mexico' Mike makes all of Mexico accessible for U.S. and Canadian tourists in an easy to read, enjoyable way. His stories tell them what they have been asking about my country better than anyone I know."

Rolando Garcia
General Director for Mexican Surface Tourism for the U.S. & Canada

"Those who know the real spirit of Mexico are enchanted by it continually. Mike Nelson is more than enchanted: he is moved to experience it. Thankfully he has shared his travels with us. *Mexico from the Driver's Seat* is must reading for those who seek to experience Mexico for themselves."

Ibarro Torres
Mexico Tourist Board

"Mexico" Mike has driven Mexico's roads for over 20 years. Unlike a "travel" writer, he tells of both known and little-known places, everyday people, and oddballs. He writes the only guide for drivers, *Sanborn's Travelog*, a weekly column for the McAllen, TX *Monitor*, the *Mexico City News*. He's written for Frommer's *Mexico On $35 A Day*, the *Dallas Morning News* and others. His factual observations have been printed in the *New York Times*, *Wall Street Journal* and others. His ramblings were chronicled in *Texas Monthly*.

Shortcuts often aren't. A pickup truck overtook us. Desperate for somebody to talk to, I motioned for it to stop.

"How far to Zacatecas?"

"Lejos, muy lejos," was the reply. (Man, it's so far you don't want to know!)

The driver saw my face fall.

"But I know a shortcut" he said. "It is only three ranches to the highway."

Aha, I thought. How far can three ranches be?

ISBN 1-878164-04-2

MEXICO TRAVELOG
Puts over 40 years of experience at your side! Copyright © Sanborn's TGP Inc.

VILLAHERMOSA (JCT HWY 195) — CARDENAS — COATZACOALCOS — 104.0 MI OR 166.4 KM — DRIVE TIME 2 – 2½ HOURS

SCENIC RATING — 1

» KAMIKAZE = Mayan word TO DRIVE — derived from Mayan rite of passage in which young men in VW's are tested for their valor in competition dedicated to god Kamikaze. ED. NOTE — as of yet unverified by any reputable source (maybe the road logger has logged one too many roads).

	MI.	KM.	
P	0.0	0.0	Starting here in **Villahermosa** at circle or "glorieta" with imposing monument to Sanchez Magallanes, and junction Hwy #195 proceed ahead on divided Hwy #180. Mgas, right.
	0.5	0.8	John Deere, left.
	0.7	1.1	Combo Arabe Taco and muffins sales at right.
Mgas	1.1	1.8	Mgas, left. Come to traffic "glorieta" (circle) and proceed halfway around (continue straight). Statue in center is of ex-Presidente Lázaro Cárdenas (1934-40), one of Mexico's most popular leaders; in 1938 he nationalized the oil industry. Farmers market and cattle expo at right.
	1.5	2.4	Cross Puente (bridge) Carrizal II over Río Carrizal.
	1.6	2.6	Pass "Retorno" (if needed for gas). **Motel Costa del Sol** at right.
H	2.2	3.5	LP gas, left. Use "Retorno" to reach it, ¼ MI farther on.
	3.5	5.6	Thru community of **Loma de Caballo** with **Motor Plaza Tabasco** (Motel de paso, not for you) at left. Then divided boulevard ends.
	5.5	8.8	Banana growing community of **Lázaro Cárdenas** at left. Many bananas sales stands.
	12.0	19.2	Side road (left) to huge Reforma oil field.
	12.5	20.0	Thru settlement of **Paso de Cunduacán**.
	13.1	21.0	Oil derrick, right and microwave relay station
	16.0	25.6	6 oil derricks on right — construction site.
	18.2	29.1	Microwave communication relay.
	20.0	32.0	Pass side road (left) to **Cucuyulapa**.
	21.5	34.4	Up over long bridge over Río Samaria.
	22.3	35.7	Thru community of **La barca de Oro** ("The Golden Boat").
	22.7	36.3	Pass another oil derrick construction site.
	26.9	43.1	Mgas at left and skirt edge of town of **Cárdenas** (population 61,017), famous for its chocolate insdustry, over to left. Pass crossroads (right) to **Comalcalco** and on to **Paraiso** and **Limon**, favorite weekend spots for locals. Left is to town and to **Huimanguillo**. Then under overpass.
Mgas	28.6	45.8	Mgas at right.
H	29.5	47.2	Pass **Hotel Tlauashco** —Mod— 92 nice a/c rooms, good restaurant, pool; AE, MC, VI. Ph: (937) 2-1940 or 2-1533. KM 120. VW agency at left. Then LP gas, right; power plant, left, and out.
	30.5	48.8	Pass **Motel Los Pilares** — not for you! Bridge under construction at right.
	34.5	55.2	57th Infantry Battalion barracks, right.
	41.0	65.6	Pass Pemex campo community of **Chontalapa**.

(Over, please)

180-N-4A
VILLAHERMOSA — COATZACOALCOS

JULY 1992

MI.	KM.	
41.8	66.9	Road narrows for bridge then widens. — A lost motorist slowed down to ask his way to the nearest town. The surly old man, whom he nearly knocked down, replied: "dunno." The motorist drove on slowly, but was soon recalled by shouts behind him. He put the car in reverse and backed until he was alongside the old man who had just been joined by another. "Well?" said the motorist. "This is m' buddy," said the old man, "an' 'e dunno either.
42.0	67.2	Pass College of Tropical Agriculture, right.
45.0	72.0	Cemetery on left.
46.0	73.6	Pass Ejido Benito Juárez, left.
48.3	77.3	Thru settlement of Pico de Oro. The Aztecs believed in the four cardinal points and the central direction (or upwards). All beings were grouped according to this. They assigned white to the west, red to east, black to north, blue to south. This may account for their acceptance of the Christian symbol of the cross, which points in all four directions.
51.6	82.6	Begin newly paved — better for about 6 miles.
52.3	83.7	Bright pink Presbyterian church, left.
55.5	88.8	Thru big Ejido Palo Mulato with little blue Pentecostal church at right.
63.8	102.1	Come now to crossroads community of Entronque (Spanish for "junction") Sanchez Magallanes at left. Sanchez Magallanes is a gulf beach layout 23 miles away, more for locals, but just off its shore is beautiful Santa Ana sandbar. No hotel evident.
76.0	121.6	Pass side road (right) to Pemex campo La Venta.

» **It was in the swamps of La Venta area where the huge (20-ton) Olmecan heads which were carved from single solid chunks of stone were discovered - and how the dickens it was managed to get 'em into the middle of these swamps miles and miles from the nearest known stone deposits, is one of the world's great mysteries. Because huge oil deposits were discovered in this immediate area, the entire site has been relocated to Villahermosa and reconstructed at La Venta Museum.**

MI.	KM.	
78.0	124.8	New 1992 immigration inspection station — have papers ready. Then pass monument to Presidente Adolfo Ruiz Cortinez (1952-58) commemorating the building of this highway at right. Then up and over bridge crossing Río Tonala which is also the state line — leave Tabasco and enter Veracruz.
80.3	128.5	Pass Rancho Hermanos ("Brothers") Graham RV Park (200 spaces, 100 with electricity and water; toilets; showers; pool; restaurant; tennis; dump station; fishing lake; very nice accommodating management) at right. KM 38.
82.0	131.2	Gas at right. Then pass side road (left) to Las Choapas.
82.4	131.8	Vibrators — Slow! — Livestock inspection station — not for you.
83.0	132.8	Pass side road (right) to Agua Dulce ("Sweet Water").
83.5	133.6	Begin 4-lane divided.
89.0	142.2	Big Silicon glass plant, left.
90.0	144.0	Another Silicon glass plant on right.
95.4	152.6	Come now to road junction.

Acayucan, veer right (curve left on overpass over old highway) and start Log 108-North-4B.

Coatzacoalcos, straight ahead and follow stub log below, although we must warn you that because of heavy industry in the area and the commercial bus and truck traffic, driving is tedious and slow.

Stub log to Coatzacoalcos

MI.	KM.	
0.0	0.0	Proceed straight ahead on 2-lane highway into Coatzacoalcos under overpass.
3.2	5.1	Note Big petro-chemical complex La Cangregera over to right. Past Instituto Mexicano del Petrolero (Mexico Institute of Petroleum) at right.
4.5	7.2	Pass turnoff (left) to Minatitlán.

(Next Page, Please)

JULY 1992
VILLAHERMOSA — COATZACOALCOS

MEXICO TRAVELOG
Puts over 40 years of experience at your side! Copyright © Sanborn's TGP Inc.

MI.	KM.	
5.0	8.0	Pass gas at right. Then pass side road (left) to Nanchital. You are now going through a major industrial zone; this general area is often called "Mexico's Houston".
5.5	8.8	Gas, no Mgas, but good carnitas (chopped pork treats, eaten with a taco). You know it's fresh 'cuz the slaughter house is behind restaurant.
7.0	11.2	Toll booth. Pay Toll, second lane from right for cars and pickups.
8.0	12.8	Up and onto big lift bridge over Río Coatzacoalcos with railroad alongside. This nice "singing" steel bridge is built so that its center span can be raised to allow ocean-bound freighters carrying oil and sulphur to proceed up river to Minatitlán which can be seen 'way off to the right.
8.8	14.1	Killer "topes".
9.2	14.7	Come to congested junction. Right is to downtown and left is to Acayucan and to Hotels Travelodge and Valgrande.

» The port of Coatzacoalcos (pronounced "kwat-zah-kwahl-koz") is a busy and growing industrial center with a population of over 500,000 (hence the aforementioned heavy commercial traffic). The City has extensive sulphur and petroleum-related operations — refineries, petro-chemical plants, etc — and is an important railhead serving as the Gulf of Mexico terminal for the Isthmus of Tehuantepec Rail Service.

End of Log.

JULY 1992   1 of 1   180-N-4B
                                                COATZACOALCOS — ACAYUCAN

MEXICO TRAVELOG
Puts over 40 years of experience at your side! Copyright © Sanborn's TGP Inc.

COATZACOALCOS JUNCTION PAST MINATITLAN TO ACAYUCAN (JCT HWY #185) — 42.5 MI OR 68.0 KM — DRIVE TIME 1 HOUR

SCENIC RATING — 0

MI.	KM.	
0.0	0.0	Having gone straight here at junction with road (left) to **Coatzacoalcos**, continue ahead up on overpass to Hwy 180, a 4-lane toll road. KM 15.
0.8	1.3	SOS phone on road. *It isn't...*
1.6	2.6	LP gas on left. Note Helaconia bright orange bracts blooming.
3.3	5.3	Pass junction to **Coatzacoalcos** and **Minatitlan**.
5.0	8.0	Uphill, speed limit 100 kmph (62 mph) maximum. *Necesary...*
5.8	9.3	Sign says Acayucan, Veracruz and Moloacan straight ahead.
6.5	10.4	Straight ahead here at junction (left) to **Ixhuatlan** and **Moloacan**.
7.5	12.0	Come to toll house — stop and pay toll. Ahead and past military base at right.
10.5	16.8	Up and over Río Coatzacoalcos on spectacular suspension bridge.
11.0	17.6	Monument to oil workers on left. *To have relatives...*
14.0	22.4	Cross bridge over San Francisco Canal.
16.0	25.6	Pass another exit (right) to **Coatzacoalcos** and oil refinery.
17.3	27.7	Past last exit to **Coatzacoalcos**, then past federal road office.
17.5	28.0	Straight ahead here — exit (right) is to **Minatitlan**.
21.0	33.6	Pemex town of **Minatitlan** on left. *In Kansas City...*
21.5	34.4	End of divided highway.
23.4	37.4	Now curve right and up thru little Pemex worker's town of **Cosoleacaque**. Slow for "topes".
25.4	40.6	Pass **Rancho Tomito** Restaurant & Mgas station (very clean restrooms at our visit). KM 34.
25.7	41.1	Pass turn off to **Oteapán**, right.
28.1	45.0	Secretary of Mines and Minerals office at right. *To be...*
28.6	45.8	Note Melaza (molasses) tank on right.
30.0	48.0	Careful for "vibradores" ahead and yellow overpass. Then past sports center at left and enter fringe of sulfur mining town of **Jaltipan** (population, 60,000) mostly to right. Sulphur mine up tracts to right.
33.0	52.8	Gas at right. *Unhappy. — Groucho Marx*
37.3	59.7	Pass side road (left) to **Texistepec**.
41.8	66.9	Mandatory immigration stop.
42.5	68.0	Come to **Acayucan** Junction (Hwy #180) with Tehuantepec Isthmus Hwy #185. Gas at right.

Mgas

Catemaco, San Andres Tuxtla, and Veracruz, continue ahead on Hwy #180 and start Log 180-North-5A. Gas ahead at end of bypass on left.

Acayucan or to La Ventosa Junction with Hwy #180, take left fork here onto old Hwy #180 into town and start Log 185-South (Tehuantepec isthmus).

H   Incidentally, the **Hotel Kinaku**, downtown a block east of main plaza, is the town's best, located at Ocampo Sur #7 (64 A/C rooms; pool; nice restaurant and bar; enclosed parking; MC, VI; Ph: 5-0466 or 5-0410 Fax: 5-3000).

End of Log.   *(Next page, please)*

SANBORN'S™
Mexico Insurance Service
P.O. Box 310 McAllen, Texas 78505-0310 (210) 686-0711

LET US EXPLAIN OUR SERVICES

INSURANCE — Recommended limits are: $50,000 property damage / $40/80,000 bodily injury liability and $2,000/10,000 medical. These coverages, added to your Fire, Total Theft and Collision coverage give you the total cost of your policy. By special arrangement with our insurance company, a Sanborn's Mexico Club member can purchase an annual policy for almost 50% less than the regular annual policy. That's right, a **50% savings.**

MEDEX — Assists you through a 24-hour phone service in locating the right kind of medical care nearest you. Directs you to a doctor who speaks your language. Monitors your progress and coordinate communication with your family and doctor in your home country and arrange for medical air evacuation if necessary

SANBORN'S MEXICO CLUB — offers you special annual vehicle insurance rates. An annual liability policy for a little more than $100. An only Sanborn's policy includes MEDEX MEDICAL ASSISTANCE SERVICE WITH EACH INSURANCE POLICY.

MEDICAL AIR EVACUATION — If you become seriously ill in Mexico, with this coverage you will be evacuated in an air ambulance to a U.S. or Canadian hospital. Do you want coverage for yourself, or your wife and family too? The individual rate is $45.00 and the family rate is $90.00 a year.

TOWING, MECHANICAL & LEGAL SERVICES — This coverage provides towing, and mechanical service and legal service up to contract limits as well as the locating and shipping of your vehicle part to you in Mexico (cost of part excluded). Choose either 6 months or a year, high limits or lower ones!

THE CLUB — Gives you a free pocket road map, a health information book on Mexico, a Hotel/RV park directory offering discounts to Club members, and of course, our famous mile-by-mile Travelog to your destination.

ALSO OFFERED TO CLUB AND NON CLUB MEMBERS: TRAVMED — It is a $100,000.00 medical policy for sickness or accident. TRAV-MED covers physicians fees and hospital expenses, emergency dental and emergency medical evacuation. TRAVMED also includes MEDEX, making it your complete medical package. Its cost — $3.00 per day through age 70 and $5.00 per day age 71-80.

MEDICAL AIR SERVICE — For #150.00 good anywhere in Canada, U.S., Mexico, and the caribbean for you and your family.

LEGAL SERVICE BY THE DAY — The Mexico auto policy DOES NOT COVER ANY LEGAL EXPENSE AS A RESULT OF AN AUTOMOBILE ACCIDENT. This service will cover your expenses for a small daily fee up to contract limits. (Show Rate Sheet)

TRAVEL WITH HEALTH TO MEXICO BOOK — Loaded with expert information on staying healthy in Mexico.

Call for current prices, There are special rates for small groups.

If you've got a minute ...

We truly hope you had a wonderful trip and that our *Travelog* helped. You can help other folks by passing on information you may have learned. It's from your feedback that we can improve, so tell us what we did right, wrong or could have done differently. If possible, please refer to a log # (ex: 180-S-1, for highway #180, the part of the log that goes South) and mile #. The upper left corner has a secret code that helps us audit distribution. Please include that. The whole *Travelog* covers all of Mexico & is 1,000 pages. Each page is

690 (secret code)	180-SOUTH-1

printed at a different time, so we need some way to track it. YOUR PHONE #, POR FAVOR! I may have a question, or want to thank you personally! Praise or complaints for Mexican individuals or companies should be sent to : Secretaria de Turismo, Direccion General de Servicios al Turismo, Presidente Masaryk — 3er Piso, C.P. 11587, Mexico D.F. Each year, the government honors a citizen who helped tourists. Your complaint will be recorded and sent to the right agency. You'd be surprised at what good it can do. *Hasta luego,* "*Mexico Mike*" *and all the staff at Sanborn's.*

Today's date: _____ Date entered Mexico _____ Exit date _____

Which Sanborn's office served you? _____

Were they friendly? ____ Helpful? ____ Knowledgeable? ____ How could they improve service? _____

_____

Did you have a good time — overall? YES! _____ NO. _____ Was any facility or individual especially helpful? (Sanborn's has a program of honoring Mexicans who go out of their way to assist our customers).

_____

Was you Travelog in order? Did it make sense? YES _____ NO _____

Excellent? _____ Good? _____ Fair? _____

Was the **HIGHWAY INFORMATION** essentially accurate? YES _____ NO _____

Do you have new info for us? _____

_____

_____

Was the **EAT & STRAY** section essentially accurate? YES _____ NO _____

Do you have new places for us, or some that should be edited? _____

_____

_____

_____

What would YOU like to see that WASN'T there? _____

Will you return to Mexico someday? _____

Name: _____

Address, City, State, Zip _____

Country _____ TELEPHONE #( ) _____

How many travelling? _____ First trip? _____ YES _____ NO _____

Where did you hear about Sanborn's? _____

Please use other side if necessary